100
SPORTS

W9-AAV-950

Rolling Thunder

The Golden Age of Roller Derby & the Rise and Fall of the L.A. T-Birds

Scott Stephens

ROLLING THUNDER
THE GOLDEN AGE OF ROLLER DERBY & THE
RISE AND FALL OF THE L.A. T-BIRDS

Copyright © 2019 Scott Stephens.

All rights reserved. No part of this book may be used or reproduced by any means, graphic, electronic, or mechanical, including photocopying, recording, taping or by any information storage retrieval system without the written permission of the author except in the case of brief quotations embodied in critical articles and reviews.

iUniverse books may be ordered through booksellers or by contacting:

iUniverse
1663 Liberty Drive
Bloomington, IN 47403
www.iuniverse.com
1-800-Authors (1-800-288-4677)

Because of the dynamic nature of the Internet, any web addresses or links contained in this book may have changed since publication and may no longer be valid. The views expressed in this work are solely those of the author and do not necessarily reflect the views of the publisher, and the publisher hereby disclaims any responsibility for them.

Any people depicted in stock imagery provided by Getty Images are models, and such images are being used for illustrative purposes only. Certain stock imagery © Getty Images.

ISBN: 978-1-5320-8472-0 (sc)
ISBN: 978-1-5320-8473-7 (hc)
ISBN: 978-1-5320-8474-4 (e)

Library of Congress Control Number: 2019915457

Print information available on the last page.

iUniverse rev. date: 10/14/2019

Contents

Section 1 – Outlaw League

Section 2 – Starting Line

Section 3 – National Skating Derby

Section 4 – International Skating Conference

Section 5 – Roller Superstars

Section 6 – International Roller Derby League

Section 7 – WAR

Section 8 – The Aftermath

Section 9 – Roller Games International

Section 10 – Postscript

"To the skaters."

Foreword by John Hall

Another SOLD-OUT house of fanatical fans! A LOUD, excited, and happy crowd! Are they at a baseball game, hockey game, football game, or boxing match? What type of event captures the hearts, minds, and spirits of fans while also bringing them endless excitement? It is the ROLLER GAMES!

Roller derby is a unique American born sport with equal squads of female and male teammates who skate against an opposing team of the same makeup. They are on roller skates. They skate on a banked track and they skate fast. They race each other in an attempt to score points. They hit with hard blocks to try to stop the opponent from scoring. They lose their tempers, often. They receive penalties. They excite their fans and irritate fans of the opposing team. These are the females and males of the exciting game called Roller Games and often referred to as Roller Derby.

Within these pages, you will learn about the entertaining sport of banked track roller skating. At one time, Roller Games was on over 120 television stations in the USA. They were also broadcast to millions of viewers in Canada, Mexico, Australia and Japan. Roller Games had teams in major USA cities of Los Angeles, Philadelphia, San Francisco, Chicago, Miami, Baltimore, Cleveland, Phoenix and Honolulu.

Scott Stephens saw the Roller Games on TV and instantly knew that he wanted to become a skater. He trained, learned and earned a tryout with a team that was skating against the home area L.A. T-birds at the Olympic Auditorium in Los Angeles. Although he was a rookie, in his first professional game, his skating, spirit, and attitude caught the attention of the L.A. T-Birds Coach, Hall of Famer, Ralph Valladares. Ralph talked to me (I was the T-Birds manager), and we signed the rookie to a T-Birds contract. As a T-Birds skater, he excelled in the game. He garnered many fans and earned the respect of his teammates. Although he relished and excelled in skating, Scott's love for music kept calling him and after just a few years, he left the world of banked track skating. Roller Games lost a wonderful skater to the music world.

Herein, Scott Stephens has recounted the story of how Roller Games began followed by its growth and rise in popularity. Scott has painstakingly researched everything about Roller Games. His dedication and motivation are inspiring. Scott is a lead performer and singer with the world-famous band Liquid Blue. While on his latest tour in Asia, Scott found the time to write this book about Roller Games. In my opinion, this is the best and most accurate book ever written about the history of the banked track sport. This former athlete has captured the heart and soul of the sport he participated in, within the pages of this book.

Reading this book brings back meaningful memories of skating events of my past. Sold-out games at the Fabulous Forum in Inglewood, California and many sold-out games at the Olympic Auditorium in Los Angeles, the L.A. Sports Arena and the San Diego Sports Arena. Scott relives so many wonderful memories such as The Roller Games' L.A. T-Birds skating before a sold-out crowd of 51,000 people at White Sox Park in Chicago against the rival Roller Derby team, The Midwest Pioneers. Scott Stephens captured the spirit of 20,000 fans every night for ten consecutive games in the Palacio Desportes in Mexico City. Scott knows the history of Roller Games. Herein he shares his recollections of the Roller Games. Thank you,

Scott Stephens. Your book gets "two thumbs up" and an M.V.B. (Most Valuable Book) award from me.

John Hall / Member- National Roller Derby Hall of Fame.
John Hall

Foreword
by Bill Griffiths, Jr.

ROLLING THUNDER, the Golden Age of Roller Derby & the Rise and Fall of the L.A. T-Birds is a book well worth reading whether you're a fan of classic American roller derby or not. Scott Stephens has gone to great lengths to bring a representative story of the Los Angeles T-Birds to life. The amount of research he's done, alone, would qualify him for a book writing Gold Medal if one existed. The story of the T-Birds and roller derby is a long and complicated one to present. Of course, there were the games and its many skaters, stars, and characters, but there was also a story of dramatics and intrigue both on and off the banked track. You cannot simply say, "oh, it's only roller derby." The story goes much, much deeper than that.

Scott has done a fine job covering the games and the teams chronologically. However, to truly understand this form of entertainment, you must also get a look inside the management of roller derby. Again, Scott's research is second to none. He has gathered the stories, facts, and opinions of what went on behind the scenes, and what it took to mount such an international phenomenon as the T-Birds and roller derby. In my view, this book is as close to T-Birds reality as you'll ever find!

You'll read about the big games and classic matchups that roller derby provided for the public's entertainment. There is humor, pathos, drama, the triumphs, and the tragedies. You'll also read about the in-fighting that took place both on the banked track as well as in Management's Boardroom- stories that are still debated today among roller derby enthusiasts.

Scott's unique perspective, as a skater himself, gives him the credibility to present such a book. He presents everything from that perspective. He didn't race to put this book out but went about collecting material in a slow, methodical way. He has put several years of hard work into it and has tried to give the reader a full on look at what, at one time, covered four continents simultaneously. This was not an easy task for him, but rather a labor of love. A book like ROLLING THUNDER, *the Golden Age of Roller Derby & the Rise and Fall of the L.A. T-Birds* has never been attempted before. I, for one, really enjoyed the read, and I'm certain you will too!

Bill Griffiths Jr.

Preface

Growing up in Los Angeles in the 1960s and 1970s, it was impossible not to be exposed to the Los Angeles Thunderbirds (L.A. T-Birds). The team was part of the L.A. culture and games were televised and shown at least every week. And unlike other sports, Roller Games were broadcast all year long, not just seasonally. Dick Lane and many of the T-Birds were household names and in the inner cities, the Thunderbirds and their stars were arguably more popular than those of the more traditional sports based in L.A. (the Dodgers, Lakers, Rams, etc.). More on that subject later.

Like so many SoCal kids, I watched the games on KTLA (5) and KCOP (13) regularly and became a devoted Thunderbirds fan. And like many of us in the suburbs, I never actually ventured to the Grand Olympic Auditorium to see a game live. The Olympic was not in the best area of the city, and it was unlikely that my father would have been willing to take me there. I didn't witness my first live Roller Game until 1978 when I skated my debut game. Very few, if any, of my friends from the San Fernando Valley ever attended a game, but most of them watched on and off throughout their childhood and early teen years.

At the time Roller Derby was conceived of by Leo Seltzer in 1935, more than 90% of Americans had roller skated at one time or another during their lives. Roller skating was still very popular in the 1960s, and I received my first set of skates at age six (in 1966). It wasn't long after that, that I was staging roller derby games in our backyard. There was a nice-sized chunk of concrete there, and we used chalk to create the lines simulating the track. We used plastic Dodgers batting helmets that were given away at Dodger Stadium on "Helmet Night" as our jamming helmets. Frankly, the helmets we wore in Roller Games were not much better than those giveaway Dodgers helmets. We created makeshift uniforms using felt pens to inscribe the name "T-Birds" in blue and red on white tees. We each pretended to be our favourite skaters (Valladares, Washington, Reilly, etc.). Our games were unorganized, out of control, and lasted about a month.

In my early teen years, I began to see through some of the theatrical aspects of the game and thoughts arose questioning the validity of the *so-called* sport. Despite my awakening, I still watched occasionally, although less and less, as sex, drugs, and rock & roll began to take centre stage in my life.

1976 was a tumultuous year for me. I founded a publication covering the Los Angeles rock & roll/punk scene (*Raw Power Magazine*), began singing in my first band (Electric Warrior), and started training with Roller Games at the new T-Bird Rollerdrome in Pico Rivera.

Initially, I started training not so much because I thought I could make the team, but because I loved roller skating on a banked track. I didn't know at the time that the Roller Games had crashed and burned and was going through a reorganization period that left them low on skaters.

The average male pro skater stands only 5'8". The added height from wearing skates and the elevated banked track gives professional skaters the illusion of much greater stature. At 5'7", my height was not a disadvantage in the derby. Five nights a week, I drove approximately an hour each way on the 101 and five freeways south from Woodland Hills to Pico Rivera to pay five dollars for the privilege of training with the masters. The masters being John Hall and Ralphie Valladares, who were trying to keep the T-Birds alive. Despite struggling with the transition to the banked track, in less than 18 months, I found myself skating my first pro game with the Detroit Devils. To this very day, the memories of training at the Rollerdrome are the most vivid of anything I have ever experienced in my life.

It was as a result of these training sessions, even more than the actual games, that I gained admiration and respect for the talented skaters of Roller Games. It was this experience that was the main inspiration for this book.

The opportunity to skate with my childhood heroes was both exciting and daunting because I had to juggle my time and responsibilities with my band, my magazine, and roller derby. And since none of those paid much at the time, I also took a gig as a lifeguard to make some money.

Of all of those things, roller derby was my first love. But needless to say, due to my schedule, I was unable to put in the proper time to become the best skater I could be, even though I loved skating on a banked track more than singing in a rock band. And being the lead vocalist of an up-and-coming band during that period of the late '70s was quite a rush. To top it off, my magazine was growing in popularity and we were scoring interviews with the biggest rock stars of the day. And I was dating a smokin' hot blonde valley girl (who not surprisingly left me since I had almost no free time to spend with her). But I can say without hesitation that the most exciting and intense moments in my life were those spent at the Pico Rivera training center and the Olympic Auditorium.

I loved the training despite the toll it took on my body. I quickly developed water on both elbows and other assorted injuries. At the end of each training session, I was battered and often bloody, only to return the following night more determined. I eventually got wise and purchased some elbow pads and rigged up a girdle with football thigh padding to protect my ass. I wasn't blessed with much natural protection, and often I could barely sit down after practice. Falling was part of the game.

The first time I ever stepped on a banked track at training, I was knocked off my skates by another trainee as I merely skated around trying not to engage anyone. I was trying to get used to the banked track. The trainee reminded me that I was a rookie and would have to earn the respect of the others before having free reign of the track. He used a dirty tactic on me that sent me flying backwards landing on my upper back and neck. At the same time, he hit me with a legal shoulder block to the chest and kicked my skates out from behind me. I don't ever recall a hit like that, even in actual games. This guy was a wannabe Psycho Rains. As it turned out, he had been training a long time and had never made a team. He was likely taking out his frustration on me and hoping I wouldn't return to lower his amount of competition. When I got back on my feet, I skated over to him and gave him the hardest shoulder/arm block I could muster. At the time, I didn't have any knowledge on proper blocking and I don't think he moved a millimeter. But after that, he never bothered me again and I kept coming to practice just about every day, eventually doing some hitting of my own.

Roller Games, like the punk rock arena I was covering through *Raw Power*, was an alternative, underground scene complete with a mix of shadowy characters and venues, adrenaline seekers, and alternative lifestyles. I loved it! Not surprisingly, the Olympic Auditorium, home of the T-Birds, eventually became a popular venue for punk rock concerts.

By the time I arrived on the scene for that first game in 1978, Roller Games was in the midst of a minor comeback. The popularity of the sport had peaked in 1972, and since then attendance, television contracts, and salaries had all dwindled. Some of the marquee skaters stayed home while a few were slightly past their prime. This created an opportunity to be called into action much sooner than would have been the norm just a few years earlier.

From 1978 to 1981, from my seat on the infield of the track and on the track itself, I witnessed the best and worst that Roller Games had to offer. Most of the teams from this era fielded 12 to 14 skaters; six or seven each for the male and female squads. Of those, about half were outstanding athletes who were bonafide stars. Another 25%

were solid pros, and the last 25% would not have qualified for a team in years prior. It was those stars, many unheralded for their greatness, which inspired this book. The speed, agility, power, and skill level of those skaters rivaled that of any other professional athlete, no matter the sport.

The top skaters usually carried the game, while the lesser skaters, although doing their very best, often fouled up jams. They also packed action with clumsy skating and showed a lack of understanding for what was happening in the game. I was often guilty of this myself. The action often went from breathtaking to laughable in the span of two jams depending on which skaters were being featured.

From the best seat in the house, I was able to witness this spectacle up close and personal. I often drifted away in thought and amazement when I watched from the bench and wasn't on the track. I was in awe of the talent of the game's stars and how they took beatings and also dished them out. Throughout my life, I have always been an avid sports fan, especially of the four major sports leagues-the MLB, NFL, NBA, and the NHL. I've also been a talent recruiter in the music industry as well as a music critic. I'm well versed in assessing talent and the top talent that Roller Games was fielding in the period I skated was simply amazing. For entertainment value and excitement, the sport of roller derby matches up with any other sport. I truly believe fans have more fun at roller derby games than that of any other sport. The excitement that the Los Angeles Thunderbirds gave to sports fans during that era cannot be underestimated.

I left Los Angeles in 1981 to join a band in Anchorage, Alaska, where I also finished college and got married. When I returned to Southern California in 1985, I took my new wife (a former Miss Alaska Teen winner and lifelong Alaskan who had never seen a game) to the Olympic to see the T-Birds in action. I was excited to catch up with former teammates and coaches. But when the men's team exited the track at the end of the second quarter, I noticed coach Ralphie Valladares wouldn't even look at me and John Hall also refused to speak to me. At first, I thought this must be the result of having left the team during the 1981 season to move to Alaska. I later found out that I was suspected of stealing a uniform following my last game. I was devastated. I had never even considered such a thing. I had the utmost respect for John and Ralphie and their efforts to bring the game back to its glorious past, but little did I realize that team uniforms were a commodity amongst skaters, and this wouldn't have been the first time someone had mistakenly taken one home (wink) following a game. Some of the skaters had known it was my last game for a while as I was departing on a Canadian tour with my band. I was easy prey and someone ended up with an original Thunderbirds green and gold uniform with the number seven. The economic reality of roller derby was part of this equation. Most skaters had little or no college education and some didn't even graduate from high school. Most came from working-class families of modest means. Petty theft was quite common in those neighborhoods and not nearly as frowned upon as it would be in other places. As a skater, I was a rare breed as a college student from an upper-middle-class family, living in the Los Angeles County suburb of Woodland Hills. And while there were certainly well-off thieves out there, it wasn't my thing. If I wanted a uniform that badly, I would have offered to buy one. Stealing is offensive to me unless it involves survival. And biting the hand that feeds you, or in this case, stealing from those that gave me the amazing opportunity to skate professionally, would have been unthinkable. Upon hearing my story, both Ralphie and John apologized for the mix-up on the uniform and I became very close with both of them in the coming years.

One of the saddest days of my life came upon hearing the news the Rollerdrome Training Center had closed in 1986. I knew that spelt the end of Roller Games. With no place for skaters to train and an aging group of talent, Roller Games limped along after 1986 and rarely held games at the Olympic. I didn't see Ralphie or John again for almost ten years until the mid-1990s. By this time, the T-Birds had skated their last game.

Unfortunately, Ralphie's life was cut short by illness. Before Ralphie's death, we became very close friends and I spent a good deal of time with him in the weeks prior to his departure. He shared with me many secrets about his life that will remain with me forever. He was candid and humble and showed genuine remorse for things that happened in his life that may have hurt others. It's rare to see someone admitting fault, but especially those individuals who are superstars in their respective pursuits. Ralphie was tough as nails but had a profoundly kind heart. He visited my home in Encinitas one day along with skater Harold Jackson, and we skated from my home to the local high school. This was the last time Ralphie ever put on a pair of skates. I also arranged the last media interview with Ralph through DJ Lynn Harper, on a local San Diego radio station.

The two most prolific Thunderbirds, John and Ralphie, had become bitter enemies later in life. They were business partners on the Thunderbird Rollerdrome skating rink, as well as minority owners of Roller Games (under Bill Griffiths). Like many business partnerships, this taxed their relationship. It's likely that the stress caused by the downfall of the entire sport of roller derby, combined with the closing of the Rollerdrome, contributed to their troubles. When I learned Ralphie was terminally ill, I approached John Hall to consider putting aside their differences and visiting Ralphie in the hospital. John agreed, and the two men once again became fast friends and spent quality time together in the hospital during the final days of Ralphie's life. In comparison to any other small contributions I made to Roller Games, I am most proud of this moment. Both John and Ralphie were heroes not only in my eyes, but also to all fans and skaters of Roller Games. They were both legends of the sport and members of the Hall of Fame. I'm glad they finished as they started; friends with mutual respect for one another.

Following Ralphie's death at such a young age, I did a lot of reflecting on Roller Games and desired to keep that history alive. So I created a website in tribute to the Thunderbirds and Roller Games: http://www.LATBirds.net. I also became heavily involved in the Thunderbirds Facebook page. These two sites have kept the T-Birds spirit alive, even while the team is dormant. I've known for a long time that the missing piece in the preservation of Roller Games history was a book dedicated to this league and its flagship team.

With my duties managing and performing with my band Liquid Blue, I didn't have the time to undertake such a venture. But recently I decided that this book needed to be completed. This was driven by several factors, the main one being that John Hall is (at the time of writing) approaching the age of 90. Bill Griffiths and Ralphie are now gone, so John is the lone remaining figure of those who worked behind the scenes in the early days of Roller Games. His wealth of knowledge is priceless.

The other driving force that led me to finally undertake this task is the surprising lack of information available on the Thunderbirds, relative to the team's impact on the sport of roller derby.

As I write this section, it is November 2017 and I'm on a flight from Manila to Singapore to meet up with my band for a show. I'm traveling in Southeast Asia most of this time, and parts of this book were written in Hong Kong, the Philippines, Brunei, Singapore, Taiwan, Australia, and Costa Rica. Ironically, I even wrote a chapter while staying at the "Thunderbird" Resort in the La Union province of the Philippines. Recently, I was going through some of my file folders and found a document from 1998 entitled "book outline". It reminded me that I had started writing this prior to Ralphie's death and just before my band Liquid Blue took off. I can't believe I waited almost 20 years to dive into this project, but that's what happened. Had I written the book back then before the turn of the century, there would have been a much higher percentage of Thunderbird fans still alive. Twenty years is a long time, and many of these folks have now departed, including Bill Griffiths and Jerry Hill. Bill took a lot of heat, but he is not here to defend himself or tell his side of the story, which is always on my mind as I fill these pages. As for my excuse, Liquid Blue took off around this time, and it was all I could do to keep up with the demands of running it as a sole proprietor and later as a solely owned corporation. Since starting the band, I have worked an average of 70 hours a week for the past 20 years. There simply wasn't enough time left outside of my obligations to properly cover this topic. Things are only slightly different now as I'm still putting in 40 to 50 hours a week but those extra 20 to 30 hours are going into this book. Finally!

My love for the skaters who gave their blood, sweat, and tears to Roller Games will be evident as you read onward. But I certainly encountered some issues and problems with various skaters and management along the way. A few examples with unnamed skaters: One of my childhood skating heroes, who was my teammate on the 1980 Thunderbirds, requested a loan from me in the 1990s under the guise that he needed the money for medical reasons resulting from a car accident. I lent him a few thousand dollars and he vanished never to repay me. The car accident was fake. I skated for years, and examples like these are few and far between and a part of life. There will be nothing derogatory written about anyone whom I felt wronged me, no matter how blatant or egregious I thought the issues were. We've all had similar experiences, and it's best to forgive and move on. My respect for these individuals, as skaters, never wavered. On personal matters involving myself off the track, skaters' names will not be mentioned. On the track is a different story.

Before embarking on this project, I understood the enormous investment of time that comes with writing any full-length work of non-fiction, and I had to come to terms with the fact that the market for this work is extremely narrow and limited. That is mainly because the Thunderbirds are no longer active and haven't had a large fan base since the 1970s. Most fans of Roller Games are now either deceased or senior citizens. And judging by the low number of followers on our Thunderbird Facebook page, many of these folks aren't online. It will not be easy to make potential readers aware that this book exists. You, who are holding this book (or Kindle version) in your hands right now can help by spreading the word to others you know who got enjoyment from watching the T-Birds battle it out with the opposing villains.

While the target audience of this work is fans of Roller Games as aforementioned, I am also hopeful that this will find its way into the hands of the current crop of Roller Derby skaters. The history of this worldwide sport, born in America, is vital to understand for many reasons. The study of history educates the reader, and there is much to be learned. It's imperative for anyone involved in the ownership or management of a current team or league to study the past to avoid making similar mistakes. Just as importantly, it's wise to learn what worked and what didn't work. And all athletes who call themselves Roller Derby skaters should be aware of the Los Angeles Thunderbirds, as well as the Bay Bombers (and their respective leagues). No skating teams, before or after, ever had the success and impact of the Bombers and T-Birds.

Of all my life's adventures, including traveling and performing all over the world with Liquid Blue, nothing has fascinated me as much as my time in the roller derby. The story of the T-Birds and the skaters of Roller Games has never been properly told. That's what this book attempts to accomplish.

Acknowledgments

I'm grateful to so many individuals who shared their time and experiences with me to help make this comprehensive work possible. During the twenty-year span in which this book was a work-in-progress, I was fortunate to interview many of the key figures of Roller Games including, Bill Griffiths, Sr., Ralph Valladares, John Hall, Bill Griffiths, Jr., and dozens of skaters. When I conceived the idea of a book on the T-Birds in 1998, I spent a lot of time with Ralphie, and he shared many stories. Unfortunately, he passed away that same year. Of all the individuals I interviewed for this book, Ralphie was the most forthcoming. I also had two brief interviews with Bill Griffiths, Sr. One was by telephone, followed by a personal meeting at his home in Granada Hills. Mr. Griffiths appeared skeptical about the prospects of a book on the Thunderbirds but took the time to grant the interview. For this, I am grateful.

Much of the credit for this book goes to John Hall. He was my primary source of information and was extremely gracious and giving of his time. Most importantly, the depth of knowledge he accumulated during his 30 plus years in the game was invaluable. We corresponded two to three times a week for several years during the writing of this book. Without John Hall, this book would not have been possible.

Another key contributor was Gary Powers, a brilliant historian who I brought onboard to fact check. He shared his wealth of knowledge up until a point where we parted ways based on creative differences. Nonetheless, I'm grateful to Gary for his contributions, which were second only to John Hall in terms of their impact on the final product.

Bill Griffiths, Jr. graciously shared his time and knowledge with me as I was nearing the finish line. He did a final fact-checking review and added some little-known facts as well.

Other key contributors include Gina Valladares, and roller derby historians Tom Wersderfer, Bill Nagy, and Phil Berrier.

Upon completion of the unedited manuscript, I approached the great derby guru Jerry Seltzer to ask if he would review specific sections of the book that pertained to his Roller Derby league and its flagship team, the Bay Bombers. Jerry was very ill at this time in late 2018, and had posted on social media he had only a few more months to live. Jerry replied, "Scott, I admire you and your work. I appreciate you contacting me for this project, but I cannot endorse the product." The rivalry between Roller Games, Roller Derby, the Thunderbirds, and the Bay Bombers was too deep; it would be taken to the grave. Jerry was one of the most forward-thinking, open-minded individuals in the sport that his family created, but he was also human. I respect his wishes.

Introduction

Roller derby's story is one of the most unique and intriguing in American sports history. Roller Games and their flagship team, the Los Angeles T-Birds, are a big part of that story.

Some of the terms and titles used in the sport and its principle leagues can often be very confusing to all but the most dedicated fans, so please allow me to clarify.

Roller derby is the name of the sport itself. Until Roller Games arrived in 1960, the sport of roller derby and the league Roller Derby were one and the same. Roller Games is the title of the rival league that is the subject of this book. But the sport is roller derby. Important: When you see the term roller derby without a capital R and D, it refers to the sport itself. When used with a capital R and D (Roller Derby), it refers to the original league started and owned by Leo Seltzer.

Definitions:

roller derby – The _sport_ or sporting event in which two teams skate on roller skates around an oval track that is often banked (elevated).

Roller Derby (1948-1973) – The name of the original roller derby league dba the National Roller Derby League that lasted 25 years.

Roller Games (1961-1993) – The name of the second and only other roller derby league that achieved success in the twentieth century. It lasted 33 years and is the subject of this book.

Transcontinental Roller Derby – The original roller derby was called Transcontinental Roller Derby and was formed in 1935 by Leo Seltzer. This is when the term "roller derby" was first used, but it was not until 1938 that modern roller derby was created when famed New York sportswriter, Damon Runyon convinced Leo Seltzer to turn Transcontinental Roller Derby into a contact sport. Over the next ten years, the game developed and then in 1948, an official league was formed.

NRDL – National Roller Derby League: The first official league for the sport of roller derby. It was founded in 1948 and run by Leo Seltzer until the late 1950s when his son, Jerry Seltzer took it over and ran it until the end of 1973. It was simply known as ROLLER DERBY.

RSC – Rollerskating Championships: the original name of ROLLER GAMES. Only used in 1960 and 1961.

NSD – National Skating Derby: The official name of the ROLLER GAMES league starting in 1962.

NRL – National Roller League: For a short time, NSD of ROLLER GAMES was changed to NRL due to pressure from Jerry Seltzer who owned the rights to the name Roller Derby.

ISC – International Skating Conference: The name ROLLER GAMES used for its league in 1974 and 1975 after the Roller Derby folded and many of their skaters were hired by Roller Games.

RSS – Roller Super Stars: The name used by John Hall and Ralphie Valladares when they resurrected ROLLER GAMES in 1976. This is not to be confused with another league that debuted in 1975 under the name *Roller Stars*.

IRDL – International Roller Derby League: The name used by ROLLER GAMES in 1985 through 1988. In '85 and '86, ESPN broadcast games of this league and called the show *Championship Roller Derby*. The IRDL was also a name Jerry Seltzer had used for his Roller Derby league.

RRG – Rockin' Rollergames: The name used for the 1989 television show that featured the Thunderbirds of ROLLER GAMES as its marquee team.

RGI – Roller Games International: The name used in the 1990s and 2000s for ROLLER GAMES.

White shirt – This term refers to the home team, which were normally portrayed as good and morally superior to their opponents.

Red-shirt – The visiting teams who were typically portrayed as evil and morally bankrupt compared to the angelic white-shirt teams.

You are about to embark on a journey that will immerse you in the history of Roller Games and its flagship team, the Los Angeles Thunderbirds. And while this is a large volume of work, there is no way to completely cover all the happenings and highlights from a sports league that lasted more than 30 years. But this should be a fun trip!

So please lace up your skates and let's roll!

Outlaw League

Chapter 1

The Thunderbirds!

"It's great entertainment. You have both men and women competing. They are highly skilled athletes. They keep things moving. And people still love the fact that good triumphs over evil." – Bill Griffiths

The Thunderbirds could be called America's team, (along with the Bay Bombers) during the heyday of roller derby in the '60s and early '70s. They were arguably the most popular and prolific international roller derby team in the history of the sport.

In the United States, the Thunderbirds were every bit as famous as the storied San Francisco Bay Bombers and New York Chiefs of the original Roller Derby league. But it should be pointed out that while the popularity of the Thunderbirds rivaled any team in roller derby history, the pure skating talent in the original Roller Derby was unsurpassed by any team or league, including the powerful Thunderbirds.

In Los Angeles and throughout Southern California, the Thunderbirds dominated the market. The top Thunderbirds skaters were household names and the team often drew more fans than the Lakers (NBA) and the Kings (NHL), both in game attendance and television ratings.

Internationally, Roller Games had no peers. The league operated highly successful leagues in both Japan and Australia that, although short-lived, are still remembered by many today.

The Thunderbirds team was loaded with exceptional skating talent on both the men's and women's squads as well as the opposition. Games were exciting, fast-paced and hard-hitting. In later years, scoring increased and there was a great deal of mayhem and showmanship on display to spice things up between jams. Never a dull moment. Fans were given a full dose of athleticism and entertainment and got their money's worth. The powerful Thunderbirds were stacked with top skaters and rarely lost a contest. They were the perennial world champions of Roller Games, winning the title twenty times.

But even with all of the championships withstanding, professional roller derby in this era was never about winning and losing; it was about the spectacle and excitement of the game itself. It was the journey, not the destination. And year after year, the Thunderbirds provided a splendid experience for their fans.

Anyone who ever attended a Thunderbirds game at the Olympic Auditorium will remember the team's diehard, rabid fans chanting,

"Go! Go! Go!" in unison as they supported their heroes onward to victory. The level of excitement inside the building was undeniable.

The Thunderbirds brought new highs as well as new lows to the sport of roller derby. The story of the rapid rise and slow, painful death of Roller Games is told within these pages.

Chapter 2

From East to West

"In Los Angeles, everyone is a star." – Denzel Washington

The West Coast was booming in the 1950s and '60s and Los Angeles was the epicenter of its growth. The allure of the West, with its vivid blue Pacific Ocean, fabulous beaches, great weather and the glitter of Hollywood did not go unnoticed by big business in the U.S., including major league sports franchises.

In 1946, pro football came to Los Angeles as the Cleveland Rams became the Los Angeles Rams and L.A.'s first pro sports franchise. Twelve years later in 1958, the Brooklyn Dodgers moved their operation to Los Angeles. Fans flocked to Dodger games in large numbers and the potential of the L.A. sports market was now well established. In 1960, the Minneapolis Lakers of the NBA became L.A.'s third pro sports team and would eventually bring more championships to Los Angeles than any other team. The fledgling American Football League (AFL) chose Los Angeles for one of their expansion franchises, as the league began operations in 1960. The Los Angeles Chargers would last only one season here before moving south to become the very first sports franchise in San Diego (the team relocated back to L.A. in 2017).

While all this was going on in Los Angeles, a similar phenomenon was occurring in another California coastal city, San Francisco. In 1946, the San Francisco 49ers were established as a charter member of the All-America Football Conference (AAFC). The AAFC merged with the NFL in 1949. Like the Rams of Los Angeles, the 49ers were the first pro sports franchise established in their city. In 1958, the New York Giants and Willie Mays made a move west to become the San Francisco Giants, the very same year the Dodgers moved west to Los Angeles. Then just two years after the Lakers moved west, the NBA's Philadelphia Warriors got on the bandwagon and moved operations to the Bay Area, becoming the San Francisco Warriors (and eventually rebranded with the geographic moniker –the Golden State Warriors). Wilt Chamberlain would become the Bay Area's first basketball star. The AFL established the Oakland Raiders in 1960 as the league began operations. The Dodgers and Giants, as well as the Chargers and Raiders, have long-standing rivalries to this day.

Chapter 3

Brave Beginnings

The Braves
DEC. 1, 1958
CHARLIE SAUNDERS   DON OLSON   PAT MURILLO   BILL BOGASH   COACH   LOU SANCHEZ   GAIL ODOM   BILL BOBO   RUSS MASSRO
CO-CO GRAVES   GLORIA SANCHEZ   RUTH CERDA   SANDRA GOLD   JULIE PATRICK   TONI TAGG   JEAN PORTER   DOLLY HANSEN
Roller Derby   JOYCE BEASLY   RED SMARTT   *Ubell Photo*

"Derby is the fastest-growing entertainment attraction in the country. It is neither sport nor show biz, but a new television art form with elements of both. It is cathartic, dramatically structured, fast-paced and as classic as a John Wayne movie." – Variety

In 1953, the National Roller Derby League began the process of moving its operations from New York to Los Angeles with the creation of two teams: the Hollywood Ravens and the Los Angeles Braves. The Ravens were soon gone, as the Braves became the premier team of the league. Yes, the Braves were L.A.'s original Derby team, not the Thunderbirds. Shortly after that, the San Francisco Bay Bombers were created, and eventually became the league's premier team. By 1954, the league had completed its shift to the West and the Braves were its top team.

The Braves had prime time T.V. coverage on KTLA, Channel 5, with Dick Lane calling the games. The team drew sell-out crowds of 9,000 fans to the Olympic Auditorium in downtown Los Angeles, as well as other venues.

Despite their enormous success, the Braves only made Los Angeles their home base for five years (1954-1958). In 1959, they were sent on the road to skate as a red-shirt team. At this time, Leo Seltzer decided to hand the reins over to his son Jerry, who pulled the plug on the Los Angeles operation and focused on the Bay Area. Jerry lived in San Francisco and was willing to give up the potentially lucrative L.A. market. When KTLA inquired about the upcoming schedule of games for 1959, they were informed there would be no L.A. Braves. After this and throughout 1963, the Braves became a road team, with only a handful of games in Los Angeles during this period. This left the door wide open for another organization to step in and capitalize on the local fan base that had become crazy for roller derby.

The two-year absence of the Braves in Los Angeles did not go unnoticed. Herb Roberts, who had not been directly involved in roller derby, but who held the lease for the parking lots at the Olympic Auditorium, realized there was a surplus of good skaters in L.A. and a strong market to support a league in Southern California. Roller Games and its premier team, the L.A. Thunderbirds, were conceived in 1960 by Roberts, with the help of many key skaters. The first games were held in early 1961.

T-Bird games were broadcast on the same L.A. network that had televised the Braves, KTLA-TV, Channel 5 and even employed the same announcer, Dick Lane to call the games. The T-Birds filled the same arenas that the Braves had filled and featured some of the same stars, including Julie Patrick, Ralphie Valladares, Jean Porter, Honey Sanchez, George Copeland and Red Smartt.

On January 20, 1961, John F. Kennedy was sworn in as the 35th President of the United States and shortly after that, the Los Angeles Thunderbirds skated their debut game. Los Angeles had the Rams (NFL), the Dodgers (MLB), the Lakers (NBA) and the Thunderbirds (NRL). The 1960s turned out to be a fascinating time to be in Los Angeles. And while the Dodgers were undeniably the darlings of the city with their amazing teams of the early to mid-1960s, the Thunderbirds began to build their loyal following and add to the excitement of the L.A. sports scene.

Chapter 4

Birth of a Rival League

"Roller Derby defers no payments, it rings bells now. It offers one-dimensional action and excitement without baseball's fabricated mythology or that increasingly suspect insistence, in all major sports, on the integrity of the game." – Robert Lipsyte, *New York Times* sports columnist

Rollerskating Championships (which would later be reorganized as National Skating Derby, Inc.) was founded in 1960 by Roller Derby announcer Herb Roberts, along with its flagship team, the Los Angeles Thunderbirds. Thus begins the storied history of Roller Games, the alternative league to Roller Derby, which eventually outlasted the famed Bay Bombers and the NRDL.

Roberts had no previous derby experience, but he had been in and around the scene at the Olympic Auditorium for boxing, wrestling and L.A. Braves Roller Derby matches. He was friends with many skaters and well liked. Some of these skaters had approached Herb about becoming an investor for a potential new league that would be based in Los Angeles and hold contests at the Olympic. Herb liked the idea and ran with it.

The new league was initially called Rollerskating Championships and was a so-called "outlaw outfit" not associated with the original league, Roller Derby. Until this time, the Seltzer family had held a monopoly on the sport of roller derby. The first games were not skated until 1961.

This precursor to the new league had its origins in Paris, France. A lovely city considered by many to be the world's most beautiful and sophisticated metropolitan area. Roberts and independent promoter, Sid Cohen, organized a two-month tour to Europe and Africa with a group of top skaters in the summer of 1960. His venture was called *Roller-Catch*: four weeks in Paris, France, two weeks in Oran, Algeria, and two weeks in Casablanca, Morocco.

On June 12, 1960, the group took off for Paris on Air Israel from LaGuardia in New York. The venue held 12,000 people and weekend attendance was a healthy 4,000/7,000 on average. The skaters were paid well on this tour, most of them making their money from Roller Derby. This tour allowed them to have a great time on and off the track. Fans in Paris were quite vocal in their appreciation for the action on the track.

Things were not as smooth when the skaters arrived in Algeria, as there was an ongoing war between France and Algeria in progress. The Algerians were fighting for independence from French rule.

The war lasted from 1954 to 1962 and led to Algeria gaining its independence from France. The Algerian National Liberation Front led the fighting against the French, and it was a brutal conflict that included guerrilla warfare, the use of torture, and internal fighting in Algeria (civil war) between various communities. There were 300,000 Algerian casualties and over a million Europeans were forced to flee the area. Games were skated under tense circumstances with soldiers armed with machine guns everywhere. Things were escalating, and the situation got very dangerous. A decision was made to not finish the remainder of the scheduled games and move on to Casablanca ahead of schedule. Skaters had several days of free time before the start of scheduled games. When the games commenced, the turnout was disappointing with only about 2,000 fans showing up per game in a 5,000-seat arena. Following the tension in Algeria and the low turnout in Morocco, skaters were anxious to return to the United States. But this unique adventure with its highs and lows had bonded many of the skaters. This bond was instrumental in forming the nucleus of skaters that followed Herb Roberts to the eventual beginning of what would become "Roller Games" with that first game in El Monte in 1961.

The home team representing Paris was called the *Diables Bleus* (French for Blue Devils) and included Coach Lewis "Punky" Gardner, Ralph Valladares, Bill Gatchell, Pat Murillo, John Hall, Ernie Lopez, and Stan Manti on the men's squad, with a women's team made up of Captain Terri Lynch, Toni Tagg, Marge Forrest, Sylvia Viramontes, Sheila McKenna, Peggy Stapleton, and Honey Sanchez.

The visiting team, *the Rangers*, included Coach Dave Pound, Chick Chakota, George Knerr, Vinnie Gandolfo, Jim Ott, Richard Seitz, and Gil Mora on the men's squad, with Captain Shirley Hardman, Liz Hernandez, Toni Gandara, Darlene Dunaway, Gail Fund, and Mary "Apache" Vasquez on the women's squad. All of these skaters who went on the trip were part of the new beginning in El Monte, except Gail Fund, who went back to Roller Derby.

Herb was well liked by the skaters of Roller Derby. He held the lease for the parking lot at the Olympic Auditorium where the

Los Angeles Braves had skated some of their games. Herb financed this venture himself. He had assistance and support from local L.A. television station KTLA and veteran announcer Dick Lane. John Hall, along with referee Al Costa and a construction friend, Steve White, built the first banked track of the new league. Most of the materials were from George Copeland's father's lumber company.

At the initial inception of this new league, there was no formal training center. The skaters were all still in top shape from recent competitions held in Paris, France and Casablanca for eight weeks. In Paris, this outlaw league skated seven days a week with two doubleheaders on Sundays. 16 games in 14 days! In Casablanca, there were four games each week for three weeks. After returning to the USA, this same group of outlaw skaters had four weeks of skating in Philadelphia, PA, Washington, DC, and Johnston, PA.

Dick Lane and Herb Roberts had worked out a deal with the Maywood Bell Ford car company to become their major TV sponsor. In the agreement it was stated that the home team be named after the popular new car from Ford Motor Company, the Thunderbird. The advertising firm that had the Maywood Bell account was Griffiths, Lilly, and Hill out of Hollywood. Jerry Hill and Bill Griffiths (the remaining partners in the firm) began associating with the skaters, considering they had a major interest in the TV deal. So, with a TV deal from KTLA and a sponsor from a local Ford dealership, the T-Birds came right out of the gate in 1961.

Starting Line

Chapter 5
The Golden Age of
Roller Games

"For almost four decades, roller derby was America's biggest indoor sport, a mid-century American staple of mobile mayhem that rewarded its participants with bruised cheeks, cracked ribs and international travel." – Los Angeles Times, 1999

With Jerry Hill and Bill Griffiths having purchased Herb Roberts' RollerSkating Championships and renaming it the National Skating Derby (dba Roller Games), the new league debuted at the Olympic Auditorium in January 1962.

Running the show was Jerry Hill and Bill Griffiths. They were a dynamic duo. Hill had experience working for the Ice Follies, the Western Hockey League, the Pan Pacific, and Olympic Auditorium in various capacities. He became very close to many of the skaters and was well liked. Griffiths, a Canadian and former child actor in vaudeville, was respected as an astute businessman. Right behind Hill and Griffiths was Dee Maresca, who was an exceptionally bright New York native. She was a nurse, which was why she was in the infield at games. She was deeply into management and was part of the upper level in decision making. Two more key insiders were Bill Haupt and Dick Lane, both of whom will be covered in an upcoming chapter on television. Another key figure during this early period was a gifted young skater named John Hall, who was heavily involved in Roller Games both on and off the track. John was one of the first African-American skaters in the league. He managed many of the duties that some of the top veteran skaters preferred not to handle such as tourist visas, transportation, and other business details. His training as a military policeman and experience traveling abroad on the "Roller-Catch" European tour made him even more valuable on overseas trips. He was also an expert in track construction from his duties with Roller Derby in New York City. John's responsibilities with the organization continued to grow in the years to come. Bonnie Nelson was another skater who, like John, was also part of the group of insiders. She often went on pre-event road trips to help set up interviews, do press releases, and other promo work. Additionally, she also wrote articles for the *Derby News* and other newspapers for publication before events.

Television announcer, Dick Lane frequently referred to the teams as the "National Roller League" and that term was used a lot in the weekly publicity newsletter, the *Roller Games Gazette*. It was sold at every game and delivered by mail. It provided fans with the most recent news, along with lineups, skater profiles, and promo for upcoming games. National Skating Derby (NSD) was renamed National Roller League (NRL) shortly after formation, because Jerry Seltzer, who held the trademark for Roller Derby, filed a legal complaint claiming copyright infringement on the trademark "Roller Derby." There was never an actual lawsuit filed and the matter was dropped once the term "derby" was removed from the official name. Both leagues carved out their own (relatively) separate territories that allowed them each to profit while rarely stepping on the toes of the other. Roller Games was the official title that was used to promote this new league and its games. There was instant success thanks to Dick Lane on KTLA, the leadership of Hill and Griffiths, and the talented group of skaters they had assembled.

Americans loved to roller skate! Young kids and teens were still roller skating in large numbers in the 1960s as smooth pavement was prevalent in cities and their adjoining suburbs. With the road building boom of the 1950s, fresh concrete was in abundance. The popularity of roller skating crossed into every sector of society. Almost everyone skated: both children and adults, regardless of color, nationality or religion. You could skate indoors or outdoors. Roller rinks were booming. Derby was the biggest sport on eight wheels; nothing else compared. When the T-Birds arrived in Los Angeles, it became even more fashionable to be a skater.

By the end of 1962, it was apparent that the Thunderbirds weren't just another typical outlaw unit destined to fail. And while at this early juncture they were still considered "second-tier" in the roller derby world, they had quickly become trendy in Southern California. With each successive year, the league grew its fan base. By the mid '60s, the Thunderbirds had established themselves as one of the most popular and well-known teams in the sport of banked track skating (roller derby) history. The best was yet to come as the partnership of Griffith and Hill ('62-'72) yielded the most successful and exciting years for the T-Birds, culminating in explosive growth during the last five years of their partnership.

No one knew it at the time, but during the Griffiths and Hill partnership, Roller Games and the T-Birds would be responsible for establishing the sport not only in multiple markets across the United

States, but around the world. The National Roller Derby League had captivated the nation during the 1950s, but it was the popularity of the T-Birds that created an audience around the globe for the sport. Even the triumphant resurgence of the original Derby league in the 1960s under Jerry Seltzer's leadership could not claim to have created legions of fans outside the United States. Only the T-Birds and Roller Games did.

This 1960's and early 1970's period, in which the Bay Bombers and L.A. T-Birds were kings of their respective leagues, was the zenith of roller derby's success throughout its history. The number of people that attended or tuned into derby games in this period exceeded even that of the 1950s.

And although the 1950s has been referred to as "The Golden Age of Roller Derby," looking back 60 years later, some might conclude that the Golden Age ran from the early 1950s through the early 1970s. Historians may debate this point for generations, but one thing is clear: The period of true "classic" banked track roller derby was led initially by the N.Y. Chiefs in the 1950s, followed by the L.A. Thunderbirds in Southern California and the S.F. Bay Bombers in Northern California, in the 1960s and 1970s.

Each of the teams above has a compelling history. None of them have survived to the present day. Much has been written about the Chiefs and Bay Bombers (both National Roller Derby League teams), but very little has been documented about the Thunderbirds. The two leagues have had a long-running feud among fans, which continues today, long after both organizations ceased to operate. Many fans of the original Derby dismiss any accomplishments achieved by the T-Birds and Roller Games as if it diminishes the original league. But this is nothing new; the T-Birds and Roller Games have been rebels since skaters jumped ship to create "another outfit," a credible alternative league, providing more regular employment and opportunity for skaters who at the time had only one option – a monopoly.

Do you love it when an underdog succeeds? If so, in this book, you'll experience how an outlaw league overcame all odds and became roller derby's most famous team!

Chapter 6

KTLA

*"Whenever and wherever the Derby is scheduled, it invariably
out rates the opposition on the other channels at that time.
It beats all its competition in about eighty percent of the
cities where it is shown. When measured against such
'respectable' sports as hockey, golf, bowling, skiing, track,
and baseball, the Derby always has higher ratings. It duels
basketball and football evenly. Every week at least three
million persons in the United States see a Derby game
on television."* – Frank DeFord, 1969

Historically, roller derby was reliant on television to promote the sport to the masses. In the late 1940s and throughout the 1950s, the kinescope method was used to preserve and rebroadcast roller derby matches. But in 1960, at the birth of Roller Games, videotape had just been perfected. This process was far superior to kinescope and brought more clarity and detail to fans witnessing the chaotic action of roller derby on television. All televised sports benefitted from this change, but maybe none more than roller derby, which was typically taped and shown at a pre-determined time slot rather than live. Videotape led the way to an unprecedented period of enormous growth for roller derby.

KTLA-VHF Channel 5 was the flagship station from the very beginning for the fledgling Thunderbirds. In 1947, KTLA was the first station to be issued a commercial broadcasting license in California; the eighth station granted one in the United States. KTLA has carried the annual Tournament of Roses Parade from Pasadena each New Year's Day since 1948. From 1964 to 1995, KTLA served as the broadcast television home of the California Angels baseball team. The station was also the home of the Los Angeles Dodgers and Los Angeles Kings. Channel 5 broadcasted as far north as Fresno and south past Tijuana, Mexico. In the 1960s, merely seven TV channels were transmitting to the Los Angeles area. To be featured on any one of those channels meant a guaranteed audience. To be carried by KTLA, the top local provider, was indeed a bonanza (pun intended; *Bonanza* was aired on the station for many years). Roller Games initially was telecast on Tuesday evenings on prime time from 8 p.m. to 10 p.m. It was the highest-rated TV show in that slot for many years. Dick Lane was the primary announcer and did the play-by-play (jam-by-jam). He was joined by color commentator and veteran broadcast journalist, Bill "Hoppy" Haupt. Bill was a SAG member under contract with Griffiths, Lilly, and Hill Advertising. Lane conducted most of the halftime interviews, but Hoppy did quite a few and more in later years. He frequently got in-between rival skaters during halftime interviews, and it often appeared he was taking his life into his hands. Hoppy was Dick Lane's loyal sidekick in the broadcast booth, where his cheap toupees were the brunt of jokes for skaters on and off camera as well as fans. But his impact on Roller Games went far beyond his television role. He was a key producer and director for Roller Games and worked tirelessly behind the scenes and wore many toupees (hats), including being responsible for most of the content in the weekly *Gazette* and programs, the sport's biggest marketing tools. His efforts were rarely adequately acknowledged, but helped keep TV ratings high in the very competitive Los Angeles market. Hoppy was with Roller Games from 1962 to 1981. Both Lane and Hoppy were extremely popular and contributed to the high ratings.

Not only were T-Bird games broadcast at prime time by KTLA in Los Angeles, but they were also shown in many other regions of the United States. In the second half of the 1960s, when Roller Games expanded internationally, games were shown in Australia, Japan, Canada, Mexico, and Puerto Rico.

In the latter part of the 1960s, KTLA requested that Roller Games switch from Tuesday nights to Sunday nights, at prime time, from 8 p.m. to 10 p.m. The station needed a rating booster for this vital prime time slot. Roller Games made the change, which helped both the station's ratings and the popularity of the Roller Games telecast. Sunday night prime time was the most sought after and viewed time slot of the week. This change was one of the factors that helped propel the popularity of the Thunderbirds to its eventual zenith in the years between 1968 to 1972. Roller Games then began making game broadcasts available to a national TV syndicate of independent stations. Soon, Roller Games, primarily featuring the Los Angeles T-Birds, appeared on over one hundred television stations around the world.

The most recognizable and beloved TV voice of the T-Birds was Dick Lane, a former actor, who first coined the phrase, "Whoa, Nellie!," before it was used by others, including Keith Jackson. KTLA's Stan Chambers commented, "He was really L.A. television's first big star." Born May 28, 1899 in Rice Lake, Wisconsin, Richard Lane began his showbiz career as a song-and-dance man in Vaudeville

Scott Stephens

before working in film, most notably in Columbia's *Boston Blackie* series of the 1940s. He would appear in more than seventy movies including *Take Me Out to the Ball Game* (1949), *The Jackie Robinson Story* (1950), *Visit to a Small Planet* (1960), *Kansas City Bomber* (1972), and *The Shaggy D.A.* (1976). Lane was one of KTLA's first on-air personalities, which began in 1947. He announced the Hot Rod Derby, professional wrestling and starting in 1951, Roller Derby. He worked for the Los Angeles Thunderbirds and Roller Games from 1961 until 1975, bringing an "Old Hollywood" gravitas to every broadcast, while casually enjoying a cigarette trackside, keeping the game at arm's length while still being fully involved. In the book, *The Box: An Oral History of Television, 1920-1961*, author Jeff Kisseloff stated, "Who cared if ninety-percent of the country never heard of Dick Lane; the people of Los Angeles had, and they loved him." Lane died on September 5, 1982, in Newport Beach, California, posthumously elected to both the Wrestling Observer Newsletter HOF and the National Roller Derby Hall of Fame.

Legendary skating star, Elmer Anderson (later the TV voice of the Philadelphia Warriors), was also a frequent guest announcer. Herb Roberts, the league's founder, was the first and chief trackside announcer for Roller Games from 1962 until the end of 1974.

With the good fortunes of having a powerhouse television station carrying their games in prime time, a syndicate of TV stations broadcasting T-Bird games around the world, first class announcers calling those games while working meticulously to "sell" the product every week, a nearly perfect venue for roller derby (the Olympic), a healthy stock of top-tier skating stars and their savvy GM's Jerry Hill and Bill Griffiths, the Thunderbirds had all the right ingredients for success. Roller Games was averaging 25,000 fans in attendance per week (50 weeks per year) and TV ratings and game attendance was often higher than the NBA Lakers and almost always higher than the NHL Kings. The large television audiences bolstered game attendance since each broadcast was fundamentally a commercial selling the upcoming week of games. Other than the San Francisco Bay Bombers

22

and the New York Chiefs of Roller Derby, no roller derby team before or after the Thunderbirds ever came close to those numbers.

In the 1960s, Roller Games would usually videotape full games of eight periods, but the first half might be broadcast one week and the second half the next. By the early 1970s, just the second half of games were taped for broadcast. A one-hour TV show seemed to work best for the networks and hold audiences better than a full-game, two-hour broadcast. Whether it was one hour or two, Roller Games was always able to perfectly tailor the broadcast to one thing - making sure to promote the upcoming week of games and match races, making sure fans were more than anxious to cheer on their favorite T-Bird skaters and see them battle whatever Roller Games skater was trying to destroy the skater or team that week.

Later, the flagship station for the T-Birds changed from KTLA (5) to KCOP (13). KCOP was also a powerful VHF station and the high ratings of Roller Games carried over to Channel 13.

Another primary VHF station, KHJ Channel 9, became the flagship station for the Thunderbirds during their rebirth period in the late 1970s. The TV show was called *Roller Superstars*. Initially, during the comeback years, a small UHF station, KBSC-TV, Channel 52, carried the T-Bird games before the contract with KHJ.

During their heyday, the Thunderbirds were broadcast by each of the three largest local L.A. TV stations on channels 5, 13, and 9. During this period, almost everyone knew of or was a fan of the T-Birds.

Chapter 7

18th & Grand

"The Olympic was a hub of violent entertainment for the better part of the 20th Century, and its history reflects the evolution of Los Angeles. Crowds were a mix of celebrity and working class; you could see Joan Jett at the T-Birds matches along with assorted punks, African-Americans and grandmas. Being L.A., a big part of the crowd was Mexican and Mexican American. The crowds came for the reliably cathartic action, be it on skates, in tights, or with gloves on— it was an exciting place to be." – Steve DeBro, director of the Olympic Auditorium Project

By the time the Thunderbirds moved into the Olympic Auditorium in 1962, the old concrete building had already seen better days. Built in 1925, at that time the Olympic was the largest indoor arena in the western United States, and for the better part of the 20th century, was the primary venue in Los Angeles for professional boxing and wrestling. It had a ubiquitous presence on local television, its phone number etched in the minds of most Los Angelino's - RI-9-5171.

A virtual den of iniquity, the Olympic Auditorium was the home of some of sports' darkest moments; it was a place of permissible violence. This "house of pain" saw more blood per square foot than any other L.A. venue. Many athletes were seriously injured there. Bodies were battered, bones were broken, hopes were dashed, and dreams realized.

For roller derby, the Olympic had a capacity of approximately 8,000. In the early years, the average attendance on Saturdays was 5,000 to 6,000 and up to 8,000 plus for significant events such as playoff games or those contests that featured halftime match races. Tuesdays were televised games and the upstairs balcony was closed. The lower level capacity was 4,500 people. The average Tuesday had about 2,000 attendees. Sundays took place downstairs at a discounted "Family Day" price, averaging approximately 3,000.

"The Olympic was totally insane. It had roller derby, it had fights where people would pee in cups and throw it at the boxers. I figure punk rock insanity they wouldn't mind, because they were already insane," said Gary Tovar, a L.A. concert promoter.

While the Olympic was the iconic, official home of the Thunderbirds, the league brought home games to other parts of Southern California, covering a territory stretching south from San Diego, north to Bakersfield.

El Monte Legion Stadium, the site of the debut of Roller Games in 1961, continued to be a regular stop. It had a capacity of 3,000. The T-Birds averaged a draw of about 2,500 and usually sold-out the stadium on Saturday nights. Regular days were Tuesdays (televised), Fridays, occasional Saturdays, and sometimes Sundays. The El Monte banked track was constructed of wood with a Masonite surface. It was brand new and rarely needed maintenance.

The San Bernardino Swing Auditorium was a regular stop on Thursday nights. Its capacity was 4,500 with the team averaging 3,000 to full house. Like the Olympic, the "Swing" was a popular place for the banked track sport. Skater Bob Lewis was responsible for the T-Birds making this such a consistently big-gate venue. Bob's wife, Georgeanna Kemp, one of three siblings who skated in the Derby (Monta Jean and Buddy were the other two), also trained many skaters during the 1960s, a behind-the-scenes dynamo who gave back much to the sport by developing new talent.

The vast outdoor Long Beach Memorial Stadium was a regular stop on Friday nights, with a capacity of 12,000. The average attendance was about half that, increasing to upwards of 9,000 for a significant event. Games were also skated at the smaller Long Beach Convention Hall with its capacity of 4,000. There the team averaged 2,500 to 3,000.

Sporadically, the Thunderbirds appeared at the Santa Monica Civic Auditorium (capacity 5,000), depending on available dates. The average draw there was 3,000 plus and games were typically held on a Friday.

In 1964, Roller Games added more home venues in Southern California, including the Earl Warren Showgrounds in Santa Barbara. Its capacity was 3,000 and the T-Birds drew an average of 2,000 fans on games mostly held Friday nights.

By '64, the Thunderbirds popularity was such that the team hosted games at the home of the L.A. Lakers, the Los Angeles Sports Arena. They often outdrew attendance of the future NBA champs. The Sports Arena could hold up to 15,500 and the T-Birds would typically draw 9,000 or more. Games were customarily held Saturday nights as an occasional alternative to the Olympic.

The T-Birds then headed south to the San Diego Convention Center (capacity of 5,000) in downtown San Diego and averaged 4,000 fans per game. In 1966, the San Diego Sports Arena was built and became the T-Birds home base in San Diego for years to come.

It could hold 15,000 attendees. The team drew large crowds with an average of 11,000 fans, even often reaching capacity.

The Bakersfield Civic Arena became an occasional Monday stop for the T-Birds in late 1963 and beyond. Games were only on Monday nights. Capacity was 6,000 with an average house of 4,800 plus. During this time, the T-Birds often skated five to six contests per week. Ouch!

To recap, the main cities hosting T-Birds home games pre-expansion (1961-1965) were Los Angeles, San Bernardino, El Monte, Long Beach, San Diego, and Santa Barbara.

The latter part of 1964 and much of 1965 saw six Roller Games teams skating every week throughout the year. The only TV game was the T-Birds telecast from the Olympic in Los Angeles. That show was shown in syndication on more than 60 stations in the USA. The show would contain ad spots for local area games, which helped draw fans to Roller Games events.

Chapter 8
Homegrown Stars

Sam Washington and Ronnie Rains of the world champion Los Angeles Thunderbirds apply double blocking pressure to keep opponent from scoring.

"Whereas every town in America has a ballfield, lots of ballfields for baseball and football, whereas in every city, within every few blocks one can always find a 'pick-up game' for basketball and even some, tennis courts and in Canada, fields of ice for hockey to be played, there were no banked tracks

*throughout America where kids, smitten with the game as I
was in Brooklyn, could learn to skate. There were no national
training schools. To skate in Roller Derby, one had to be where
the game was played in order to participate in the training
school. And there were no minor leagues, no place for the kids
to learn the intricacies of the game."* – Alan Ebert, *The History
of Early Roller Derby*

Nearly every city that boasted a successful roller derby home team operation had a training center at the core of its success. For Roller Games, the hallowed ground of future superstars was the Olympic Auditorium, where training sessions were conducted every Saturday with games scheduled for the same evening. Beginners trained in the early afternoon and the advanced class was held later in the afternoon. Very often there was training on the following Sunday morning as well, running from 10 a.m. to noon for beginners and 6-8 p.m. for advanced. On Monday nights from 7-10 p.m. there was an additional advanced class.

The headquarters of the National Skating Derby Training School was the Olympic. It operated from the start of Roller Games in 1961 through its eventual demise in 1974. After that, John Hall and Ralph Valladares hosted training at their roller rink in Pico Rivera from 1976 until it closed in 1985. From 1982 to 1985, training was held at both the Olympic and the Rollerdrome in Pico Rivera depending on the game schedule. After 1985, it was once again only conducted at the Olympic, up until the last training sessions in 1988.

For a one-hour training session, costing one dollar, prospective talent received instruction from well-known professionals at the venerable Olympic Auditorium. Each trainee was issued a photo ID card valid for six months. Every six months, each trainee had to have his or her parents sign a waiver which had to be notarized. The doorman at each session was usually one of Bill Griffiths, Sr.'s sons, Jay or Bill, Jr. On any given weekend morning, young skaters might be instructed by the likes of Terri Lynch, Ralphie Valladares, Danny

Reilly, Charlie "Specs" Saunders, Georgeanna Kemp, George Vogt, or John Hall.

Roller Games was the first roller derby operation to feature a "minor league" program as a means of developing talent for the NSD. It was called the "Jet League" and training was held at the Olympic. Jet Leaguers trained in the advanced classes. The Jet League came about during the winter of '69 - '70 when National Skating Derby created the Florida Jets to skate home games in the "Sunshine State", requiring a need for more well-trained newcomers. Before the start of a regular pro game, two Jet League teams skated a four-period game usually once a week. Pro skaters coached the Jet League teams during the contest. Because of the popularity of the contests, during the early 1970s, Jet League games occurred a few times each week. Teams included the L.A. Dons, Texas Mustangs, New York Bullets, Detroit Little Devils, Chicago Jet Hawks, Renegade Rebels, and Australian Wallabies. If you skated for the Dons and did a good job, you might have ended up on the T-Birds one day. If you did a good job with the Mustangs, you might have been with the Outlaws one day.

As a result of these training sessions, Roller Games developed a long list of talented homegrown skaters. In the early days of Roller Games, every team consisted entirely of skaters trained in the original Roller Derby. With the success of the training school, eventually NSD lineups had nearly an even ration of "Derby" and "Games" trained pros. By the end of the 1960s, skaters trained exclusively in Roller Games became stars of the league as more and more skaters, taught in the original Roller Derby, retired.

It would be nearly impossible to list every skater who started their careers at the Olympic Auditorium training program, but below is a few of those who created a strong foundation for Roller Games; including a couple that were eventually enshrine into the National Roller Derby Hall of Fame. Note: There is an upcoming chapter that names some of the skaters who "graduated" from the training program at the T-Bird Rollerdrome during the rebirth period who are not listed here.

Ana Anaya
Baby Rocco
Barbara Jacobs
Barbara Williams
Bernie Jackson
Betty Brown
Betty Stone
Bill de Phillipi
Bill Fitzgerald
Billy Marshall
Brenda DeShields
Candi Mitchell
Carlos Marquez
Carmen Gomez
Carmen Thompson
Carol Kruse
Carolyn Kruse
Charlie Mitchell
Charlie Saunders Jr.
Dallas Everitt
Danny Reilly
Debbie Douglas
Diane Syverson
Donna Young
Ed Dresser
Eddie Williams
Ernie Lopez
Erwin Miller
Frank Martinez
Gail Bowers
Gail Farrell
Gary Bickford
George Fernandez
Greg Quinn
Greg Robertson

Gwen Miller
Harold Jackson
Jean Welch
Jennifer Marshall
Jennifer Richards
Jerry Reilly
Jim Terrigno
Jim Trotter
John Drew
John Johnson
Johnny Chavez
Juan Molano
Judy Woodard
Kenny Sanders
Larry Hamilton
Larry Lewis (HOF)
Lena McBride
Lenny Silverman
Leon Jackson
Manny Servin
Mark D'Amato
Mary Ann Carr
Mike Adame
Mike Garcia
Mike Gochnaur
Otis Williams
Patti Cavin
Paul Rupert
Rachel Sarabia
Rick West
Rita Stroska
Rosalie Bardwell
Sally Vega
Sandy Young
Sonja Sims

Terri Toldeo   Vicky Steppe
Toni Kadrmas   Yolanda Trevino

Because Roller Games had more squads than "Derby," operating in more markets where the opportunity for work was steadier, there was a greater need for new talent. Trainees could excel in Roller Games in a much shorter period than in the original Derby. For example, Danny Reilly's career, from rookie to Men's Coach of the T-Birds, happened very quickly compared to how it would likely have occurred in Derby.

Besides the Olympic, beginners were often trained at Valley Gardens Arena in North Hollywood. The training sessions at Valley Gardens were held three times a week, on Thursday Nights (6-8 p.m.), Saturday afternoons (2-4 p.m.) and Sundays (2-4 p.m.). The trainers were George Vogt and Charlie "Specs" Saunders. Trainee and fan Jim Winstead remembers:

"A typical beginners' class at Valley Gardens consisted of pacing... LOTS of pacing... blocking techniques... "sit out" drills (i.e. falling onto one's ass and getting back up every time the trainer blew his whistle... Everyone HATED those drills... I couldn't feel my ass for days afterward! LOL)... speed drills...How to go over the rail and survive! And learning the five-stride. In early 1970, the training school at Valley Gardens closed its doors and was moved to the Olympic Auditorium. George Vogt and "Spec" Saunders were no longer our trainers. It was strictly Ralphie or Danny, but mostly Ralphie. The move from the Gardens to the Olympic brought with it some new challenges. The main challenge was the track. The track at the Gardens was a small "training" track with low banks. The track at the Olympic was the professional track used by the T-Birds for the TV game and all the other games. The track was longer and the banks steep. For most of us, we had to learn how to skate on the banked track all over again! LOL... Ralphie's classes (like "Specs" and Vogt's classes) were centered around the basics (i.e. pacing... LOTS of pacing... sometimes for 45 minutes... blocking, etc.). Riley's were more unstructured... Sometimes he'd put on skates and demonstrate how to block... Man could he hit! LOL... How to do a three to five man whip (I went over the rail the first time I got a four man whip!) and how to skate backward and balance on one leg. He also introduced us to the theatrical side of Roller Games, stating that the fans come to see the games to be entertained and it was our jobs as skaters to give the fans a good show and leave them wanting more... When I was promoted to the Advanced Class (May of '71), the classes focused more on working together in pack formations... How to break away from the pack on jams... developing showmanship skills, and participating in mini-games. In these mini-games, sometimes pro skaters would skate with us... That is how I got injured. "Jumping" Charlie Mitchell bounced me over the rail (injuring my collarbone) during one of those games. Other pros would sit trackside and watch us skate, no doubt keeping an eye out for new talent. The Advanced Class skaters also made up the roster for the Jet League games skated on Tuesday nights and Sundays before the regular games. Besides being trained by Ralphie and Danny, the Advanced Class sometimes had a guest trainer. I remember Billy Marshall, Shirley Hardman, John Parker, Terri Lynch, and John Hall to name a few."

In the early days, there was training at the Swing Auditorium in San Bernardino. It was conducted by Georgeanna Kemp, who skated in the late 1940s until the mid 1960s. She skated with Roller Games in the early 1960s with the Outlaws, Bobcats and Falcons, as late as 1963. She was one of three siblings who skated on the banked track. She married a star skater, Bob Lewis. Bob operated the Swing Auditorium for all events including Roller Games on regular Thursdays. For a while, there was midweek training in Burbank at the Valley Gardens Arena. Roller Games also held some games there. Both Australia and Japan had training centers run by Ralph Valladares. Peter Kelly helped develop many of the skaters in Australia in the early 1970s, not only for the traveling Kangaroos, an All-Star team of the best skaters from "Down Under," but most of the talent on all the rosters in the Australian Roller Games league, which operated in the 1970s. In 1974, John Hall conducted a training program in Chicago when the Thunderbirds had a team based there. Philadelphia had a training program at the Philadelphia Arena run by Buddy Atkinson, Jr. and his wife, Dru Scott.

But for all the years of training, at this time only two homegrown Roller Games skaters have ever been inducted into the Roller Derby Hall of Fame: Larry Lewis and Ronnie Rains.

Larry Lewis started his career in 1965 at the age of 14, with the Hawaiian Warriors skating under coach Dave Pound. If you've ever seen Larry skate, you know that he possesses natural talent and grace beyond any other Roller Games skaters and perhaps in the history of roller derby. Not many started their careers at this age, but Larry's talent made this possible. Larry signed his first pro contract on October 12, 1965, with Detroit, that fateful night when John Hall broke his neck. At the end of June 1966, he quit the Devils mid-game and joined the T-Birds, where he spent four memorable years from 1966 through to 1969. Then at the end of '69, he went off to Florida to be the premier jamming star of the Jets. After this, he became a villainous red-shirt skater for numerous NSD teams. He continued skating into the new millennium and despite his 50 plus years of age, was still one of the best skaters on the track. I was privileged to skate for and against Larry. He was the coach of the 1978 Detroit Devils when I was called up to skate my first game as a rookie. I floundered all over the track and obviously wasn't ready for prime time. In '78 there was no Jet League, so rookies had to jump right into "The Bigs." I must have tripped over my skates three or four times, but Larry never expressed any anger or frustration with me. I feel certain John Hall, Ralph Valladares, and Mr. Griffiths were not happy as I fouled up jams and other actions. But Larry encouraged me to keep training and assured me I'd feel much more comfortable in future contests. This was his nature, and I was fortunate he was my coach on this first day in action. Two years later, I skated with Larry again, but this time as an opposing skater with the T-Birds. I recall going out on a couple of jams with him and being taken down with a solid legal block, perfectly-timed, making it easy to absorb. Larry never tried to injure or embarrass other skaters. He skated fast and hit hard, but always worked within the ability of the opposing jammer, whether that was a rookie or future Hall of Famer.

"On Friday night, May 28, 1965, in Bakersfield, California, Coach Dave Pound of the Hawaiian Warriors learned that three of his men hadn't arrived for a game. Pound discussed the situation with his new Women's Captain, Judy Arnold, then asked the fourteen-year-old skate boy, Larry Lewis, to skate for Hawaii that night. Despite concerns from Red Smartt, the T-Birds' General Manager, who thought it too dangerous for the 'kid' to be out there with the pros, Larry Lewis skated his first game wearing Eddie Payne's skates. Larry and the Warriors may have lost the game to the T-Birds that night, 77-71, but Lewis scored his first points and would never forget to take his skates with him again, no matter where he was. Now, almost fifty years later, Larry Lewis joins Pound, Arnold, and Smartt in Roller Derby's illustrious Hall of Fame. Born January 16, 1951, Larry Lewis was raised by his godmother, Billie Christian, in Los Angeles where he spent his youth on wheels, religiously roller skating at a rink or in the neighborhood. On Tuesday night at his best friend Lloyd's house, Larry was captivated by a program Lloyd's Aunt Eloise was watching on TV: The Roller Games. The following Saturday night, the three of them were sitting in the first row of the balcony at the Olympic Auditorium where the L.A. T-Birds hosted the Detroit Devils with Darlene Anderson and Ruberta Mitchell battling each other. All Larry could think about was how to get onto the track. He heard an announcement about a training school and the next day, he and Lloyd showed up at the Olympic ready to train. After getting signed releases, Larry began training, soon becoming a favorite of T-Bird Women's Captain, Terri Lynch, his mentor and primary trainer. Almost overnight, Lewis became the new skate boy when Manny Servin became a full-time skater. Larry was in junior high school during the day, then on the infield every night working the T-Birds' game, putting on a jersey every time an extra skater was needed. Larry's favorite skaters were Dave Pound and Judy Arnold, but with Joe Foster's San Francisco Shamrocks, he'd make a strong impression on the T-Birds. Although Larry would fill in with every team that came to town, including the IRDL Northwest Cardinals, Larry signed his first professional contract with the Detroit Devils, on October 12, 1965, when Coach John Hall was rushed to the hospital with a broken neck following a freak accident. At the end of June '66, in a classic Games' scenario, Larry quit the Devils mid-game, tearing off his jersey and joining the hometown T-Birds, then scoring the winning points over his former teammates. He'd spend the next three years wearing jersey #5 with partner Judy Sowinski for the T-Birds. Larry made his first East Coast appearance in Philly with the Chicago Hawks (May 1968) alongside Sowinski and Midge Brasuhn, the legendary Toughie's final series. When Sowinski departed the T-Birds to become Women's Captain of the New York Bombers, announcer Dick Lane famously called him "Lonesome Larry Lewis." He'd return to Philly a year later, skating with the "traveling" T-Birds. Larry, still a teenager but now a veteran speedster, traveled to the Sunshine State in 1970 when the Florida Jets were created, becoming Coach John Parker's primary offensive weapon. When the Jets disbanded six months later, Larry was again back with the Devils, this time as the league-leading scorer, then jumping between the Texas Outlaws and New York Bombers, eventually coaching both teams. Lewis could do it all, using his lightning-fast speed with bursts of precise blocking, to knock opponents off their skates. Larry would instinctively do whatever was required to sell the game, series or match race. When the ISC was created in '74, Larry found himself on the New York Chiefs, a team comprised of former skaters from the recently-disbanded IRDL. Jamming with Mike Gammon, Derby's legendary scoring superstar, fans witnessed, on one team, two of the fastest, savviest performers in the history of the game. Both men respected and admired each other's abilities, relishing the opportunity to work together, while pushing each other to even greater heights. In 1975, Larry was the only skater from National to skate with the "Roller Stars" league, a short-lived, legit version of Derby. He'd skate with Roller Games on both the East and West Coasts during the late '70s, then was asked to skate for Alfonso Reyes' Jolters during the '81 IRSL playoffs. The following season, Larry had his own IRSL team, the Northeast Braves with two other Games stars, Diane Syverson and B.J. Peterson, showing off his amazing speed and talent. San Francisco Bay Bombers' coach Bill Groll jumped at the chance to add Larry to his roster; Lewis responded by dazzling IRSL fans from coast to coast, winning MVP honors and a scoring title, thrilling everyone. After the IRSL ended in '87, Larry would skate with various West Coast teams. He even trained actors to skate on the stage in New York City during *Roller Derby: The Musical*. Those who saw the show wondered how the producers had found skaters who could act, rather it was the other way around, such was Larry's expert training of the actors. Off the track, Lewis worked for the IRS for many years, retiring on Nov. 9, 2009, and yep, Larry Lewis still makes sure to have his skates with him wherever he goes… 'cause you never know. On the banked track, Larry Lewis has been impressing teammates and fans for years with his lightning-fast speed and his genuine humility, and now finally, he takes his place in the Roller Derby Hall of Fame, as one of the greatest skaters of all time, epitomizing the best of the banked track sport."

– Excerpt from Larry Lewis' 2012 Hall of Fame induction biography by Gary Powers

Ronnie Rains started skating pro in 1963 with the New York Bombers of the National Skating Derby (Roller Games), a team that he would be associated with on and off for many years. He excelled in the role of red-shirt desperado, but also spent many years skating "white" for the Los Angeles Thunderbirds. Rains spent the prime of his career with Roller Games, although in later years he skated intermittently in various other leagues.

Ronnie was not only a phenomenally talented banked track performer, he was also an intelligent skater. Rains earned his "red shirt stripes" by exhibiting an on-track persona, which was often described as "mean" and "nasty". He was roller derby's version of NFL intimidators, Conrad Dobler or Bill Romanowski. Like these two, Rains was often feared by opponents for good reason. Anyone who ever skated against red shirt Ronnie understands why he was nicknamed "Psycho." Nearly forty years after receiving it, I still have a discernible scar, courtesy of "Pyscho" Ronnie Rains. Although he was a remarkable skater, he could be unpredictable, able to strike havoc at any time, whether on the jam, blocking, or even in the pack where few could witness his mayhem. If Rains didn't like or respect an opponent, or didn't feel the skater was putting the game before individual glory, that skater was in danger of being seriously injured. But when he admired an opposing skater, he worked with them masterfully to make sure both he and his opponent performed to the fullest of their abilities, giving fans countless memories. Ronnie Rains was truly one of the most unique and exciting characters in the history of the sport. His antics were what fans remembered, but everyone on the track knew he was the best skater out there.

"Born January 4, 1944, in Los Angeles, California, Ronnie Rains was a flat-track speedster (seven national flat-track titles), discovered by Hall-of-Famer Charlie "Specs" Saunders and legendary skating star, Lou Sanchez. Both immediately recognized Ronnie was destined for greatness. Bypassing the training school, one of a few skaters ever to do so, Ronnie skated his first game in 1963 with the New York Bombers, and then was signed by the L.A. Thunderbirds in January, '64. Rains perfected his skills in the sport with the T-Birds, then because of his fearless skating style, became a fan-favorite with the Australian Thunderbirds for the next three years. While in Australia, he married blonde Colleen Murrell, the biggest female skating star "Down Under." Ronnie was back with the L.A. T-Birds wearing jersey number one in 1968, no longer a new kid, but a veteran star. Within a few months, he was skating "red" for Jim Trotter's Texas Outlaws, exhibiting an unpredictability and rough style never before seen, almost as if he was destined to skate red. Stunning the league with his brilliant style of skating, Rains was awarded National's MVP trophy in 1968. Management immediately named him Coach of the New York Bombers. He immediately named Judy Sowinski Women's Captain and the two former T-Bird stars quickly became Roller Games' most electrifying "red shirt" duo. Ronnie's bizarre antics on the track earned him the nickname "Psycho," but his showmanship was solidly-based upon his brilliant skating style. No one could sell a game, match race or series better than Rains. His talent in knowing exactly what to do, combined with his legendary athleticism, made him National's premier skating star during the 1970s. Dramatically, he would return to the T-Birds again in 1973, from villain to hero overnight, soon becoming the T-Birds' new coach, a startling turn of events, as he wore T-Bird red-white-and-blue, making former distractors his most loyal fans. Rains continued skating on and off over the next seventeen years, never losing the spark and showmanship which continually thrilled fans. He became a NRD Hall of Fame inductee in 2006. These days, Rains is a husband, father and grandfather, but still remembered as one of the most electrifying performers in the history of the sport." – Ronnie Rains 2006 Hall of Fame induction biography by Gary Powers.

Chapter 9

Bird Watchers

"Roller Derby rooters react more personally to their sport. They are involved with it, not students of it. There is a minimum of interest in standings, records, and other cold statistical formalities that are so important to other modern sports." –
Frank DeFord, *Sports Illustrated*

The Los Angeles Thunderbirds had a vast legion of followers in Southern California, who either tuned-in to KTLA game broadcasts or attended the live action at the Olympic Auditorium (and other venues), or both. The Olympic wasn't situated in one of L.A.'s best areas, but die-hard fans packed the old sports arena two or three nights a week. Fans came from all parts of Los Angeles County, but the majority of them were minorities from the inner city. Compared to more conventional sports, a higher percentage of these fans were women.

In a town symbolized as home to the most popular of celebrities in the world, with its movie and television industry, the Olympic Auditorium was the place to be when the Thunderbirds were skating, even for some of those famous celebrities. The original Roller Derby had attracted many celebrities during its initial engagements in Los Angeles, but having Dick Lane, an established figure in Old Hollywood announcing the games every week on TV was a huge stamp of approval. This allowed many in the entertainment industry to head to the Olympic, paying no mind to its location.

Legendary singer, Ray Charles was a big fan of one of the game's first African-American superstars, George Copeland. A lifelong friendship developed. Charles attended T-Birds games at the Olympic starting in 1962, and the two spent time at each other's homes over the years. Ray Charles' wife and son also became T-Bird fans. Copeland attended Ray's funeral in 2004.

Another Olympic regular was Puerto Rican singer and songwriter Jose Feliciano (*Light My Fire* and the best-selling Christmas single, *Feliz Navidad*), who attended many games during the 1960s as a fan and friend of Ralph Valladares. British singing superstar Dusty Springfield (*Son of a Preacher Man*) was often seen at the Olympic and had a close personal relationship with the T-Birds' Julie Patrick. Other musical stars who found their way to the Olympic included Elton John, Lionel Richie, Johnny Otis, and the Fifth Dimension, plus countless others.

Naturally, because it was Hollywood, many actors would be seen trackside at the Olympic, including Norm Alden, who would later play a skater, Horrible Hank, in MGM's 1972 big-budget film, *Kansas City Bomber*, starring Raquel Welch and Kevin McCarthy, supported by a cast of Roller Games' most well-known skating stars. Norm was trained by John Hall to portray a skater in the movie. An actual T-Bird veteran skater, Tom Crews, was brought to Portland to double for Alden's skating in KCB, but Norm was so proficient on the banked track, Crews was not needed. Another TV star, Judy Norton Taylor of *The Waltons*, was often seen at Thunderbird games, as well as Willie Ames of *Eight is Enough*. American songwriter and singer Joan Jett was a huge Thunderbirds fan and often attended games. Other notable names who attended T-Birds games included Farrah Fawcett, Lee Majors, Jackie Chan, Ricardo Montalban, Sarah Purcell, Heather Thomas, and Antonio Fargas, among many others.

The Thunderbirds, decked out in their patriotic red, white and blue uniforms, were the embodiment of everything decent, fair, and just. They seemed brave and courageous and were often heroic in battle. In the United States and much of the world, those characteristics were usually depicted in the media by white males. This often included Presidents and high-level political figures, CEO's, movie stars, and others in high society. And despite being from the Middle East, even Jesus was typically portrayed as white.

Up until the 1960s, with the exception of Roller Derby's Midge "Toughie" Brasuhn and Gerry Murray, nearly all other national sports heroes were white and male. This started to change in the 1960s, but it was still a world dominated by white males. Los Angeles led the way in celebrating non-white athletes with their support for the T-Birds. L.A. was a melting pot of cultures and ethnicities with blacks and Hispanics being the predominant minority populations. The Thunderbirds represented these cultures better than any sports team in the City of Angels. The team's biggest star was an immigrant from Guatemala, Ralphie Valladares. Other Hispanic stars of Roller Games included Leroy Gonzales, Lou Sanchez, Honey Sanchez, Liz Hernandez, Ernie Lopez, Bertha Ruiz, Carmen Gomez, Lydia and Johnny Rodriguez, Dee Guerrero, Tino Galindo, Sylvia Viramontes, Toni Gandara, Sally Vega, Ana Anaya, Henry Sahagun, and George

Fernandez. One of the Thunderbirds' first mega-stars was black, George Copeland. John Hall, a black man, would become General Manager of the T-Birds and a well-known spokesperson for Roller Games. Other African American stars of the 1960s included Richard Brown, Larry Lewis, Carmen "Sugar" Thompson, Darlene Anderson (first black female team captain and a Hall of Fame member), Ruberta Mitchell, Fletcher Sanders, Jim Trotter, Lester Quarles, and Barbara Williams. Moving into the '70s, more African-American stars arrived on the scene, including Greg Robertson, Sam Washington, Billy Marshall, "Big John" Johnson, Olympic medalist Earlene "747" Brown, Eddie Williams (American Indian and black), Jennifer Marshall, Greg Quinn, brothers Leon, Burnett, and Harold Jackson, along with Hall of Famer Ronnie Robinson (son of legendary boxer "Sugar Ray"), a star in the original Derby who skated with the T-Birds in 1974. The team was loaded with Hispanic and black talent on both the male and female squads.

During the late 1960s and 1970s, Derby's last decade, the top jamming stars in the IRDL were Mike Gammon, Judi McGuire, Tony Roman, Carol Meyer, Larry Smith, and Francine Cochu; all white skaters. On the West Coast, Roller Games' premier scoring star, Ralph Valladares, a Hispanic man, began developing National's top jamming stars, black and Hispanic: Richard Brown, Carmen Thompson, Larry Lewis, Gwen Miller, Greg Robertson, Juan Molano, and George Fernandez. Even though the top stars were based upon talent and expertise, it's clear that in many ways, the IRDL was playing to Middle America while the NSD was playing to inner cities.

The Dodgers of Major League Baseball were known for breaking the color barrier with Jackie Robinson (in Brooklyn) and featured African-American stars like Maury Wills, Willie Davis, and Tommy Davis. The Lakers of the National Basketball Association featured future Hall of Famer, Elgin Baylor. But tickets to see these players in action at Dodger Stadium or the Los Angeles Sports Arena were more than double what it cost to witness the Thunderbirds at the Olympic, plus neither of those teams featured a single female athlete. Half of the T-Birds team consisted of females, and the ladies received equal airtime, equal billing, and equal pay! All of these attributes were traditional aspects, not only of the T-Birds, but the sport of roller derby in general.

One of the skaters who had the most personal impact on fans, because of her talent and personality, was Gwen "Skinny Minnie" Miller. By the time Gwen came along in 1970, the walls of the color barrier in sports had all been demolished, but fans connected with her in a way that was unprecedented. Gwen was diminutive; five-foot-four and ninety-eight pounds and immediately called "Skinny Minnie." Legendary Roller Games announcer Elmer Anderson often said, "Out on the jam is Skinny Minnie, Gwen Miller. She's so thin, she looks like she's advertising for a famine!" Gwen was born on September 12, 1951, and raised in the Pacoima neighborhood of Los Angeles, which at the time was known more for gangs and crime than anything else. The town has long had a large minority population. In the 1950s and 1960s it was mostly populated by African Americans, although by the 1970s its population had shifted to a majority of Hispanics. She was an immediate favorite with fans because her size was an asset, not a hindrance.

Gwen was a fast and intelligent skater. Her personality and charisma shined through with every appearance, even on a T-Bird women's team heavy with veteran talent. And it was clear her "star quality" could be utilized throughout the league. In 1972, she became the premier scoring star of the newly-former Cleveland Bucks, then added her expertise to one team after another including the Baltimore-Washington Cats (after the Bucks folded), finally landing on Team Canada where she thrilled fans north of the border. By the time she was skating again with the T-Birds in the mid '70s, she was one of the biggest names in the game and continued to give back to the sport over the next three decades. When she returned home to Los Angeles and the T-Birds, the area of Pacoima was facing a crime epidemic. But due to civic involvement in what the *Los Angeles Times* described as an "unprecedented wave of activism," the city countered the crime surge. During this time, Gwen may have been the most well known and loved citizen of Pacoima due mostly to her celebrity stature with the T-Birds, but also due to the example she set for others in the community. She stayed clear of crime, gangs, and drugs as she focused on achieving goals both on and off the track. Regrettably, Gwen passed away before this book was completed. She died May 9, 2018.

In the 1970s, Roller Games continued its tradition of not only hiring minority skater, but often placing them in leadership roles. John Hall and Ralphie Valladares eventually became minority owners of the league. Not necessarily a pun but the word "minority" takes on two meanings in the last sentence.

From a socio-economic standpoint, the Los Angeles Thunderbirds uniquely represented inner-city minorities. Anyone who ever attended a Roller Game at the Olympic can attest to the deep connection these fans felt for their heroes. It was perceptible, tangible, and palpable. For these city folks, the T-Birds were "the real deal." Even a relatively inexpensive ticket to witness a T-Bird game was a significant outlay for those on limited, fixed incomes. Many who frequented the Olympic were elderly. For many of these folks, a night out at the Olympic may have been their only source of affordable entertainment, other than their home TV screens. But for most, it was more than a night out. The performers on the track were much like them. They weren't wealthy and most had no college education. They performed in a dingy old building and also came from the inner cities. This connection to inner city minorities was apparent not only in L.A. but in every big city they visited. Of course, fans of the Thunderbirds were not limited to minorities. Another demographic who followed the team, both in Southern California or wherever they ventured, were blue collar workers. Long before Roller Games, this class of society followed roller derby from the very start.

In the culture of professional sports, homosexuals are the one segment of society who have never been fully accepted even to the present day (with a few notable exceptions). Only a few brave souls have risked the backlash associated with "coming out." By the 1960s, openly gay athletes in sports were unheard of. Roller Derby had a large percentage of gay men and lesbians within their ranks. Off the track, Roller Games skaters were often open about their sexuality and were rarely subjected to intolerance from fellow skaters within the Derby family. On the track, in front of fans, sexuality was never discussed unless someone was straight. If an announcer knew a skater was gay, male or female, they were often said to be dating an opposite-sex skater or simply categorized as "never married". Even in the locker room among heterosexual skaters, dressing and undressing, gay skaters felt the freedom to express themselves openly without fear of retaliation. Over-the-top personalities and the light-hearted good humor of certain individuals, usually gay skaters in my experience, added an upbeat, jovial ambiance to the locker room. During the era I participated in Roller Games, the most colorful and interesting characters, on and off the track, were usually gay. In their lives, they had learned to handle discrimination with humor. Most could have made a living doing stand-up comedy and they certainly kept those in the locker rooms rolling with laughter.

Conversely, T-Birds contests attracted gay fans in much higher percentages than other L.A. sports teams, and although this could be said for roller derby in general, it was more apparent in progressive-minded Los Angeles, the home of Hollywood, as well as the glam rock culture. Roller Games attracted a large gay audience since, without knowing it, those in the gay community were seeing role models, something they rarely saw on TV. The role models were never identified, but there was an unspoken bond that homosexuals could see but couldn't articulate. The sport was colorful and theatrical, over-the-top, at times bizarre, and similar to the grand opera with its soap opera storylines; but what always attracted the gay community was the morality play elements. Imagine the idea of a good person, battling society's bigotry and intolerance and being victorious in the end?

Attending a Thunderbirds contest at the Olympic, one could have easily imagined they had stepped into the Democratic National Convention. Every segment of society was represented: women, minorities, immigrants, musicians, artists, white and blue collar workers, rich, poor, every nationality, every religion, gay, straight, suburban white males and even conservative Republicans who loved the "good triumphing over evil" mantra, were espoused by the sport.

Often, when I was participating in a game, my thoughts and attention drifted to the reactions of fans. When I looked into the eyes of a fan and saw their facial expressions, their smiles, scorn, and fear, I gained insight into what they might be feeling inside. There was something extraordinary about the relationship between the fans and their Thunderbird heroes. From my viewpoint, there was no greater bond than that of "Skinny Minnie" Miller and her fans. Nothing compelled me to write this book more than those longing eyes I witnessed casting their hopeful gaze on Gwen, as she sped around the track looking to score points and survive attacks from bigger, meaner opponents out to stop her. I'm not sure Gwen or other skaters understood the impact they were having at the time. Gwen, like other skaters, was doing what she was paid to do: skate and entertain fans, hopefully putting more butts in the seats at future games. Their jobs were not to understand the impact they were having, although many did when their skating days were over. Of course, I should not have been drifting off during a game, but I was genuinely fascinated by all of it.

From its earliest existence, Roller Derby was a morality play. Gwen and the rest of her Thunderbird teammates were always cast as underdogs. Yes, the T-Birds were nearly victorious in every contest, but not until after overcoming enormous obstacles. It seems as if everyone was out to get them, analogous to the real lives of those inner-city Angelenos attending or watching on TV. Good versus evil. From the start of nearly every contest, they were taunted, threatened, disrespected, illegally kicked, punched, and humiliated. Despite the one-sided onslaught, they tried to keep their composure and play by the rules. It often seemed they had no support as even the refs appeared helpless (or blind) to stop these illegal and immoral actions against them. Similar to what fans might have been experiencing in their own lives, with regards to the police, landlords, and other figures of authority.

But the Thunderbirds pushed onward against all odds. They kept getting back up after being knocked down. Amongst the faithful, there was always hope that the T-Birds could have risen to tame those unscrupulous beasts, be they Devils, Bombers, Outlaws or Hawks. By the final period, having seen their heroes beaten and battered throughout the contest, fans were often so emotionally attached to what was occurring on the track, some had to be restrained from instigating violence upon unsuspecting visiting skaters. This was a common occurrence, and it was often more dangerous for red-shirt skaters to be near the audience than to be on the track facing Danny Reilly or "Psycho" Rains. No one knew what might occur when a skater went over the rail and got too close to fans, as well as when teams went to the locker room. At the Olympic, skaters (both home and away) had to walk right through the fans to make their way to the locker room.

Although the occasional fan got so wrapped up in the game and took matters into their own hands, everyone was riveted by the action on the track. Those die-hard fans felt every blow their favorite skaters absorbed. They felt the oppression being heaped upon the well-meaning innocent skaters and they knew the police (the refs) weren't going to do a thing about it. Their hearts were racing, and the anger and anxiety was shown plainly on their faces. By this time, with the crowd so emotionally involved, when things started to turn around, and the T-Birds rebounded, there was a tremendous release of energy and excitement that is hard to describe unless you witnessed a game in person. And it didn't matter if you read between the lines and understood it was part of the show or if you believed it was real; no matter what, you were having the time of your life. Moments one would never forget. It wasn't just a T-Bird victory. It was a triumph of good over evil. It was a demonstration to everyone there that there was always hope. Everyone in the audience was part of a family who had made it through the storm together. Things would be okay. There would always be hope.

Much of this drama occurred at the Olympic Auditorium, which was never a mainstream venue. The Thunderbirds brought a sense of pride and joy to a segment of the population which was not fully represented in many ways. After 1985, when the team no longer performed in downtown Los Angeles, eventually folding completely, many fans were heartbroken since their lives had paralleled their now forgotten T-Bird heroes. With the T-Birds gone, broken dreams, disillusionment, and disappointment followed.

Chapter 10

Showstoppers

"The Derby is most similar to the routine that a good, established comedian depends on. The act includes many popular and familiar bits that are scattered amidst new material and clever ad-libs." – Frank DeFord, *Sports Illustrated*

In 1960's Roller Games, skating still took front and center stage. Roller Games featured a more scripted, theatrical version of roller derby, as compared to the Seltzer operation in the Bay Area, but the "show" portions were well executed and not overdone as compared to later years. The top skaters knew how to "sell the game" to fans; the majority of action was on the track rather than on the infield. Scores were generally low with each team scoring twenty or thirty points, as opposed to games a decade later when each team would score over a hundred points per game. Defense was a big part of the game early on.

As the years rolled on, Roller Games broke from roller derby tradition, and the theatrical side of the events grew in prominence to a level in which they often upstaged the athletic performances on the track. Highly scripted "dramas" were played out, mostly from the infield area in the center of the oval banked track. It was here that former skaters, with no formal performance arts training, became acting stars and often household names. As the stagecraft evolved (or devolved depending on which side of the fence you're on), audiences grew as well. These dramatic interludes filled the gaps between jams so there was rarely an idle moment once the game began. Some of the main characters of derby drama showed considerable depth in their roles while others were one-dimensional. If Academy Awards had been given to Roller Games participants, likely winners might have included Shirley Hardman, Ronnie Rains, Judy Sowinski, and Danny Reilly, with the Golden Globe going the Dave Pound.

When all aspects of a Roller Games presentation were properly executed, it could be argued this version of roller derby was, for some fans more exciting and entertaining compared to any other format of roller derby either before or after Roller Games. Throughout its history and up until the end of the last century, roller derby was a unique combination of sport and entertainment. Thus the term "sports entertainment" has often been used to describe roller derby. From its very earliest days, roller derby included elements of showmanship, including pre-determined winners.

On the track, feuding skaters battled intensely until the score had to be settled via a "match race," a one-on-one battle between two or four skaters, usually five laps, usually "anything goes," sometimes "blocking only". More often than not, the skaters involved were good friends off the track. The fights, good versus evil drama, and skater showmanship increased ticket sales and allowed the sport to prosper at even higher levels. Match races, unlike the more impromptu nature of action on the track during games, were highly-choreographed. The Sunday telecast was one extended advertisement for the week's upcoming match races, which were never televised. Match races were a bonus for fans attending live games during the week. The philosophy of Jerry Seltzer's Roller Derby was to keep the focus on the competition between the two teams. Match races happened during a series, but it was never the focus of television broadcasts. The purpose of the syndicated telecasts was to sell the national tour when Derby would crisscross the nation playing live contests. The color displayed by skaters played into the morality play elements of the contest. Nevertheless, because Seltzer's Derby was considered "worked," his version, like Roller Games, was never considered a legitimate sport by the mainstream press.

Bill Griffiths took a different approach and placed a greater emphasis on the "show." For this, he is often criticized by derby purists. But one has to ponder whether or not this is hypocritical. After all, both leagues had pre-determined winners, heroes, and champions. Both leagues featured and promoted one or two home teams (the T-Birds and Warriors in Roller Games) based in their respective cities, but the opposition teams (and their skaters) were also based in the same town as the home team. Both leagues promoted battles-to-the-death between opposing skaters (Weston vs. Calvello, Hardman vs. Lynch, O'Connell vs. Monte, Valladares vs. Gonzales) when none existed in reality. Each of the two major derby leagues promoted a traveling show in which skaters of both teams often traveled and roomed together. Because of this, neither league was seen as legitimate by the mainstream media. Of course, both leagues attempted to present a spectacle that was believable; at least to a majority of those coming in the turnstiles. The difference between Roller Games and Roller Derby is that Griffiths took the showmanship portion to the extreme.

Much of the reason the Thunderbirds achieved such unprecedented international success was due to the high-level combination of sport and show, executed by skillful performers. The original Derby let the skating speak for itself. Roller Games embellished what was happening on the track with non-skating personalities, whether they were general managers, infield managers, team owners, mascots, representatives from the Commissioner's Office, referees, or announcers. At halftime, during interviews, there were often grand pronouncements from the Commissioners' Office, but rarely did this person ever make an appearance since, if truth be told, they didn't exist. The Commissioners, if there were any, were Griffiths and Hill, owners of the league. Often the role of infield manager or representative was given to a former skater who, because of injuries, could be useful even if their skating careers were over. And if you're presenting a "show," you'd better have good performers. Owner Bill Griffiths' tactics were akin to Bill Veeck of Major League Baseball, circa 1940s to 1970s, who always seemed to push boundaries with America's pastime, once even sending a dwarf to bat for his struggling St. Louis Browns. In this chapter, we'll take a brief look at some of the most memorable non-skating performers.

The first Thunderbird infield manager was Marion "Red" Smartt, who became general manager at the end of summer 1963, after serving as T-Birds skating coach since March 1962, succeeding Ralph Valladares. A native of Chattanooga, Tennessee, Smartt joined the Derby in 1947 and had been a huge star and fan-favorite with the L.A. Braves during the 1950s. After he became T-Birds G.M., he often supervised the team from the infield, did interviews, wrote a column in the weekly *Gazette*, and skated the occasional match race until his permanent retirement in June 1968. His involvement off the track was used to increase attendance at games, but did not compare to what would come later as non-skating personnel became more prominent to the show. Red Smartt died July 13, 1987.

While Red was a reassuring presence on the infield during games, the Thunderbird mascot, "Little Angie," a dwarf, wreaked havoc on the infield with opposing skaters to the delight of fans. He often shouted through a large megaphone and carried a T-Bird pennant. Angelo Rossitto stood only 2'11", but he was adored by T-Bird fans everywhere. An American dwarf actor and voice artist, Little Angie had appeared in over seventy feature films during his long career, but may best be known for his tenure in Roller Games. The appearance of Little Angie on the infield during the 1960s was the first sign of things to come from the mind of "Little Billy Sunshine," the former stage name of former-Vaudevillian Bill Griffiths, Sr. Another dwarf, Leroy Lambert, was on the infield in the 1970s, disrupting the action for various red shirt teams. In the comeback era of the late '70s and '80s, the T-Bird mascot was no longer a dwarf but the "T-Bird Chicken," to the delight of younger fans. The person inside the costume was usually Scott Ferguson, who became my best buddy in Roller Games. We often roomed together on road trips. Even though he was the team mascot, Scott was highly critical of what he viewed on the track when skating talent was thin. He never followed Roller Games before working on the infield, thus never witnessed the game when it shined.

In 1968, Bob Lewis, a former skater and successful Southern California concert promoter, became general manager of the T-Birds. Lewis was another Derby star who joined the league in 1947 and had also been a fan-favorite with the L.A. Braves in the 1950s. Working for the NSD, he created Roller Games Hall in San Bernardino, a weekly Thursday night sell-out for the T-Birds, and also operated a training school with his wife, Georgeanna Kemp, another former skater. Until 1971, during Bob Lewis' tenure as general manager, the mayhem in games escalated as match races and storylines became more pronounced. High-scoring games were prevalent, but it was still non-offensive to all but the most orthodox fans. Attendance increased based on the success of the weekly promotion. Fans in the glam capital of L.A. seemed to enjoy this version of the game.

After breaking his neck during a freak accident on October 12, 1965, John Hall's skating career was over, although he would reinvent himself as Roller Games' first active infield manager with the Detroit Devils. Following the unscripted, surprise victory of the Devils over the T-Birds in the 1968 Roller Games World Series, Hall was named T-Birds assistant general manager in March 1969, when G.M. Bob Lewis decided he wanted to focus more on being a concert promoter. After two white G.M.s, a black man, John Hall, became the public face of the T-Birds. A fan favorite, Hall's promotions drew significantly higher attendance than ever before. Rival managers often challenged Hall, eventually culminating in an "anything goes" match race with the former Devils coach lacing up his skates and donning the red-white-and-blue jersey of the T-Birds to oppose his distractor. John endured great battles with skating greats Leroy Gonzales, Ronnie Rains, John Parker, and John Gautieri, who was a former referee turned infield manager. John's tough yet classy demeanor, plus being someone who had overcome a career-ending injury, which was apparent even during tumultuous battles, led to endearment from fans.

In the Spring of '71, General Manager Lester Quarles of the Texas Outlaws cited a little-known rule prohibiting assistant general managers from being on the infield during games, systematically barring Hall from the infield. During a momentous halftime interview when Quarles seemed to have succeeded in eliminating Hall's influence, John offered his resignation, which was followed by the announcement that G.M. Bob Lewis had also resigned and that John Hall was being named new general manager of the team; everyone watching was stunned and delighted. Hall's tenure as G.M. was the T-Birds' zenith in both popularity and profitability. His contribution to the team's success is indisputable.

Fans couldn't have been more thrilled that John Hall was now general manager of the Thunderbirds. Little did they know what was already being planned to take Roller Games and the T-Birds to new heights. Roller Games was preparing to develop a new territory in Ohio and Michigan with the creation of the Cleveland Bucks. Hall's expertise was needed with the Bucks. So two other former greats of the game, who no longer actively skated night after night followed in his footsteps.

Born June 7, 1939 in Seattle, Washington, Shirley Hardman made her debut in the original Derby in 1956. When Roller Games was created in 1961, Shirley was a pillar of the new league and became the most prominent female draw of the league as Women's Captain of the Texas Outlaws. Whenever the league ventured into a new market, Hardman and her Outlaws were the first team sent in to draw the ire of fans, making them Roller Games converts instantly. Her rough, no-holds-barred style of skating resulted in many serious injuries. In 1968, she broke her back in an inter-league series in San Francisco. Her doctors told her never to skate again, but Griffiths had another role for her in mind. In May 1971, with Hall named G.M., the long-loathed Hardman was named Assistant G.M. of the T-Birds. When Hall departed for Cleveland at the end of '71, Shirley assumed Hall's responsibilities with the team. Fans couldn't be more thrilled. When things got rough, Hardman was known to pull out a baseball bat that she kept in the penalty box. She was adored by Southern California fans who had once vociferously hated her. Hardman tragically died on August 1, 1973 as a result of a reported drowning incident at the age of 34, a significant loss for the T-Birds and the game.

Dave Pound was another skater whose status in the game became even more significant when he hung up his skates and became an infield manager. A Los Angeles native, born June 3, 1937, Pound joined the original Derby in San Diego in 1955. He left the IRDL in 1963, joining the NSD, and became the first coach of the Chicago Hawks. Because Pound was such a phenomenal skater and beloved by colleagues, he went freely from one league to another, but his brutal style of play resulted in numerous debilitating injuries. With Hall working for the Bucks in Cleveland at the start of '72, it seemed as if the T-Birds were not about to promote an accomplished woman to be their new general manager. Pound, a long-time archenemy of the T-Birds, was brought in to be the new general manager, but management had grand plans for this storyline. Hardman would remain Assistant G.M., but was fired within a week by Pound as he remade the team firing one skater after another, colluding with the T-Birds' most vociferous enemies, as if he was determined to destroy the team from within.

Pound was undoubtedly the most effective general manager in Roller Games in regard to box office draws. His match races and promotions always attracted huge crowds. John Hall returned from Cleveland for a match race with Pound to determine who would own the T-Birds. If Pound defeated Hall, he could buy the team; if he lost, he was banished from the team. The Inglewood Forum was sold out for the match race. Ticket scalpers were getting up to $200 for tickets, unheard of for Roller Games. Hall won the match race and the T-Birds survived, but knowing full well how successful the promotion had been and sensing another chance for big-ticket sales, the humiliated Pound was brought back, this time skating for the T-Birds. In a match race to decide the '72 President's Cup, Pound defeated Ronnie Rains, coach of the New York Bombers. He later clashed with referee Bob Martin, who suspended him, citing another obscure rule from the never-seen rulebook. Pound came back at the time of the World Series to help the T-Birds to another championship title.

Of course, a year later, the exact same promotion occurred with Pound as general manager of the Philadelphia Warriors, destroying the team from within. It took place on the East Coast and broke attendance records, the likes of which the Warriors had never before experienced. Back on the West Coast, Hardman was the new G.M. of the T-Birds, former nemesis Ronnie Rains was in T-Birds' red white-and-blue, and another former skater, Jess Adams, was brought in as a "Special Representative of the Commission," to prove Rains was indeed psychotic; another successful promotion of an outside force trying to destroy the T-Birds. The result was even bigger crowds in every place the T-Birds skated.

In any given Roller Games season, there was always an ongoing battle of good versus evil, which featured an ever-changing, long list of characters representing their teams. The most stunning (and popular) developments occurred when a long-time enemy of the team quit his team mid-game and joined the home team sending fans into ecstasy. Often some obscure rule was discovered (more like conveniently created), and forced a newly signed skater to don the jersey of the opposing team, then participate in a match race to win their contract. Or sometimes a manager objected to an announcer and took him off the air, forcing a skater to race another in order to save the announcer's job. Anything could happen in Roller Games and often the more bizarre it became, the more fans ate it up.

National Skating Derby

Chapter 11

Rollerskating Championships (1961)

1961 THUNDERBIRDS
Honey Sanchez, Marge Forrest, Terri Lynch, Julie Patrick, Pat Kennedy, Jean Porter
Red Smartt, Ralph Valladares, George Knerr, George Copeland, Punky Gardner, Julian Silva, Abel Lara

"(Roller derby) had grown tired by 1961, the year California promoter Bill Griffiths spiced it up and created the Roller Games circuit. In it, opposing teams and skaters feuded in a way that presaged the modern world of professional wrestling.

Storylines became part of the game. Referees were urged to look the other way when fights broke out." – David Block, *Philadelphia Inquirer*

The first Rollerskating Championships game was at the El Monte Legion Stadium (capacity 2,500) in March 1961. It was televised live on KTLA with Dick Lane announcing. The home team, Thunderbirds, skated against the Detroit Devils, which was led by Captains Roger Schroeder and Toni Tagg. The initial televised game was a big hit. The Thunderbirds became an instant sensation, and the TV games garnered top ratings and very good crowds. There were three additional teams originally. The Detroit Devils, Texas Outlaws and the Chicago Cyclones. Each team skated a three-week series with a TV game and also games on Friday and Saturday nights. Venues in San Bernardino and Long Beach were added later in the 1961 season.

The very first T-Birds men's team consisted of Captain Red Smartt, Coach Ralph Valladares, Julian Silva, George Knerr, Ernie Lopez, George Copeland, and Abel Lara. The debut women's team featured Captain Terri Lynch, Honey Sanchez, Jean Porter, Marge Forrest, Sylvia Viramontes, Julie Patrick, and Sheila McKenna. The team was loaded with veteran stars and even a few future Hall of Fame inductees.

George Copeland was the first black American skater to gain fame in the Roller Derby. He had great skating talents- tricky, agile, and very fast. He had tremendous knowledge of the game and was a scoring star for the L.A. Braves in Roller Derby. George also had many associates and friends in the movie industry. Ray Charles was a close family friend. George chose not to relocate with the Roller Derby as his family and friends were in Los Angeles and he was an automatic selection for the T-Birds. George had a large fan base among banked track fans, and he quickly became a favorite of T-Birds enthusiasts. George has been inducted into the National Roller Derby Hall of Fame.

The coaches and captains of the first Roller Games teams were as follows:

Los Angeles Thunderbirds: Coach Ralph Valladares, Men's Captain Red Smartt and Women's Captain Terri Lynch.

Detroit Devils: Coach Roger Schroeder, Women's Captain: Toni Tagg, and Gerry Rapp was also an assistant coach integral to the Devils.

Texas Outlaws: Coach Bucky Buckholtz and Women's Captain Shirley Hardman.

Chicago Cyclones. Coach Charlie "Specs" Saunders and Women's Captain Mary Gardner. Cecil Hatfield was Charlie's second in command.

Herb Roberts began to incur financial difficulties that included unpaid payroll taxes, and the IRS was in hot pursuit. Herb Roberts offered to sell the National Skating Derby to skater Bert Wall for $2,000. Wall contacted Jerry Seltzer to see if he was interested but Seltzer declined as he wanted to focus on the Bay Area. Advertising Executives Jerry Hill and Bill Griffiths, who had represented Maywood Bell Ford on KTLA, stepped in and offered to buy Herb out. The skaters had a meeting that resulted in a stamp of approval for the new owners.

Upon selling, Herb was guaranteed a position as the head trackside announcer with a yearly salary. That 1961 season finished under the leadership of Jerry Hill and Bill Griffiths. The two new league owners decided that the Olympic Auditorium (the former home of the Los Angeles Braves of Roller Derby) would become the official home of the Thunderbirds, as well as the home base of Roller Games and the official training center. Training was normally held on both Saturday and Sunday afternoons. The majority of Thunderbird home games were skated in this building for the next 25 years.

Jerry and Bill had a 50/50 partnership with the company. They moved operations from El Monte to Los Angeles and had a suite of offices at 1717 N. Highland Ave. (which is now the home of the Academy Awards). Eventually, the offices were relocated to the Olympic Auditorium. Jerry and Bill were very hands-on business owners. They held monthly meetings with the coach and captain of each team to discuss details and plans for the league. They had an efficient office

Scott Stephens

staff with a CPA, lawyer, and administrative staff. Their business principles and work ethic set the stage for great success to come.

Early Roller Games contests were low scoring affairs, rarely exceeding 30 or 40 points per team; similar to the original Roller Derby and very much in contrast to the high scoring of later Roller Games. There was no championship series in 1961 nor a President's Cup mid-season contest.

64

Chapter 12

Texas Try (1962)

"Everyone with a TV set remembers Roller Derby, the alternative sports television event of the 1950s, '60s and '70s that packed such venues as New York's Madison Square Garden, San Francisco's Cow Palace and Pasadena's Rose Bowl with heckling, horn-blowing, beer-chugging, decidedly blue-collar fans who screamed for blood and worse." – Los Angeles Times, 1995

he Texas Outlaws were one of the top teams in Roller Games in the early '60s, along with the Detroit Devils. League officials even tried to base the Outlaws in the Lone Star state in 1963. They were coached by the industrious Lou Sanchez, who later made several attempts to break away to form leagues of his own. His '62 and '63 Outlaws teams were solid, featuring a young John Hall in his skating prime before his serious neck injury in 1965. Other stars included Vinnie Gandolfo, Fletcher Sanders, Jim Trotter, Bill Gatchell, and a very young Ronnie Rains. The women's team was led by Shirley Hardman, a fixture with the Outlaws throughout the decade and one of the toughest and most feared skaters in the league. Other notable women included Adeline Hocker, Olympic medalist Earlene Brown, Norma Rossner, and rookie Barbara Williams.

Many of these skaters remained with the team and in 1967 challenged the T-Birds again for the championship, but lost. In 1967, Diane Syverson was added to the team. Jim Trotter was assigned the coaching job in 1966 when the Outlaws opened in Australia and would soon go on to Philadelphia to lead the Warriors for many years. All in all, the Outlaws would go on to compete for the World Series title seven times, a number only matched by the Detroit Devils.

It is worth mentioning that opposition teams that reached the Roller Games World Series were almost always teams that were the strongest that particular year and who had the biggest draw. So although winners and losers were often pre-determined, reaching the finals was earned.

One of the most significant events of 1962 was the arrival of Judy Sowinski. She was the up-and-coming star of the San Francisco Bay Bombers in 1961, having been plucked out of obscurity in Chicago two years earlier by superstar Charlie O'Connell and trained by the cream-of-the-crop. Sowinski had won *Rookie of the Year* honors in the NRDL in 1960, made the All-Star team in '61, and was destined to be one of Derby's biggest distaff stars. After the '61 campaign, Sowinski was scheduled to travel with Derby for a series in Hawaii, but was unceremoniously dumped from the trip. Unsure what to do, she called her friend Terri Lynch in Los Angeles, who suggested she come south to skate with National. Sowinski made her debut with the T-Birds in March 1962 wearing jersey number five, and over the next eleven seasons, would become one of the premier female stars in the history of the sport.

In this series, the T-Birds were led by their coach Red Smartt. He was the first coach of the Thunderbirds and later became manager in March 1962. Prior to coaching the T-Birds, he skated for the Roller Derby's Los Angeles home team, the L.A. Braves. Red was primarily a blocker and one of the team's leaders. He was also an occasional jammer and was a fan favorite. After the Roller Derby vacated Los Angeles in 1960, Red didn't care to relocate to Northern California, as he had a business in L.A. called Red Cap Sign Company, which needed his attention. Red was married to Joyce Beasely, a skater on the L.A. Braves, who elected to stay at home and raise their children when the T-Birds formed. Red led the T-Birds to their very first world championship in 1962 at the expense of the Outlaws and again in 1963. He was inducted into the National Roller Derby Hall of Fame some years after his death.

There was an attempt in 1963 to make the Texas Outlaws a home team based in the unlikely, mid-size city of El Paso, Texas. Initially, a local promoter wanted to co-promote games at the 6,000 seat El Paso Coliseum on Friday, Saturday, and Sunday with the Outlaws skating against the Detroit Devils. He paid all costs and Roller Games was to receive 30% of the profits. However, this arrangement was unsuccessful. Attendance was about 800 at all three dates with most of the crowd chanting "T-Birds! T-Birds!" which led to Roller Games saying goodbye to El Paso. It would be the last time the Outlaws were based in their namesake state. Despite their failed attempt at expansion, the Outlaws were the top foe for the Thunderbirds in the early years of the NRL.

This same year, Roller Games also attempted to establish another home team in the Southwest, as the Arizona Raiders were founded in Phoenix. There was a co-promotional agreement with promoter Ernie Mohammed, who owned South Mountain Speedway on the outskirts of Phoenix.

The Arizona Raiders featured men's coach Bill Gatchell, women's captain Darlene Anderson, men's captain Ronnie Kolsoozian along with George Vogt, Betty Boyd, Barbara Williams, Johnny Rodriguez, and Toni Gandara.

The first series in Phoenix took place over three games on April 25, 26, and 27 between Arizona and Texas. The games were held in an outdoor race arena with a capacity of 5,000, which had an excellent turnout with near capacity crowds both nights. Roller Games and Mohammed then made arrangements to have the home team Raiders host a short nine-week season in Phoenix against other Roller Games teams. The nine-week series in Phoenix, which was usually three games a week, ended at the beginning of July when the Raiders faced the newly organized and rarely known Jersey Jets with Mary Gardner, Gerry Murray, Norma Rossner, and Lillian Sugasawara (the only Japanese-American girl in the history of the sport), who lasted only one month. The Raiders skated a few more games in July and September in Phoenix, usually on Saturday nights. Typically, there were four games scheduled per week with the weekend games held at South Mountain and weekday games held in smaller venues. The weekend games had decent turnouts, but did not sell out and the weekday games did not draw well. After one season, the experiment in Phoenix ended and the team was disbanded. In later years, after TV tapes of the T-Birds began showing in Arizona, Roller Games returned to Phoenix with the Thunderbirds as the home team and did well.

Despite these early failures of the league trying to establish teams in the nearby Southwest region, Griffiths and Jerry Hill would try their hand again very soon, with much better results.

Chapter 13
Aloha! (1963)

1963 Thunderbirds
Left to right: Ralph Valladares, Danny Miller, Sharon Ozeki, Julian Silva, Jeannie Porter, Abel Lara, Carmen Gomez, Danny Reilly, Judy Sowinski, Bertha Ruiz, Ernie Lopez, Terri Lynch, George Copeland, Ruberta Mitchell

"The put-on actually consumes only a small portion of the play, and really seldom intrudes on the bona fide action itself, but, of course, as long as it exists at all, it manages to discredit the Derby's generally honest posture." – Frank DeFord, *Sports Illustrated*

side from the T-Birds, the most successful home team operation in Roller Games was the Warriors, a team formed in Hawaii in 1963. Leo Seltzer's original National Roller Derby League debuted in Hawaii in 1954 and ran through the 1950s before it became the 50th state of the United States. The crimson-and-gold Honolulu Hawaiians eventually became a part of the league, but when Jerry Seltzer took over the NRDL in 1959, he lost interest in cultivating the Hawaiian market.

Griffiths and Hill took notice, making sure T-Birds games were shown in Hawaii, then sending the team to the Islands during the earliest years of the NSD. Roller Games was required to uphold their obligation to KTLA TV, so televised home games needed to continue. This requirement was fulfilled by creating the Long Beach Falcons. The popularity of Gerry Murray was the primary factor for KTLA accepting the Falcons as a temporary replacement. Murray's Falcons started play on May 25, 1963, in San Bernardino with Bob Satterfield as coach, Jerry Rapp and Gerry Murray as captains, and Georgeanna Kemp also on the team. Despite the star power of the Falcons, fans missed the home team Thunderbirds and after they returned to their regular schedule, the Falcons were disbanded.

The tours featuring the Thunderbirds in Hawaii were so successful that NSD decided to form a home base in Honolulu. T-Bird star George Copeland stayed over in Hawaii to help organize the team. The Hawaiian Warriors were established in 1963 and skated in the 4,000 seat Civic Center Arena. The Warriors opened play there on June 20, 1963. Fans in Honolulu loved the games and attendance was usually upwards of 3,500 with many sellouts in a city whose population was approximately 300,000. The operation was co-promoted with Ralph Yempuku, the owner of the Civic Auditorium. Games were skated Thursday through Saturday with an occasional game scheduled on Monday in Maui. The average attendance in Maui was 3,000 plus, which was near capacity. The Warriors season lasted nine to twelve weeks during the summer months.

The Hawaiian Warriors were led by coach George Copeland and women's captain Liz Hernandez. Over the years, numerous great skating stars like Red Smartt, Mary Lou Palermo, Norma Rossner, Dave Pound, Fred Noa, and Dolores Doss skated with the Warriors who appeared live on the Islands over the next two years, eventually taking on the T-Birds in Southern California in '65. The Warriors participated in the '65 NSD World Series, winning the Consolation Championship game, third place, over the Detroit Devils.

In 1965, when the NSD created the San Francisco Shamrocks, skating home games in Northern California, the league realized they were resilient enough to manage other operations outside Los Angeles. Roller Games in Hawaii was doing fine during the Warriors' sporadic seasons, but Jerry Hill noticed an outlaw league skating games every Friday, Saturday, and Sunday nights at the Cherry Hill Arena in the Delaware Valley on the East Coast. The league was called RollerRama and was staffed with many skaters who wished to remain in the East. However, the league had little television coverage and no money, and was disbanded. Hill recognized an opportunity and suggested moving the part-time Warriors' Hawaii operation to the East Coast, although the team did return to Hawaii frequently including in '68, '70, '71, and '72, for mostly short series following the season in Philadelphia.

Chapter 14
Detroit Wheels (1964)

Carmen Gomez, Ruberta Mitchell, Terri Toledo, Little Angie, Kay Finlay, Honey Sanchez, Judy Sowinski, Terri Lynch
Don Chambers, Eddie Payne, Jerry Reilly, Danny Reilly, Ralph Valladares, Roger Schroeder, Punky Gardner

"I've made some excellent money, and I've lost excellent money." – Bill Griffiths

In 1964, the effort continued to turn the red-shirt Detroit Devils into a home team based in Detroit. This plan began in 1963 when a nine-week series was held over the summer that pitted the Devils against the Texas Outlaws and Chicago Hawks. There were five games a week, Wednesday through Sunday, mostly held at the Michigan State Fairgrounds. It had a capacity of 5,000 with the Devils averaging 3,500 to 4,000. On the final Saturday of each series, there was a special event at the new Cobo Hall Arena, home of the NBA Detroit Pistons, with a capacity of 12,000. The Devils drew a respectable 8,000 to 9,000 fans; league officials were optimistic. No actual attendance figures are available, but those skating during the games have estimated these crowd figures. This is the case not only for the aforementioned games but throughout much of this book.

In 1964, the Devils continued to skate home games in the motor city. Attendance was up and down. The effort continued as late as 1965 when a three-week series with the Texas Outlaws was held at the State Fair Coliseum. Games were conducted five nights a week, Tuesday through Saturday evenings. Plans were made to host more games in 1966, but with energy shifting towards the new venture in Australia, the Devils returned to their original role as a visiting team and became the number one challenger for the Thunderbirds.

In 1964, the Detroit Devils finished the regular season ahead of the competition, even winning the final series against the T-Birds. Los Angeles beat Texas to face Detroit in the World Series. The Devils team reached the Roller Games Finals, only to face a Thunderbirds team with seven future Hall of Famers anchored by G.M. Red Smartt. In the '64 World Series, the Devils' roster consisted of Men's Coach John Hall, Women's Captain Toni Tagg, Men's Captain Vinnie Gandolfo, Adeline Hocker, Ernie Lopez, Bill Fitzgerald, Charlie Mitchell, Tom Raffety, Johnny Chavez, Rita Stroska, Toni Gandara, Katie Kolbus, Marlene Perales, and Carmen Thompson.

At the beginning of '64, the T-Birds roster was Coach George Copeland, Captain Terri Lynch, Captain Ralph Valladares, Julian Silva, George Knerr, Eddie Payne, Bob Roberts, Judy Sowinski, Liz Hernandez, Ruberta Mitchell, Honey Sanchez, Bertha Ruiz (Mrs.

Copeland), Carmen Gomez, and Sally Vega. Mary Lou Palermo joined the team at the beginning of the summer when her girls were on school break, then left the squad at the end of the summer.

The President's Cup was held on August 15 at Veterans Memorial Stadium. A record crowd of 13,873 showed up to cheer on the Thunderbirds.

As the season progressed, there were roster changes and by the '64 World Series the T-Birds lineup featured Ralph Valladares, Punky Gardner, Danny Reilly, Judy Sowinski, Liz Hernandez, Ruberta Mitchell, Roger Schroeder, Eddie Payne, Danny Miller, Donnie Chambers, Terri Toledo, Sally Vega, Carmen Gomez, and Kay Finlay. Terri Lynch did not skate in the World Series because of an injury.

Lewis "Punky" Gardner was one of four siblings from Knoxville, Tennessee who joined the original Derby. Lewis debuted in 1950 and would become a fan favorite with the L.A. Braves in the 1950s. He was married to Julie Patrick. His sister, Mary, would be inducted into the Hall of Fame. Punky was men's captain of the Blue Devils in Roller Catch in Europe in 1960. He was a fan favorite in Paris and Casablanca and joined the T-Birds in 1962. Punky and Valladares had similar skating styles and were roughly the same size. After Coach George Copeland left the T-Birds midway through the '64 season, Punky was given more responsibility on the track. He was named men's coach in 1965, but left at the end of the season, as his family had family ties in Northern California. Later, Punky was involved in an auto accident while driving for UPS where he sustained head injuries. He was hospitalized and died on the day he was to be discharged.

The 1964 Devils were outmatched, and the T-Birds won the World Series, 4 games to 2, winning the title in the sixth game. The Devils would eventually qualify for the Roller Games Finals seven times (equaled only by the Outlaws) and became one of only two opposing teams to win a World Series title. They are arguably the most famous rival of the Thunderbirds in Roller Games history.

Prosperity

Roller Games was started by a group of skaters, many unhappy with Jerry Seltzer's decision to move his league to Northern California rather than remain in Southern California. Moving north with the new Derby would mean finding new homes, moving the few belongings they owned to another part of the state, dragging children out of school, creating brand new worlds for their families, while not being assured steady employment. Many major Derby stars opted to leave the NRDL rather than accept secondary roles up North. One could easily make the case that Roller Games was born and flourished as a direct result of decisions made by the Seltzer family.

Bill Griffiths and Jerry Hill had very different management styles. Bill was generally more vocal and gave direction in many areas, especially in regards to promotion. Jerry Hill maintained a personal involvement with the skaters and was involved in the game. He was trusted and well-liked by all. He was also friendly, but very businesslike and somewhat aloof. Despite different styles and approaches, Bill and Jerry worked well together. They were both jointly involved in booking buildings and opening new areas. They structured a pay system based on the one that Herb Roberts had initially implemented and took inspiration from Jerry Hill's plea for more equitable pay for skaters. Only star skaters had guaranteed contracts. In the off-season, the other skaters who were employees of the company would often collect unemployment. It was nearly impossible to get a similar job as a roller derby skater as there were only two leagues whose off-seasons often coincided. Hill pointed out that the stars on the visiting teams were not compensated commensurate with the home team stars. The home team Thunderbird skaters were performing on a more consistent basis while the visiting skaters were essentially unemployed during off weeks. Hill implemented a guarantee for some of the major stars, which eventually led to a guaranteed weekly salary for all skaters that were willing to make a full commitment to Roller Games. The skaters had to commit to going anywhere at any time, regardless of whether they were white or red shirt performers. Roller Games was the first league to establish a salary guarantee, and it attracted skaters from Roller Derby to jump ship to Roller Games.

While the better pay was often the number one reason skaters made the jump from Derby to Roller Games, another consideration was the opportunity to travel and see the world. Roller Games had significant operations on three continents in the late '60s, which aside from North America included Asia and Australia. Word was getting out about the good times being had overseas, and indeed, some Derby skaters were tempted to consider Roller Games.

In an interview published on former skater Loretta Behrens' *Derby Memories* website, Buddy Atkinson, Jr. was quoted as saying, "I had more enjoyment with National (Roller Games) because we were treated better and the skaters got along really well together. There was a time when Roller Games was higher paying and had more benefits than Roller Derby." Buddy Jr., son of two Derby Hall of Famers and nephew of Uncle Tommie, spent the first ten years of his career in the original Derby, mostly with the New York Chiefs (1958-1967). He won two consecutive MVP awards (1965-1966), then moved to National, coaching the Philadelphia Warriors from the Fall of '67 over the next seven years.

The arrival of former Roller Derby stars was a big selling point for fans. Roller Games grew, but Hill never personally credited himself with formulating and implementing the new pay status. When he announced this news to team leaders at the monthly meeting, he used the term *we*, crediting both Bill and himself despite being the one who had pushed for this change that benefitted both the skaters and league. John Hall commented, "Jerry Hill was the main reason that the skaters prospered and were treated in a fair and professional manner."

The biggest news to rock the world of professional roller derby occurred at the start of 1965 when iconic Derby star, Ann Calvello, in a dispute with Ken Monte and Seltzer, quit the IRDL and signed with the NSD Shamrocks in her hometown of San Francisco. She had been rejected by management five years earlier and now returned the favor. Calvello's departure stunned everyone in both leagues and made it clear that skating for Roller Games was a clear alternative to the original Derby. Calvello, the sport's most dynamic personality and performer, was now with National and it lead the way for other big stars of Roller Games, who had always been on the fence, to jump ship. The likes of John Parker, Jan Vallow, Leroy Gonzales, "Toughie" Brasuhn, Nick Scopas, Frankie Macedo, Lester Quarles, Joan Kazmerski, Bob Hein, George Adams, and Judy Arnold made their way south to the National Skating Derby (Roller Games).

The growth and expansion of Roller Games brought with it increased prosperity for the league and higher salaries for the skaters. Previously, a solid skater might have drawn a yearly salary of $10,000. Now a few of the stars were making $50,000. Some select skaters became enrolled in the new league profit sharing plan. The profit sharing began with Roller Derby in 1968 and National Skating Derby, Inc. (Roller Games) followed suit with its profit-sharing plan in 1969 to keep up. Both Leagues were doing great. Following the implementation of profit sharing, there were much fewer defections from one league to another. Roller derby was the first sport to provide this benefit to its athletes.

Comparing the pay scales for the two leagues is problematic as much of this information was only known by top executives. However, fewer Roller Games skaters were defecting to Roller Derby than vice-versa.

Chapter 15

Bad Boy Bombers (1965)

1965 LOS ANGELES THUNDERBIRDS
Ralph Valladares, Red Smartt, Danny Reilly, Richard Brown, Jess Adams, Roger Schroeder, Eddie Payne, Jerry Reilly
Dick Lane, Ruberta Mitchell, Liz Hernandez, Carmen Gomez, Terri Lynch, Judy Sowinski, Honey Sanchez, Terri Toledo, Little Angie

"Without Roller Derby as competition (Seltzer had folded the L.A. Braves to concentrate on the Bombers in Northern California), and with KTLA's backing, plus a move from El Monte to the spacious Olympic Auditorium in downtown Los Angeles, the unit, now owned by Jerry Hill and Bill Griffiths, became the hugely successful six-team National

Skating Derby. At long last, skaters had bargaining power.
There was Roller Derby in Northern California and beyond,
and Roller Games in Southern California. With a choice,
skaters finally could negotiate for the best deal." – Alan Ebert,
The History of Early Roller Derby.

In 1965, the New York Bombers made their first appearance in a Roller Games World Series. It was also the first time for Leroy "Bad-Boy" Gonzales to reach the Finals. Leroy was known for wreaking havoc and chaos in every game he skated or coached. Gonzales would go on to represent three different teams in the Finals (Bombers, Outlaws and Devils). In 1965, he was establishing himself as the league's number one unpredictable bully and bad boy. It was a role he relished and thrived in. The only skater in the league who would go on to challenge his title of the "baddest of the bad" was Ronnie "Psycho" Rains who would later go on to lead the Bombers in a similar disorderly and menacing manner. But in this 1965 season, Leroy led his Bombers squad to the coveted throne of being T-Bird fans "most hated team."

Leroy Gonzales was born in Brownsville, Texas on October 17, 1937. His skating debut was in 1955 with the hallowed New York Chiefs. One of the first Latino stars, he was named Rookie of the Year in '56. Leroy skated with the Brooklyn Red Devils in '57, then spent four years in the U.S. Navy before returning to Derby in '62. He made his move to the NSD at the beginning of '65, skating with the Chicago Hawks, and then was named men's coach of the Bombers. His departure from the IRDL (Roller Derby) to NSD (Roller Games) was big news in the sport. After leading New York to the NRL pennant in '65 and being named runner-up finalist in the World Series, he then skated with the IRDL Cardinals in the 1965 Derby World Series finals, becoming the only skater to ever participate in both playoff finals of two pro leagues in the same year.

The New York Bombers made their debut in the NSD at the beginning of 1963 with Coach Charlie "Specs" Saunders, Women's Captain Loretta Behrens, plus Don Rixman, George Adams, Joanne

Koons, and Bonnie Nelson. Veteran skaters, husband and wife Jan Vallow and Nick Scopas would join the Bombers during the summer of '63. George Vogt became men's coach in September '63. Dave Pound became interim coach in September '64 after Vogt was suspended. Don Rixman was chosen as men's coach in December '64. Gonzales was designated men's coach in February '65. Midge "Toughie" Brasuhn was appointed women's captain in the same month. Brasuhn resigned from her role as captain in May '65 and Jan Vallow was selected as the new captain.

At the beginning of the year, the '65 NY Bombers featured Coach Leroy Gonzales, Women's Captain Jan Vallow, Nick Scopas, Midge "Toughie" Brasuhn, Jim Trotter, Toni Dare, Bob Roberts, Judy Woodard, Joanne Koons, and Cal Valentine. In June, Trotter, already destined for stardom, was sent to Texas. He was named coach of the Outlaws seven months later. Gonzales and Scopas were the heart of the men's team and worked exceptionally well together. Brasuhn did a lot of the color (showmanship) for the women while Vallow did the brunt of the heavy skating and took her place as one of the premier stars of National.

The Los Angeles T-Birds' lineup at the start of '65 was Men's Coach Punky Gardner, Women's Captain Terri Lynch, Ralph Valladares, Judy Sowinski, Liz Hernandez, Ruberta Mitchell, Danny Reilly, Roger Schroeder, Honey Sanchez, Sally Vega, Eddie Payne, Danny Miller, Donnie Chambers, Jerry Reilly, Kay Finlay, and Carmen Gomez. By April, Terri Toledo was added to the team and Danny Miller was gone. Mike Garcia was inserted in June. Kay Finlay was gone during the summer and Richard Brown, wearing jersey number nine, was added to the men's team after graduating high school. Ralph, Punky, and Danny Reilly were the core of the men's team for L.A. and promoted Richard Brown late in the summer as a rookie scoring sensation, which he was.

During the regular season, there were some classic battles between the teams with Gonzales and Vallow taking out their aggression on the home team T-Birds in typical Roller Games style. Thunderbird fans were served a heaping measure of excitement by the likes of speedsters Valladares and Brown. For the women, Lynch, Mitchell, Hernandez, Sowinski, and Sanchez were equally compelling.

The New York Bombers won the NRL pennant for the '65 season. In November, the T-Birds beat the Bombers for the World Series title as 13,187 fans attended the Long Beach Arena for the Finals. The Bombers would come back even stronger in 1966 to make a second consecutive series appearance.

On October 12, 1965, the T-Birds were hosting John Hall's Detroit Devils in a Tuesday night game taped for broadcast on KTLA at the Olympic Auditorium. This was the scene of one of the worst injuries to ever occur, that would change the course of Hall's career in Roller Games forever. In a freak event, Hall severely fractured his neck.

The injury occurred during the Devils warm-up at approximately 7:05 p.m. After the Devils had warmed up, trackside host Herb Roberts, after being briefed by Coach John Hall and Captain Toni Tagg, announced to the Olympic crowd of Thunderbird fans, "The Detroit Devils duo of John Hall and Jumpin' Charlie Mitchell are going to show you T-Bird fans some spectacular skating."

While the rest of the Devils team went to the infield, John and Charlie made their way to the starting line on the banked track. Charlie and John had performed this stunt a few times at Devils' practice sessions but never in front of fans; it was never taught in training classes due to the danger involved. Upon the signal to start skating, Charlie skated the normal direction while John skated in the opposite direction. Both started at full speed and passed each other once. On the second round, John squatted like a ball as Charlie came directly at him but Charlie also squatted instead of remaining upright. At the last second, Charlie attempted to rise from his hunched position and leap over Hall, but his knee struck Hall square in the head. Fans cheered as they were unaware at the time that it wasn't planned this way.

Charlie landed about 19 feet down the track and sustained jaw and shoulder injuries. While his injuries were severe, he was fortunate to be able to resume skating in just three weeks; John Hall was not as lucky. Charlie's violent strike to his head had broken his neck and a doctor and paramedics arrived on the scene. Fans cheered even louder as they realized that the top two skaters on the Detroit team would not be in action against the T-Birds. Hall and Mitchell were taken to the Orthopedic Hospital in Los Angeles.

Charlie was treated and released the following day. John Hall had a cervical fusion of C-3, 4, and 5 vertebrae in his neck. He left the hospital wearing a brace on his shoulder and chest areas up to the front and back of his head. The injury would leave him with mild, partial paralysis and reduced agility. The reduction of movement would stay with him the remainder of his life.

The skate boy, Larry Lewis, who had filled in at various times with different teams during the year, was called into service for the Devils, with both Hall and Mitchell injured. The fourteen-year-old Lewis would carry the race for Detroit on this fateful evening. The home team Thunderbirds took the game and fans went home happy, but Jerry Hill and Bill Griffiths were concerned as one of their top stars appeared to be severely injured.

During his recovery, John worked at the league office and began his new role with Roller Games. John had previously been a United States military policeman, spending time overseas in Germany. Jerry Hill and Bill Griffiths certainly utilized John's "off the track" skills as the league was expanding to Australia.

John became operations vice president and continued as Detroit Devils (non-skating) coach. By early January of 1966, John had recovered enough to get back onto the track as a trainer. At this time, the T-Birds' training school had been moved to the Costa Mesa Fairgrounds. The current trainer, Ralph Valladares, was going to Australia, so John was assigned to train new trainees and pros in Costa Mesa. John felt he taught others more effectively when he was on skates and proceeded to lace up his skates for the first time since his neck injury. He made his way to the banked track and purposefully took a fall. The experiment, which would not have been approved by a medical doctor, was a success and John had no ill effects. He now felt confident that he could train skaters and personally demonstrate to them the drills and techniques he was teaching. He even believed he was fit enough to skate in game action, but not everyone agreed. The league's insurance company had inserted a clause into their contract that stated that if John Hall performed in game competition, it would violate the terms of the contact, thus providing no insurance protection to league owners in the event of an accident. Hall was forbidden to skate in Roller Games competitions, thus effectively ending his skating career. John was then promoted to general manager of the Devils.

Officially, during the remaining years of National Skating Derby, Inc. (Roller Games), he did not skate in a regular game.

"I missed being on the track and did skate in games when I felt it would not be seen or discovered by the insurance company. But officially, my skating in league games was over," said John Hall

In Australia in 1966, John skated in game action for the first time following his accident in a match race against Ralphie Valladares, who skated for the Australian home team. John defeated Ralph in the match race and decided to skate in the second half of the game to promote a rematch with Valladares the following Saturday night; that game was a sell-out.

John never skated regularly in any season again, but after the league was reformed in 1976, he skated anytime the team was short on skaters and for special promotional appearances and match races.

Chapter 16

Thunder Down Under (1966)

1966 Thunderbirds
Red Smartt, Carmen Thompson, Ruberta Mitchell, Liz Hernandez, Honey Sanchez, Judy Sowinski, Eddie Payne, Terri Lynch
Danny Reilly, Roger Schroeder, Betty Stone, Richard Brown, Gary Bickford, Larry Lewis, Abel Lara
Little Angie

"The Roller Game first came to Australia as a taped TV show from America in 1964 and became one of the most

popular sports on TV. Bill Griffiths, executive director of
International Roller Games, who runs six teams on the U.S.
West Coast, figured that perhaps Australia might be interested
in seeing the sport 'live.' So he flew here in July last year,
and enthusiastic TV managements convinced him Australia
was right for the action. Two teams rolled in this January,
the Los Angeles Thunderbirds and the Texas Outlaws. They
broke all attendance records at stadiums in Melbourne,
Sydney, and Brisbane, even outselling the Beatles. What
was to have been a ten-week season hasn't stopped. The
Roller Game is here to stay." – New South Wales TV WEEK
magazine, October 8, 1966

The original Roller Derby debuted in Sydney, Australia on August 26, 1955 during a six-week tour named *Brought to Australia* by legendary rock promoter, Lee Gordon, whose program, *The Big Show* was a huge hit presenting the greatest music acts across the country. The Seltzers provided the skaters but had little to do with the tour. Team Australia featured Gerry Murray, Fred Noa, Dolores Doss, Lou Guzman, Joan Kazmerski, Beverly Wallace, Peggy Conlon, and Bob Sumsky, facing Team America with Roger Schroeder, Loretta Behrens, George Vogt, Norma Rossner, Charlie O'Connell, Lee Frodelli, Jimmy Ciota, and the sophomore-year sensation, Joan Weston, whose photo appeared on the souvenir program's front cover. This premier series of games in a foreign country received almost no coverage in Derby publications, and it was clear the Seltzers had little interest in developing a market eight thousand miles away from Los Angeles.

Two years after its syndicated telecasts had become a smash hit down under, Roller Games began operations in Australia at the beginning of 1966 under the name, *The Roller Game*. The run would last three years through 1968. The first series ran from January 20 to April 4 and featured the Texas Outlaws and Los Angeles T-Birds in Brisbane, with later games in Sydney and Melbourne. Ralph Valladares and Liz Hernandez were coach and captain of L.A. along with Danny Reilly, Jerry Reilly, JoJo Stafford, Jess Adams,

Terri Toledo, and Carmen Gomez. Ann Calvello was brought to the T-Birds from the Shamrocks while Texas coach Vinnie Gandolfo was assigned to the T-Birds for the series as well. Texas had the NSD's premier female star, Shirley Hardman, leading the team along with new Outlaws coach Jim Trotter. This pair would make Texas one of the most feared teams in the NSD through the end of the 1960s. Also skating for Texas was Art Salaiz, Paul Rupert, Bob Roberts, Baby Rocco, Sandy Young, Jean Welch, and Nancy Gagnon.

On the initial tour, almost every game sold out. On Wednesdays and Saturdays, games were held at the 6,000 seat Sydney Stadium and were televised. On Thursdays, the teams flew on a charter jet to Brisbane for games on Thursdays and Fridays at the Brisbane Festival Hall Arena which seated 4,800. It was sold out every game during the initial tour. Following the Friday contest, there was a flight back to Sydney for the Saturday game. On Sunday the teams flew to Melbourne for a match at the Melbourne Festival Hall, which also sold out during the initial tour. Mondays and Tuesdays were days off, but top skaters rarely rested or relaxed as they were acquired to attend many interviews and make personal promotional appearances. Roller Games skaters were very popular; fans wanted contact with them off the track, especially with Ralphie, Calvello, Liz Hernandez, Shirley Hardman, and Jim Trotter. Australians seemed to be fascinated by Jim Trotter, who was black. One photo in a magazine was captioned, "Negro Jimmy Trotter posed with green-haired Ann Calvello for what the lady called a 'color' picture." The skaters loved all the attention as they were treated more like rock stars in this country, lavished with attention. It seemed as if everyone wanted to be near these American athletes, exotic in a country which had always appeared exotic to much of the rest of the world. There were additional perks provided to the skaters from some of the TV show sponsors and nightclubs pleaded for appearances by the skaters. Clubs that spread the word about Roller Games stars being in attendance were guaranteed a packed venue with almost everything being complimentary for the skaters. The male skaters were surrounded by adoring female fans and the female skaters even had marriage proposals.

Each team would also travel once during the 90-day tour to Perth and stay for a week. Perth is a beautiful coastal city located on the other side of the country with a travel distance similar to going from New York to Los Angeles. Teams were flown on commercial airlines such as TAA or Qantas. Games were scheduled Thursdays through Sundays and almost always sold-out with 6,000 attending each game. Perth was one of the skaters' favorite cities. It featured weather similar to Hawaii and had an abundance of beaches and fantastic nightlife. Skaters received star treatment to an even greater extent than in Sydney. In the USA, the skaters were familiar with being adored by fans, but in Australia, it was significantly magnified, especially on this initial tour.

After the initial three-month series between the T-Birds and Outlaws, the Hawaiian Warriors, San Francisco Shamrocks, Detroit Devils, and New York Bombers were flown into Australia, usually for a five to six-week series against the Aussie T-Birds.

Schedule for Thunderbirds and their opponents in 1966

Jan. 20-April 4: Texas Outlaws with Hardman and Trotter

April 13-May 22: Hawaiian Warriors with Dave Pound and Toni Tagg

May 25-July 3: San Francisco Shamrocks with John Parker and Adeline Hocker

July 6-August 7: Detroit Devils with Adeline Hocker, Charlie Mitchell and John Hall (infield)

Aug. 10-Sept 18: New York Bombers with Leroy Gonzales, Jan Vallow, Midge Brasuhn, and Nick Scopas

Sept. 21-Oct. 30: Hawaiian Warriors with John Parker, Toni Tagg, and Bobbie Velasco

Nov. 2-Dec. 11: Texas Outlaws with Shirley Hardman, Jim Trotter, and Vinnie Gandolfo

In late 1966, an official Roller Games league office was set up and staffed by Jerry Hill, followed later by Bill Griffiths and Red Smartt. Also, the league's medical officer, Ms. Dee Maresca, would manage the office for different periods of time. An Australian TV executive, John Frank, was hired to do promotions, booking, and other functions. He arranged for a regular Monday game in Adelaide in an arena seating 4,000, which was regularly sold-out.

The 1967 season began on January 18 in Perth. At the end of '66, Manny Servin and Ronnie Rains were touted as the renewing of their contracts with the Aussies were announced, plus the resignation of six Australian born skaters, John Single, Peter Kelly, Colleen Richardson, Colleen Murrell, Karen Steven, and Lynn Stephenson, was announced. Calvello left Australia, returning to the States, and was replaced as women's captain by Adeline Hocker. Valladares remained as coach and was joined by wife Honey Sanchez and their two daughters. Dave Cox, JoJo Stafford, and Toni Gandara were again with the team in '67, joined by Carol Phillips, who had skated the '66 season with the IRDL Bay Bombers. Darlene Anderson would join the team later in the year; everything was looking up.

Going into 1967, with a home team being there almost year-round, fans and skaters became very familiar. Details began to circulate about the game and how the skaters didn't hate each other. Skaters from visiting teams were frequently seen socializing with members of the Aussie T-Birds, their supposed enemies. The legitimacy of the games started to be questioned. Attendance dropped and games were no longer automatic sell-outs.

Some fans and the media were beginning to question the legitimacy of *The Roller Game* despite it still being popular and profitable, as this quote from the November 11, 1967, *Tasmania TV WEEK* suggests: "Brutal, phony, violent, disgusting. These are just some of the criticisms leveled at that most maligned of television programs, *The Roller Game*. It has been shown for less than two years, but in that time it has achieved a notoriety unparalleled in the eleven-year history of Australian TV. The Australian Broadcasting Control Board looks upon it with growing disfavor, and television critics have a caustic field day with the program's violence. But at trackside in Brisbane, Melbourne, and Sydney the promoters of *The Roller Game* are laughing up their financial sleeves - for this incredible display of mayhem on wheels is big business with a capital $. The Australian tracks costing $10,000 at Sydney Stadium, and the Festival Halls in Melbourne and Brisbane have attracted crowds. Sydney draws the biggest Roller Game TV audience - between 230,000 and 300,000 each Saturday afternoon. As many as 156,000 watch it on Melbourne's GTV9 and 70,000 on Adelaide's NWS9. Pro rata, the biggest audience is in Brisbane, where up to 150,000 tune-in to the show."

To compensate for the diminished attendance, match races between star skaters were implemented which began to sell-out again. Some of these battles featured new Women's Captain Adeline Hocker battling Shirley Hardman, Jan Vallow, or Ann Calvello, now leading the Shamrocks, along with Men's Coach Ralph Valladares against Jim Trotter, John Parker, or Leroy Gonzales, to name a few. With these added promotions, things quickly got back to normal and 1967 was another excellent year for Roller Games in Australia. Ralph Valladares was put in charge of training Australian skaters to supplement both the visiting teams and the T-Birds.

Tall and lanky Peter Kelly was the best homegrown Australian male skater. Promoted by John Parker to the big leagues, Kelly was a fan favorite and exhibited remarkable athleticism for a tall skater. One of his specialty moves was to appear off balance with one leg high in the air and then jump onto the rail, recover his balance, and jump onto the track, skating faster than ever. He would later become the primary trainer for all new kids in Australia and then coach the Australian Kangaroos in 1972. The Kangaroos were an All-Star team of the best skaters from Australia facing the best of the NSD in the States. Kelly would later skate for the Warriors, Cats, and Team Canada, marrying skater Marti Zinni. The best female star from Australia was blonde and perky Colleen Murrell, an intelligent speedster, who endeared herself to fans everywhere. She married Ronnie Rains while both were skating in Australia. Colleen would become a fan favorite in Southern California.

Adeline Hocker made her pro debut with Roller Derby in 1956, but serious injuries forced her to retire two years later. After being out of the game for four years, she made a comeback in 1962, joining the NSD Texas Outlaws, where she would become a major star with the league. She came to Australia at the beginning of the summer in 1966 and fell in love with the country and its people, eventually becoming Aussie women's captain when Calvello returned to the States. After the Aussie T-Birds ended, Hocker would lead the Devils and Florida Jets, but often skate for the L.A. T-Birds, being women's captain of the Traveling T-Birds on numerous occasions. She eventually relocated to Australia and lived there until her death in June 2010.

In 1968, attendance dipped again even with the match races. Roller Games may have been spread too thin to give proper attention to the operation in Australia as both Japan and Philadelphia were new start-ups. At the beginning of '68, the Los Angeles T-Birds skated "Down Under" against the Australia T-Birds. L.A. had Coach Reilly, Captain Lynch, Liz Hernandez, Carol Choyce, Ana Anaya, Ernie Lopez, Bob Corbin, and Greg Robertson. Australia had Coach Valladares, Captain Hocker, Darlene Anderson, Honey Sanchez, Colleen Murrell, Ronnie Rains, Manny Servin, JoJo Stafford, Dave Cox, and Peter Kelly. These same two teams met for ten games in February in Southern California. The Saturday night game on Febuary 17 at the Olympic was the last game in the USA for the Aussies. During the L.A. series, the T-Birds stars also featured Julie Patrick, Judy Sowinski, Sally Vega, Carmen Thompson, Roger Schroeder, Larry Lewis, and George Adams.

Revenue kept tumbling, but Australia continued as it was convenient and fiscally beneficial to combine tours to include both Japan and Australia and sometimes Hawaii. From an accounting standpoint, these three operations were looked upon as one and the numbers worked. It was a way to salvage Australia while the league attempted to regain its huge following. However, attendance stayed low with no signs of improving. As Japan became very profitable, the league began to withdraw from being a full-time operation in Australia and many original skaters returned to Los Angeles. Profits were marginal compared to 1966 and 1967. At the same time, Japan, Los Angeles, and Philadelphia were all doing well. The decision was finally made to close home team operations in Australia and dismantle the Australian Thunderbirds. The tracks were placed in storage with plans to do occasional tours. It was a sad moment for many skaters who had fallen in love with the land down under. The three-year period of 1966 to 1968 had brought roller derby to Australia, and for two of those years (1966 and 1977), it was the hottest ticket in the country. Those years were monumental and historical, developing a market for roller derby in Australia for the first time.

Looking back, John Hall laments, "If there had been adequate management to staff all the areas, it might have continued. So many of the skaters and I loved Australia." Bill Griffiths did take Roller Games back there in 1981 for a three-city tour of Perth, Sydney, and Brisbane, but an airline strike put a damper on the plans to re-establish the game. The T-Birds and Texas Outlaws returned to Australia in 1984 between April 23 through July 4 in Perth, Adelaide, Brisbane, and Sydney.

During this time in the United States, circa 1966, the league was still expanding and the Thunderbirds popularity grew both in game attendance and TV ratings, despite the loss of talent to Australia.

The Shamrocks were created at the end of 1965 to skate home games in the heart of the Bay Bombers' home territory (Roller Derby). Games were held at the 5,600 seat Winterland Ballroom. The Shamrocks were loaded with former Roller Derby stars such as Ann Calvello, Annis Jensen, Joe Foster, and many others. Griffiths and Hill offered these Derby skaters more money to make them jump to Roller Games. The games were held at the 6,000 seat Wintergarden Arena. Despite the star power the Shamrocks had acquired, they averaged only about 3,500 fans a game. The Bay Area was not ready to abandon their beloved Bombers and rejected both the Shamrocks and the Roller Games style of skating. After one season of the Shamrocks skating in the Bay Area, Jerry Seltzer and Bill Griffiths decided that the Shamrocks would stop skating home games in Northern California and would become a traveling team; Roller Games would stay in Southern California and the two leagues would begin hosting inter-league series.

In 1966, Leroy Gonzales once again led the New York Bombers to the finals to face the T-Birds. His team included Jan Vallow, Nick Scopas, Adeline Hocker, Lydia Rodriguez, J.J. Burton, Joe Guiterrez, Toni Dare, Larry Graham, Mary Holland, Tim Brown, Jim Williams, Barbara Gonzalez, Roger Hambrick, Judy Woodard, Richard Haffke, Lucy Chavarria, Bob Curry, Yolanda Trevino, Bob Mills, Carol Galindo, Dave Cannella, Don Oleson, Sandy Oleson, and Midge Brasuhn.

1966 also saw significant changes in management roles for the T-Birds. Bob Lewis was designated a unit manager for the NSD and would later become T-Birds G.M. in 1968. Danny Reilly was designated as the team's new head coach. Reilly was coming into his own as one of the league's top defensive skaters and had a knack for precise timing and showmanship. He would go on to become one of the biggest draws in the league. Bob Lewis was from Chicago, a former star with the original Derby and a fan-favorite with the L.A. Braves in the 1950s. He was involved with Roller Games from 1966 to 1971. Lewis was a Roller Games executive and a rock n' roll promoter. He arranged the very first Rolling Stones concert in the United States in 1964 at the Swing Auditorium in San Bernardino, a venue that the Thunderbirds also skated in. He also worked with Elvis Presley for three years in the 1970s.

In addition to the loss of Smartt and Gardner, Ralphie Valladares and an exciting young speedster, Ronnie Rains, were assigned to Australia to assist with the fledgling Australian Thunderbirds. With Ralphie gone, the '66 T-Birds were not quite as dominant as the team of 1965. But up-and-coming youngsters like Richard Brown, Sally Vega, and Larry Lewis picked up the slack. The women's team retained their dominance and even added Sugar Thompson, a terrific skater who would eventually go on to skate pro longer than almost anyone else.

With such a bolstered team facing a T-Bird squad devoid of two of its biggest stars, Bad-Boy Leroy had his best chance to date to win a championship. But despite his knack for inflaming fans and instigating trouble, league officials deemed it more beneficial to continue the reign of the Thunderbirds and the home team once again prevailed. Leroy wasn't pleased and felt somewhat disrespected by management. He would later express these feelings in shocking fashion.

Chapter 17

Brotherly Love (1967)

THUNDERBIRDS
Little Angie, Linda Moody, Judy Sowinski, Julie Patrick, Terri Lynch, Liz Hernandez, Carol Choyce, Sally Vega, Carmen Thompson
Bob Corbin, Greg Robertson, Larry Lewis, Danny Reilly, Eddie Payne, Roger Schroeder, George Adams, Gary Bickford

"Anyone who watched roller derby at the old Arena or saw their wild games on Channel 48 will recall that the Philadelphia Warriors had a thirst for mayhem. 'I had three bodyguards whenever I came to Philadelphia,' said Gootch Gautieri, a former player and official with the New York Bombers." –
David Block, *Philadelphia Inquirer*

967 was the year Roller Games said goodbye to Hawaii and hello to Philadelphia. Philadelphia had always been a popular market for the original Derby. The "City of Brotherly Love" had one of the original six teams called the Panthers when the NRDL was created in 1949. The team was led by Coach Elmer "Elbows" Anderson, Women's Captain Bobbie Johnstone (mother of Buddy, Jr.), with Buddy Atkinson, Sr., Hal Janowitz, Dolores Doss (who was destined to become one of the most popular female skating stars in Hawaii), Ann Calvello, and Jimmy Ciota (long-time veteran star from the East Coast). The Panthers were wildly popular with fans and were a staple at the Philly Arena, lasting until the mid-1950s when Derby moved West.

The NSD recognized Philly as being potentially profitable once again, something Hawaii was not capable of being, and the risky decision was made to move the Warriors to the East Coast. However, everything fell into place for the NSD in 1967 when a series of fortunate events took place. During the IRDL season, Jerry Seltzer learned that two of his best skaters, Buddy Atkinson, Jr. and Mike Gammon of the New York Chiefs, were talking about starting up a new outlaw league. Rather than disciplining them, Seltzer disbanded the Chiefs mid-season, sending Atkinson and Gammon and their two talented wives to National. Missing one team for the IRDL playoffs, Seltzer asked Griffiths to allow an NSD team, John Hall's Detroit Devils, to compete in his championship playoffs.

Atkinson, Gammon, and their wives Dru Scott and Judi McGuire were now the drawing cards for the Warriors' move east to Philly in the Fall of '67. Buddy, Jr. had been the MVP of the '65 and '66 IRDL season. Gammon was also the son of two Hall of Famers (Gerry Murray and Paul Milane), the league's MVP in 1960, and its top scorer. McGuire was the top female scorer in the IRDL. Roller Games had signed some of Derby's brightest new stars.

The Hawaiian Warriors were now the Philadelphia Warriors, often referred to as the Eastern Warriors, since not only were they skating in the Delaware Valley, they also ventured north to Boston and Braintree, Massachusetts and as far south as Baltimore and Washington, DC. The Warriors debuted on the East Coast in October 1967 against Shirley Hardman and Jim Trotter's Texas Outlaws. The second series featured the IRDL Midwest Pioneers, followed by the Detroit Devils with Midge "Toughie" Brasuhn and John Parker. Jan Vallow and Nick Scopas' New York Bombers would close out '67 and open '68.

The home base for the Warriors was the 5,500 seat Philly Arena, which first opened in 1920 (five years ahead of the Olympic Auditorium). It had been the home of the NBA Philadelphia Warriors up until 1962. Like many other teams, the Warriors moved west to San Francisco to eventually become the Golden State Warriors. The Warriors packed the Arena usually two or three times a week, almost always on Fridays. Sunday evening games started at 7:30 p.m. from the Camden Convention Center and would be televised live at 8 p.m. for two hours on WKBS, Channel 48, a UHF station in Philly. Within a few years, the Sunday evening game was held at the Arena and eventually moved to Sunday afternoons with the telecast shown on Sunday from 4 to 6 p.m., then re-broadcast on Saturday afternoons with some new commentary.

"When we got to Philadelphia in '67, we had very good TV ratings. But the first few months, we had small audiences. After a few months, we started selling out the Philadelphia Arena," said Buddy Atkinson, Jr.

The voice of the Warriors was Elmer "Elbows" Anderson, former Philly Panthers' coach. Elmer became as important to the team's success as any of the skaters, knowing instinctively how to sell the upcoming games to the viewing audience and becoming his own animated character in the banked track drama. When the team debuted, Buddy Atkinson, Jr., whose parents had been stars with the Panthers, was men's coach. The original Warriors team in Philly had Captain Judy Arnold, Mike Gammon, Judi McGuire, Dru Scott, Richard Brown, Harlean Khien, Yolanda Trevino, Lena McBride, Irene Maldinado, Erwin Miller, Ernie Lopez, and John Jimmerson. Within a few years, former Warriors coach, Vinnie Gandolfo would be back with the team, along with flat track champion Harry Morgan. Veteran skater, Pete Boyd filled in for an injured Atkinson at the start of '68.

During the first couple of years, attendance at Warriors games was low, but the NSD was patient. By 1969, the game telecasts were becoming quite popular and the live audience was growing. The local media was fascinated, covering the team at every opportunity. The Warriors were becoming the "in thing" to do in Philly on the weekends. The Arena was usually packed on Friday, Saturday, and Sunday evenings, with Sunday evenings attracting rabid fans from Philly's inner city as the T-Birds had done in L.A. African-American skaters like "Lefty Lena" McBride, Yvonne Riggins, Richard Brown, and Otis Williams became fan favorites and were featured prominently during games and in match races. Former coach Vinnie Gandolfo returned to the team in '69 and in '71, Jim Trotter and Ruberta Mitchell thrilled fans by joining the team; the Warriors were much stronger now.

Jerry Hill ran the Warriors on the East Coast from the start in October 1967 through September 1972 and they were regarded as one of the greatest teams in the history of the sport by historians and purists. The style of Roller Games in Philly was less-theatrical than its Southern California counterpart. The Warriors were the most "Derby" team in National since they skated a mix of both versions of the sport. Because of this, Derby purists viewed the Warriors more kindly than the T-Birds.

Jerry Hill allowed the skaters to supervise what happened on the track while he took care of the business. Judy Sowinski, New York Bombers' captain, noted her team always had to "up" their game when coming to Philly to skate the Warriors. Fans loved an intriguing drama, of course, but for them, it was secondary to the fast, hard-hitting skating. Scripted promotions and over-the-top theatrics didn't play as well in Philly as in glitzy Southern California. There was a mild attempt by Bill to move the games to more of an L.A. style when he visited eastern areas but since the revenues were healthy, he didn't push hard for many changes. The East Coast games were easier to skate with less intricate promotions to facilitate. The game itself was the primary draw for most fans in eastern cities. Philadelphia audiences had a thirst for blood.

"The Philly crowds always wanted us to smash someone. You could only do so much," said Judy Arnold. "One time, I was in a grudge-match race against Ruberta Mitchell, and an idiot fan jumped on the track and attacked me. I kicked him in the face with my skates and put him in the hospital. He had no business assaulting me," said Gootch Gautieri. "Fan attendance jumped, and it increased further with the halftime 'match race,' an anything-and-everything-goes street fight on wheels. The match races, unlike the games, were never televised, the better to sell tickets," said David Block of the *Philadelphia Inquirer.*

A traveling team of L.A. T-Birds made appearances in Philly starting in 1968. Ralph Valladares and Liz Hernandez, along with Ronnie Rains, Colleen Murrell, and Honey Sanchez, led the T-Birds to the East Coast, while the regular T-Birds still skated in Southern California. Over the years, Adeline Hocker and Danny Reilly became the most visible leaders of the traveling T-Birds in Philly. During one series in December 1969, Jan Vallow and John Parker were captain and coach of the team, archenemies of the team in L.A. In December 1973, the final series for the NSD on the East Coast featured the Warriors and T-Birds.

The Warriors skated their first game at the new 16,000-seat Philadelphia Spectrum during the Eastern Regional Playoffs in June 1970. Some called it *Judy's Place* after the Warriors' women's captain, and the Spectrum would eventually become the Tuesday evening site for most games. Over the years, the Warriors averaged 7,000 to 12,000 with occasional sell-outs. In October 1970, the Warriors hosted a three game series against the T-Birds with Terri Lynch and Danny Reilly, the first and only time Lynch skated for the T-Birds in Philly.

Buddy Atkinson was named general manager in 1971 and would skate less often now that Jim Trotter was with the team. The Warriors became so popular that the team was split in two during the summer of 1971, with one Warrior team on the Eastern Seaboard and the other in Hawaii. At the end of 1971, a decision was made to make this split permanent with the creation of the Baltimore-Washington Cats. Richard Brown, Vinnie Gandolfo, Ruberta Mitchell, and Yolanda

Trevino became the centerpiece of the Cats, along with Sonja Sims, a relatively unknown skater who became a huge star with the team.

By 1973, the Warriors were branching out into newer markets all across Pennsylvania and New Jersey, often selling out all six games during the week, particularly during the Dave Pound saga. It appeared as if nothing could stop the team's success. In the summer of '73, the Baltimore Cats and Philadelphia Warriors combined and became known as the War-Cats, skating in resort cities along the Atlantic Coast. When the original Roller Derby folded in '73, the War-Cats ventured into some of the former Seltzer territories. One of the best old Derby cities for the War-Cats was Atlanta. The Omni Arena held 12,000, and the War-Cats averaged over 9,000 there.

The Warriors were also very popular in Puerto Rico, eventually skating a home series on the island that was the catalyst for the creation of the Latin Libertadores, Roller Games' first all-Latin team led by Leroy Gonzales and Sally Vega. The Libs would eventually host a series against the Warriors in Puerto Rico in 1974.

Cindy Ogbin, Lynn Congleton, and Bessie Gonzales became fan favorites in the early 1970s along with Carey "Butch" McCrae, Al Candolero, Jeff Hart, Roger McLeod, and Sammy Evans. Jess Adams, a former skater, would become the team's general manager in '74 as Buddy Jr. returned to skating full time. The Warriors even won the very first ISC World Series Championship playoffs in August 1974.

But with the National Skating Derby's closing, the tried-and-true routine that fans came to know ended. For years, the Warriors would skate October to June, then spend a couple of months in Hawaii or on the Eastern Seaboard. September meant a trip to Southern California (the Warriors participated in the '71 NSD World Series, placing third) or to Florida in 1969, creating a foundation for the Florida Jets or in Puerto Rico ('73). Fans could always find the Warriors on Friday nights and Sunday afternoons at the Philly Arena, but all of a sudden, this was no longer the case.

By 1974, the Warriors could be anywhere except the Philly Arena. Fans were watching a team with many new members skate "red" on TV. Fans witnessed the Warriors skating as villains against the Cats during the ISC and against the T-Birds in L.A., something never seen before. The usual cast of characters of Outlaws, Bombers, Hawks, and Devils were replaced by the Chiefs, Team Canada, and more games with the T-Birds. The ISC couldn't find the appropriate balance between pure skating and theatrics. To the dismay of fans, more over-the-top antics transpired.

The team's biggest star, Judy Arnold, then decided to retire at the end of the summer in 1975. Judy Sowinski would leave the T-Birds and skate for the Warriors at the end of '74, in preparation for Arnold's retirement. Some experts considered Judy to be one of the top-five best all-around women skaters in the history of the sport. Fans worshipped her. There were occasions when during an interview, "Pretty Judy" would get so upset and begin to cry, endearing herself to more and more fans, showing emotions never typically displayed in Roller Games. Once Judy Arnold was gone at the end of the summer in 1975, many fans saw no reason to watch.

The Warriors would lose the second ISC World Series Championship playoffs to the T-Birds in 1975, but by then, the entire league was limping along. When Bill Griffith shut down Roller Games in the middle of '75, there was no longer any television coverage and attendance suffered. Ed Derian, who was the house announcer and assistant unit manager, purchased the rights to Roller Games-East, Inc. when the NSD decided to vacate the area. He soon sold the rights to John Hall, who closed the entire Warriors operation in late 1975. John still maintains the rights to this day. The team fans loved was gone but is still fondly remembered. The Warriors (Hawaii and Philadelphia) operated successfully from 1963 to 1975.

In 1967, while the Warriors were being established in Philadelphia, Roller Games' popularity was leveling off, but still firm in Australia. In January the very first NFL Super Bowl was held at the Los Angeles Memorial Coliseum with Vince Lombardi's Green Bay Packers taking the game over the AFL's Kansas City Chiefs. Just two miles down the road from the Coliseum, the Thunderbirds were continuing to build their well-established following in Los Angeles at the Olympic Auditorium.

1967 may be remembered as the "Summer of Love," but for Roller Games purists, it was the year of #17, the number worn by one of the greatest female skaters of all-time, Shirley Hardman. Hardman was the leader of the Texas Outlaws for many years and came to epitomize what a red-shirt skater can do to terrorize opposing skaters and bolster league attendance. Hardman was a rough and tumble skater as well as a colorful, tough team leader. Because of her rugged style of skating, Hardman suffered career-ending injuries, but reinvented herself in 1972 as the first female manager in the history of the sport with the T-Birds, endearing herself to fans who had booed her mercilessly for a decade. But for longtime fans of Roller Games, she is best remembered as the villainous skater from the Texas Outlaws. In the year of 1967, the Hardman/Lynch rivalry reached its zenith. The pair had worked together (as opposing skaters) for many years and knew each other's moves instinctively. Fans had relished the rivalry for seven years, but sadly Hardman was severely injured the next year in an interleague game with the San Francisco Bay Bombers and never fully recovered. The rivalry was never the same again.

Terri Lynch was one of the first women's captains of the original T-Birds team. To her teammates, Terri was a strict disciplinarian, but also a well-respected captain and fierce skater. She was a fan favorite as she was fiery, temperamental, and had tremendous skating abilities. Terri led the T-Birds from their beginning in 1961 until she retired in early 1973. When the Outlaw league went to Europe in June of 1960, they didn't have any idea that they were going to be the precursor of Roller Games. Terri Lynch spearheaded getting this outlaw group to Paris and Casablanca. It was natural she would be named the inaugural coach of the T-Birds. Terri Lynch was the first female star of the Thunderbirds. The fiery redheaded captain of the Thunderbird women had a long-running feud with Shirley Hardman of the Texas Outlaws. Their rivalry was analogous to that of Roller Derby's Weston and Calvello and their legendary battles. In 1967, both skaters were at their very best and fighting for the championship. Terri Lynch retired in June 1972 because of extreme fatigue. After leaving Roller Games in 1972, Lynch became a social worker in L.A.

before retiring to Hawaii in 1999. She was inducted into the National Roller Derby Hall of Fame before her death on June 21, 2015.

Facing this talented '67 Outlaws team, the "Summer of Love" had little relevance to the T-Birds on the track, as they confronted a war whenever Shirley and her Outlaws came to town. But off the track, the Civil Rights Movement was making strides that impacted the lives of African Americans, Hispanics, and other minorities across the U.S. The Women's Movement was making similar gains for women across America. These movements happening across America reflected what the banked track sport had been doing for years. Women played by the same rules as men in Roller Games. Blacks, Hispanics, and other minorities were already making their mark on the banked track. By virtue of these facts, Roller Games had already sustained a cultural impact across America and especially in Los Angeles.

For the entire '67 season, Texas women consisted of Hardman, Norma Rossner, Jean Welch, Sandy Young, Baby Rocco, and Syverson. The Texas men at the start of the season consisted of Jim Trotter, Bob Roberts, Art Salaiz, Dave Cannella, Larry Graham, and Rick West. Only Trotter and Salaiz were with the team at the end of the season with Lou Sanchez, Bob Mayo, Tom Crews, Johnny Velez, and Irwin Miller. Miller went to the Warriors in the Fall, and Rick West rejoined the team. These Outlaws skated the Bay Bombers in April '67 in an interleague series. The Thunderbirds of '67 were similar to '66 with Ralphie and Ronnie Rains still in Australia. They started '67 with Coach Reilly, Roger Schroeder, Richard Brown, Eddie Payne, Larry Lewis, Gary Bickford, Johnny Chavez, Captain Lynch, Sowinski, Hernandez, Sanchez, Carmen Thompson, Betty Stone, and Carol Choyce. Richard Brown left the team in the summer, going to the Warriors along with Bob Corbin, Sally Vega, and rookie Greg Robertson. Julie Patrick also skated part of the season and Red Smartt was the general manager. The team had a half-dozen future Hall of Fame inductees.

Though they tried, the Outlaws were unable to unseat the T-Birds from their throne, but 1967 was another big year for Roller Games and a good one for positive social change.

Chapter 18

Sympathy for the Devil (1968)

1968 LOS ANGELES THUNDERBIRDS
JULIE PATRICK, CARMEN THOMPSON, SALLY VEGA, TOMMY MYAMOTO, SALLY JIMMERSON, LINDA MOODY, MARGARET SMITH
GARY BICKFORD, LARRY LEWIS, ROGER SCHROEDER, WALT GOODWIN, EDDIE PAYNE, GEORGE ADAMS

"The athlete who catches the imagination is the individualist, the free soul who challenges not only the opposition but the generally accepted rules of behavior. Essentially, he should be uncivilized. Untamed." – Bill Veeck, owner, Chicago White Sox

The Detroit Devils were consistently one of the top rivals for the Thunderbirds. John Hall's skating time was virtually eliminated since he had broken his neck in that unfortunate pre-game accident in 1965, but his role as Devils infield manger became magnified. In 1968, the already strong Devils were bolstered by the addition of superstar Leroy "Bad-Boy" Gonzales, who until then had served as the coach of the New York Bombers.

Fans were very familiar with Gonzales, and he was one of the most feared skaters in the entire league. Leroy was psycho even before Ronnie Rains laid claim to the title. Leroy was often unpredictable on the track and opposition skaters had to be aware of where he was at all times. Off the track, because of his personality and warmth, skaters were fond of Leroy and he was extremely popular. They recognized and respected his talent, even if his behavior on the track often veered to the unpredictable. His on-track persona in Southern California, especially regarding T-Birds fans, was undoubtedly as "red" as any skater could be; that was his role and he played it well. He was a talented skater, a good interview, and a huge box office draw. Leroy was as intelligent as anyone skating in the game at the time. From his earliest days around the sport, Leroy was noted for being introspective, and often seen intensely studying the game trackside, often alone. He was a great student of the game, somewhat rare in roller derby. When he returned from the military, he exhibited a newfound discipline that many admired and when he was back in the IRDL in '63, he was encouraged by Ken Monte to skate more aggressively. Almost overnight, Gonzales exhibited a fiery temper and unforgiving nature on the track, something not appreciated by Charlie O'Connell, Derby's premier star. During an interleague series against the Bay Bombers in '66, he clocked O'Connell with his skate, breaking Charlie's nose and making it clear that Roller Games was not going to take the brush off from the IRDL. More importantly, Leroy made it clear that he wouldn't back down from anyone. With Leroy as coach and Hall serving as infield manager, the Devils stormed into the playoffs and eventually the 1968 Roller Games World Series.

In a preview of a storyline which would eventually be taken to its natural conclusion, John Hall was named probationary general manager of the T-Birds, replacing Red Smartt who retired. The T-Birds' archenemy was now part of the home team. But then in April, Hall was fired as T-Birds G.M. and returned to the Devils. Smartt returned to the T-Birds. The whole episode was to promote a match race between Smartt and Hall at the Los Angeles Sports Arena on June 15 during the President's Cup Championship. Hall was victorious over Smartt in the match race, and the New York Bombers beat the T-Birds for the Cup. Red Smartt announced his permanent retirement because of injuries suffered in the match race. Hall was now once again a brutal competitor and a lethal personality, capable of destroying the T-Birds, even if he wasn't skating in games. This would serve him well when he'd once again join the T-Birds the following year.

The '68 Series had been scripted for the T-Birds to take the title once again. Posters and other promotional items had already been produced before the final game declaring the T-Birds were seven-time World Champions. They had been the champions every year except 1961 when no official championship was held. The Detroit Devils won the very first President's Cup playoffs in '62. No team to this point, other than the Thunderbirds, had ever won the championship title. Everyone knew what would happen and everyone was naturally committed to making sure it happened, except Leroy.

Leroy took it upon himself to change history. The final World Series game was in double overtime with only the last jam remaining and Detroit was ahead. Leroy took the jamming helmet for the Devils and Danny Reilly for the T-Birds. Reilly and Gonzales were long-time rivals and had been battling it out the entire game. At the start of the final jam, Gonzales sprinted ahead of Reilly and made it past three T-Birds skaters to score go-ahead points. Reilly came up from behind with the possibility of scoring to win the game, as planned, but Leroy put his hands on his hips to call off the jam. There were only a few seconds left on the clock without enough time for another jam and the Detroit Devils were the World Champions.

"Danny Reilly was on the last jam (wearing his wooden wheels), not Valladares. Leroy called the jam off as time was close to running out. I was on the infield and I'll always have a vivid memory of that," said John Hall

The Devils became the first team other than the T-Birds to win the world title. They would never win another. It was just too profitable to promote the Thunderbirds as the World Champs when they embarked on their annual exhibition tour to cities where the TV ratings were strong. Also, Championship titles were important in the sense that the T-Birds always had to win the big games in order to fully complete the morality play elements of the sport. Simply put, Roller Games was sports entertainment. In Roller Games, there was never ever any doubt the T-Birds would win. This certainly played into the "fake" adjective that always followed Roller Games. However, to management, all that mattered was that the T-Birds won, especially the big games. What Leroy did in '68 was stunning and a complete "middle finger" to the establishment.

Why did Leroy go against the wishes of management and single-handedly change the course of the 1968 World Series? It's one of the most intriguing stories in the history of Roller Games. There were likely several reasons, but some who knew him personally have speculated that it all came down to one thing: not being appreciated and properly respected for his contributions. Leroy had taken the New York Bombers and turned them into one of the best red-shirt teams in the history of the sport. With Leroy leading the way, the Bombers went to the finals in 1965 and 1966, but both times came up empty. Now he had turned the Devils into the league's biggest draw, and he made sure they went down in history.

Following the unplanned debacle, Leroy was summoned to the office of Griffiths and Hill. He would likely be banished from the league. And there was no guarantee he would be welcomed back by Roller Derby either since some were upset when he broke the nose of superstar Charlie O'Connell. But Leroy was friends with John Hall, who was respected by league owners and one of their most loyal associates. John lobbied on behalf of Leroy and rather than being fired he walked out of that meeting the new coach of the Detroit

Devils for 1969, replacing Hall who was named general manager and infield coach of the home team Thunderbirds. For the most part with only one exception, John remained in that position for the rest of his career in Roller Games until 1986.

This was a significant event in the timeline of the T-Birds. John would go on to become loved by T-Bird fans everywhere and, along with Ralphie, was the face of the franchise.

So was it John's persuasive argument that saved Leroy or the timing of John being moved to the home team? Or was Leroy just too valuable to lose? Maybe a bit of both. Only Bill Griffiths and Jerry Hill would know for sure.

In 1969, Leroy coached the Devils as he had done in 1968 and fans packed the Olympic and other venues to see the World Champs and their hated coach/former player. However, the Devils were not part of the Finals that year. Leroy continued to coach the Devils into the 1972 season until he was recruited to coach the young Australian Devils.

Chapter 19

Jamming in Japan (1969)

LOS ANGELES THUNDERBIRDS

Angie Rositto, Terry Lynch, Ralph Valladares, Bill Griffiths, Sr., John Hall
Bob Corbin, Evangelena Horne, Danny Reilly, Julie Patrick, Betty Stone, Greg Robertson, Barbara Jacobs,
Lennie Silverman, Larry Lewis, Honey Sanchez, Mannie Servin, Carmen Thompson, Colleen Murrell, George Fernandez

*"The Roller Derby is the panacea of the proletariat, the great
Un-sport, a smash-and-crash arena of spills where the most
triumphant moment means watching good broad Joanie Weston
bump bad broad Ann Calvello hard enough in the boobs to
drive her over the rail. Mr. Deford presents a lively picture of all*

this, but the real story should lie in the hands of the sociologists and analysts, an interesting study of America the Violent in Five Strides." – Kirkus Reviews.

Roller Games had several big years in Japan, but 1969 was likely the biggest of all. Having successfully introduced Roller Games to Australia, establishing the sport "Down Under" for an entirely new continent of fans, by 1968, Bill Griffiths was focused on Japan, setting up a sweetheart deal for a new market for his Roller Games empire. The first exhibition games took place September 10-23, 1968, with the T-Bird All-Stars facing the Devils at the Korakuen Ice Arena in Tokyo. The ten-game series played to capacity crowds every game in the 16,000-seat arena.

In 1968, the Philadelphia Warriors, with a lineup of top stars rivaling the T-Birds, had returned for a summer season in Hawaii and were not due back in the Delaware Valley until October; so it was decided to bring many of the team's skaters to Japan to supplement the T-Birds and Devils. The T-Birds debuted in Japan with a team led by Coach Danny Reilly, Captain Judy Sowinski, Liz Hernandez, Julie Patrick, Ronnie Rains, Colleen Murrell, Peter Kelly, and Greg Robertson, along with Warriors' Richard Brown, Erwin Miller, Harlean Khien, and Lena McBride. The Devils had Coach Art Salaiz, Captain Adeline Hocker, Sally Vega, Lester Quarles, Paul Rupert, Diane Syverson, along with Buddy Atkinson, Jr., Judy Arnold, Mike Gammon, Judi McGuire, Otis Williams, and Dru Scott from the Warriors.

The Japanese fans loved the game and conventionally showed their appreciation with enthusiastic, polite applause. "Oohs and aahs" rang out from many younger fans. Broadcasts of Thunderbirds' games from Los Angeles were top-rated in Japan on one of the major stations in the country, Channel 12. When the team arrived in Tokyo, they already had a legion of hardcore fans awaiting them. Getting to the arena on private buses presented no problems for both squads, but following the game, it was mayhem. Younger fans surrounded the bus carrying the T-Birds, climbing on it and blocking it from leaving the arena. Extra police had to be called in to clear a pathway for the bus. The police prevented many fans from following the bus to the hotel.

The first series in Tokyo proved to be wildly successful beyond anyone's expectations. All ten games were sold out, and fans couldn't get enough. The Japanese promoters were overjoyed. They had a big hit on their hands and wanted more games scheduled. Bill Griffiths was also thrilled because he knew he would have the upper hand in negotiations for future exhibitions. Everyone involved couldn't be more excited about the future of Roller Games in Japan.

A second Japanese exhibition series, which lasted three weeks, took place in February 1969 between the T-Bird All-Stars and New York Bomber. The New York Bombers lineup at the time was John Parker, Jan Vallow, Nick Scopas, B.J. Peterson, Charlie Mitchell, Dave Cox, Leon Jackson, Bob Mayo, Carol Phillips, Diane Syverson, and Barbara Williams.

The third Japanese exhibition series, another ten games, took place June 4-15, 1969, between the T-Bird All-Stars and Texas Outlaws. Skating for the T-Birds was Coach Ralph Valladares, Captain Terri Lynch, Bob Corbin, Ernie Lopez, Larry Lewis, Lenny Silverman, Greg Robertson, Julie Patrick, Lena McBride, Renee Hall, Colleen Murrell, and Marti Rueda. Listed as skating for the Texas Outlaws were Shirley Hardman, Jim Trotter, Norma Rossner, Adeline Hocker, Baby Rocco, Toni Kadrmas, Jean Welch, JoJo Stafford, Dave Cox, Bob Mayo, Ernie Rodriguez, and Tom Alcott.

By the middle of 1969, after three successful series, expectations for the growth of Roller Games in Japan couldn't have been higher. T-Bird broadcasts were popular on Channel 12 and a training center, headed by Ralph Valladares, was opened to cultivate local talent. Many young Japanese locals wanted to become professional Roller Games skaters and worked diligently to master the game. Valladares quickly recognized and developed several solid skaters including Miki Tsunoda, Yoko Sasaki, Kaz Kawano, and Keiko Ayabe, who occasionally skated with the T-Birds in Los Angeles and competed against American skaters, in addition to cultivating the Asian market in Southern California. The Japanese trainees were proving to be hard-working, intelligent athletes who wanted nothing more than to succeed and become professional skaters.

One of the most thrilling skating stars to come out of Japan was speedster, Hiroshi Koizumi. Hiroshi would captivate fans in both Japan and the United States with his talent and expertise, becoming the most enduring figure in the history of the sport in Japan. Hiroshi has been promoting both flat track and banked track Derby events around the world over the past four decades and today is still the driving force behind Roller Games in Japan.

Jerry Hill focused his attention on Philadelphia, making the Warriors a powerful addition to the National Skating Derby, while Bill Griffiths was solely responsible for the Japanese operation. Plans were made to skate live games to other cities in Japan like Osaka, Kyoto, and Nagoya among others. Exhibitions in Japan continued in 1970 with everyone expecting the market to continue to proliferate.

Initially, Griffith had cut a great deal in Japan with most of the profits going to Roller Games. The Tokyo TV station was running the business on the Japanese side of things, an integral part of the overall success, and wanted a more equitable split of profits. With the success of the training program, more Japanese skaters filled out rosters, meaning fewer U.S. skaters were needed in Japan. This reduced Roller Games' expenses, but Griffiths was familiar with Japanese culture and knew they would honor the original contract. He listened to their requests, but did not offer to alter the existing agreements. At the end of 1970, talks once again began for a new deal between both parties.

As negotiations continued, the local promoters felt Roller Games was prospering in the country because of television exposure, while Griffiths felt the Japanese wanted too much of the profits for a product he had introduced and cultivated. The talks went nowhere, with both sides unwilling to budge. For some unexplainable reason, negotiations ended with no compromise and the future of Roller Games in Japan began to appear doomed. To most people other than Griffith and the Japanese promoters, the impasse and the lack of compromise could not be explained. Expanding Roller Games in Japan was an unfulfilled opportunity and still to this day remains a mystery since the principal negotiators are no longer alive, and no one understands why an agreement could not be made. The training school continued operating, but the future of live games and a fully realized Japanese league never materialized.

Even with the pause, the Tokyo Bombers debuted in the United States in 1973 with a complete all-Japanese roster of the best skaters from the island. Usually competing around the USA in the first game of doubleheaders, the Tokyo team's entry into the NSD necessitated the New York Bombers to change its nickname to the "Bears" to avoid any confusion with the Tokyo squad. Wearing red, white, and blue uniforms, similar to the T-Birds, Miki Tsunoda and Yoko Sasaki led this team of extraordinarily resilient and talented skaters, who often out-skated the more experienced US teams. Valladares managed the Bombers on the infield while Colleen Murrell assisted the women.

The Tokyo Bombers skated in the U.S. while skating the occasional series in Japan, too. The Northern Hawks with John Parker, Betty Brown, Juan Molano, and E.G. Miller traveled to Japan at the end of 1973 to skate the Bombers. When the International Skating Conference was created in 1974, the Tokyo Bombers were part of the new ISC. The Los Angeles T-Birds, lead by Danny Reilly and Gwen Miller, even skated a series against the Tokyo Bombers in Japan in 1974. The team continued into 1975, demonstrating a polished style and expertise against the best teams in the United States. A *Samura Sword* tournament was even held on the East Coast in February 1975, featuring the Bombers against the Warriors and NY Chiefs.

For years, Roller Games had been the biggest craze in Japan. The T-Birds were treated like rock stars during their first appearances, and American skaters loved being exposed to a new culture with polite, adoring Japanese fans. Arenas were often sold out. It lasted nearly eight years from 1968 to 1975. The T-Birds were famous and revered and they were even invited to meet the Emperor Showa of Japan. Why Roller Games did not continue developing the market is one of the sport's great mysteries.

In 1969, while Roller Games was busy making their mark in "The Land of the Rising Sun," the Thunderbirds were packing fans into the Olympic Auditorium in Los Angeles. Then on March 3, 1969, *Sports Illustrated* published an article penned by legendary writer, Frank Deford, simply titled *The Roller Derby*. The 15-page feature was the longest story ever to appear in a single issue of SI up to that time and was the basis for DeFord's first book (of many), *Five Strides on the Banked Track*, which was released two years following the article, in 1971. A feature of this length, published in the world's largest and most respected sports publication, showed just how popular roller derby had become by 1969. It also introduced the sport to a new legion of potential fans. DeFord personally accompanied the Bay Bombers on a portion of their 1968 Fall Tour, getting to know the game and its participants up close. While there have been countless articles written on classic roller derby over the years, this was the first and only time a significant sportswriter traveled with a roller derby team, which is why it was so important. In his writings, DeFord was candid and honest in his portrayal of roller derby without a hint of the snobbery often found from writers who covered more traditional sports. He didn't endorse roller derby as a sport per say, but he appreciated the entertainment value. His curiosity and occasional intrigue are evident throughout his writings. Everyone felt this mainstream press writer from Sports Illustrated was going to do a "hit job" on the sport, but instead, he fell in love with it in its purity and simplicity, especially its skaters. The significance of Deford's SI article and book, was it offered admiration and respect from the mainstream press for a popular sports entertainment phenomenon, making it okay for all sports fans to acknowledge the banked track game without fear of ridicule.

Like roller derby, the article was highly controversial, and SI took a fair amount of heat for publishing it. Many sports traditionalists were outraged that America's premier sports mag would give roller derby such glorified coverage. But on the other hand, some readers wrote reviews in support of the article.

DeFord's SI feature bolstered the already strong fan support of the Bay Bombers, as well as provided a smaller bump for the Thunderbirds. It was good for the game in general. Frank DeFord was inducted into the Roller Derby Hall of Fame in November of 2012. He died on May 28, 2017.

The 1969 Roller Games season was the most successful to date, with attendance soaring and viewership on television at an all-time high. The New York Bombers, now led by former T-Bird greats, Ronnie Rains and Judy Sowinski, were the best, most exciting red shirt team in Roller Games. The Bombers would compete in their third World Series finals against the Thunderbirds.

In 1969, some top skaters returned from Australia to Los Angeles, while others were temporarily relocated to Japan. So there was a lot of roster shuffling and those who started with one team at the beginning of the season, often did not finish the season with that same team. This started in 1966 due to the expansion to Australia, skating in Japan and the Warriors skating a full season on the East Coast. So, rosters were fluid and skaters went where they were needed.

In April 1969, the New York Bombers had Coach Rains, Captain Sowinski, Charlie Mitchell, B.J. Peterson, Lester Quarles, Carol Phillips, Buddy Redoble, Terri Toledo, Leon Jackson, Ruberta Mitchell, Vinnie Gandolfo, Barbara Williams, and Jess Adams. They basically had the same roster in October, at the end of the season, before the World Series, although Gandolfo had rejoined the Warriors, Redoble was gone, and Abel Lara was added to the men's team. Rachel Sarabia was added to the women's squad as well.

As for the Thunderbirds, the 1969 team was another powerhouse featuring a veritable all-star team. Ralph Valladares returned to Los Angeles to coach the team, alongside Bob Lewis. Veteran Terri Lynch captained the women's team. Aside from Ralphie's return, the biggest news was that John Hall returned to L.A., this time permanently, making his Thunderbird debut as assistant general manager. John had made a significant impact as a red-shirt skater and team manager, as well as a member of the Detroit Devils, but his influence during his tenure with the Thunderbirds was even more significant. John would remain a T-Bird until 1986. The men's team also added three young speedsters in Sam "The Man" Washington, Billy "Hot Wheels" Marshall, and George Fernandez. And this was a team that already had one of the fastest, smoothest, pure skaters of all-time, Larry Lewis. Fernandez was a graceful skater in the Lewis mold and stuck around a long time as well. Danny Reilly again led the men's defense, with able assistance from Greg Robertson and Lenny Silverman. Other talented men included Manny Servin, Eddie Payne, Mike Gochnaur, and Bob Corbin. Lynch's women featured Julie Patrick, Honey Sanchez, Carmen Thompson, Colleen Murrell (a recent import from Australia), Barbara Jacobs, Betty Stone, Evangelina Horne, Margaret Smith, Renee Hall, Karen Grant, and twin sisters Carolyn and Carol Kruse.

The T-Birds and Detroit Devils visited Mexico City on September 6, 1969 and drew a capacity crowd of 22,121 at Palacio de Los Deportes Arena. This was a record crowd for Roller Games at the time and led to the scheduling of a ten-game series the following year.

The '69 season was one of the best. The Thunderbirds retained their title as World Champions and from the evidence of record attendance and TV ratings that often eclipsed the numbers put up by other L.A. teams in more traditional sports, it didn't appear that fans cared much that their team never seemed to lose. At this point, everything was working.

As the 1960s ended, the league and its flagship team were the toast of Los Angeles, and there was no shortage of optimism. On the eastern side of the country, the popularity of the Philadelphia Warriors was now well rooted and rivaled that of even the T-Birds. It would later be considered the greatest decade ever for Roller Games!

Chapter 20
Devil's Advocate (1970)

Thunderbirds

Sam Washington, Henry Sahagun, Ralph Valladares, Danny Reilly, Billy Marshall, Greg Robertson, George Fernandez
Lena Horne, Carolyn Kruse, Carol Kruse, Gwen Miller, Terri Lynch, Honey Sanchez, Barbara Jacobs, Carmen Thompson

"Roller Games was a world-wide phenomenon for a reason; you don't get that popular that fast on fighting and hair-pulling alone." – WindyCityRD

A s Roller Games entered its second decade of operation, the country was going through seismic social and political changes. As the T-Birds battled old foes and new and some from within their own ranks, the country was experiencing something similar, as even fathers and sons found themselves on different sides of the political spectrum. The social optimism that emanated in the '60s also carried into the early '70s, but differently. The wannabe hippies who latched onto the crusade for the abundance of free love and drugs started to peel off and the movement, although reduced in size, began to evolve in new ways. Those that remained were the same dedicated folks that started it. Highly educated and motivated to make a real difference. And they did. Women, minorities, homosexuals, and the environment all benefitted. The driving forces behind the Vietnam War succumbed to public pressure and the reigning U.S. President was forced to step down. This post-'60s period brought with it a more educated and aware society. The music of this period reflected a nation with a higher consciousness. Prevalent music of the day, which had been basic rock and roll since the late 1950s, began to evolve into more intricate compositions featuring expanded musical pieces with profound lyrics and instrumental talent rarely seen in the rock field years prior. The Beatles had led us to the promised land of musicality, and new groups like Yes, Genesis and Pink Floyd took that a step further. The early '70s was a time of robust economics and more leisure time. The middle class was expanding and many of these people attended roller derby games for the first time as the popularity of the sport was growing. The fact that both leagues featured a highly athletic game with an emphasis on speed and hitting didn't hurt.

Roller Games had experienced great success internationally during the 1960s, but as those operations wound down, the expansion of the league began to be focused locally in the United States. The second deck of the Olympic was now routinely packed and T-Bird skaters were household names in Los Angeles and surrounding areas. TV ratings were sky high and everyone seemed to be tuned-in.

Hollywood was in the process of making a blockbuster movie based on Roller Games. There was no end in sight.

When the '70s rolled around, there was a slight, yet deliberate increase in the game's theatrics and with it came a corresponding boom in attendance. The difference between this period and later periods with elevated mayhem was the fact these skaters had the talent, training, and conditioning to pull off the required stunts. The game itself was still the focus and the draw but the storylines, often scripted by Bill "Hoppy" Haupt, added the icing to the cake. Intrigued fans ate it up.

Because of the expanded TV ratings and attendance to live games, the Thunderbird skaters of the early 1970s were the best remembered, even today. In the early '70s, the most familiar faces to fans were General Manager John Hall along with Coaches Shirley Hardman, Terri Lynch, Ralph Valladares, and Danny Reilly. In 1970, Liz Hernandez, the Hispanic darling of Southern California who had gone into semi-retirement in '69, re-emerged skating for the Chicago Hawks, alongside Norma Rossner. The "Big Three" of the T-Birds during the 1960s: Lynch, Sowinski, and Hernandez were then skating with three different teams.

Although they didn't make it to the 1970 World Series, the Chicago Hawks were back, bigger and better than ever; with the emergence of Lester Quarles as men's coach and big, beautiful orange-and-brown uniforms with numbers in the '30s. Trained with brother DeWitt in the original Derby, Lester Quarles had been with the NY Bombers in '69, but then had his own team and took his place as one of the most prominent figures in Roller Games during the first half of the 1970s.

In the 1970 World Series, the Thunderbirds squared off against their then decade-old rivals, the Detroit Devils, and their notorious coach, the devil's advocate, Leroy Gonzales. The Devils had recently won the President's Cup and looked very strong. Gonzales was assisted by Paul Rupert, Lenny "Chicken Man" Silverman, Bob Mayo, and "Big" Bill DePhilippis; a product of the George Vogt's L.A. Training School. He then got Larry Lewis in the summer after the Florida Jets folded. Lewis began skating "red" and was viewed by T-Birds fans as a traitor. For the Devils' women, Sally Vega was gone and was replaced by Diane Syverson, who eventually became a major player in the women's field over the next decade. Syverson was leading a team for the first time, ably assisted by a number of women who also became big stars in the 1970s; B.J. Peterson, Peggy Fowler, and Betty Brown, along with Cindy Ogbin, who became a big star with the Warriors on the East Coast.

Over the winter of '69, Sally Vega announced she no longer wanted to be women's captain of the Devils. She wanted to skate with the T-Birds, but Devils' coach, Leroy Gonzales did not allow it. This was a long-running saga all season. Barbara Jacobs and Sam Washington, who were named the '69 Rookies of the Year, played a bigger role with the team in 1970. Newcomers George Fernandez, Henry Sahagun, and Gwen Miller were added to the team in '70. Yet the big news was the addition of "Big Man" John Johnson in the summer, along with Japanese skaters, Miki Tsunoda and Yoko Sasaki. Vega was back with the team in the summer too. The addition of Johnson and Vega was a big complication during the season with Quarles (Outlaws), Gonzales (Devils), and Rains (Bombers), who worked overtime to keep Vega and Johnson out of the World Series. Others who participated with the T-Birds in 1971 included Honey Sanchez, Collene Murrell, Carmen Thompson, Jennifer Marshall, Adeline Hocker, twins Carolyn and Carol Kruse, "The Roadrunner" Jim Terrigno, Billy Marshall, Greg Robertson, Greg Quinn, Luther Matthews, Ed Dresser, Bob Corbin, and speedy Juan Molano.

The T-Birds roster in the 1970 World Series was Coach Valladares, Captain Lynch, Danny Reilly, John Johnson, Greg Robertson, Sam Washington, Frank Martinez, Billy Marshall, Henry Sahagun, Miki Tsunoda, George Fernandez, Sally Vega, Honey Sanchez, Gwen Miller, Carmen Thompson, Colleen Murrell, Barbara Jacobs, Carol and Carolyn Kruse, Jo Lindsay, Yoko Sasaki, and Lena Horne.

Texas had Coach Trotter, Captain Hardman, Norma Rossner, Jean Welch, Rosalie Bardwell, Toni Kadrmas, Bob Mayo, Dave Cox, WIllie Grace, Lenny Silverman, Tom Crews, and Bill Ehrgott. The Thunderbirds ultimately prevailed in the World Series, but not until they survived numerous losses, beatings, and humiliations at the hands of Syverson and Gonzales.

Roller Games did a highly successful stop in Mexico City in 1970 with the T-Birds vs. Texas Outlaws at the Palacio de los Deportes Arena. The copper-domed arena was the host of the 1968 Summer Olympics basketball tournament just two years prior. Mr. Totts, a Japanese-Mexican businessman with TV connections, was the co-promoter along with Enrique Rivadeneyra, Jose Maria Perez, and Jose Luis Vial. Ralph Valladares and Liz Hernandez led the T-Birds as coach and captain. Shirley Hardman and Jim Trotter led the Outlaws. There were some game tapes aired for weeks before the scheduled games. A team was sent to Mexico City and built a banked track. The Palacio's capacity was 20,800, and all ten games were sold-out! Fans were turned away. It was a huge success. Despite this, there was not any mention of forming a home team operation. Fans there loved the T-Birds so it wasn't necessary to create a Mexico City-based team. Surprisingly, Roller Games didn't return to Mexico for ten years until 1980.

Florida Jets

In the summer of 1969, the Philadelphia Warriors traveled to Florida to begin a ten-week exhibition series of games against Shirley Hardman and Jim Trotter's Texas Outlaws, Leroy Gonzales and Sally Vega's Detroit Devils, and Ronnie Rains and Judy Sowinski's New York Bombers. The ten weeks of games took place from the end of June until the first week of September. Games were held Five nights a week, Wednesday through Sunday at the Miami Beach Convention Hall (the site of the Muhammad Ali vs. Sonny Liston boxing match in 1964), Fort Lauderdale War Memorial Auditorium (2100 capacity), West Palm Beach Auditorium (5000 capacity), and at the Dinner Key Auditorium in Miami, later known as the Coconut Grove Convention Center (6900 capacity). The Dinner Key had no air conditioning, which league officials considered detrimental to attendance. The short-lived Miami Floridians of the American Basketball Association played at the auditorium between 1969-1970. It was demolished in 2013.

The first series in Miami was June 29 through July 26, 1969, and saw the Warriors take 14 games with Texas with five games won. Then the Detroit Devils came into town July 27 through August 16, winning five of 15 games. The next series started the following day and ran August 17 to September 6 with the New York Bombers also winning just five of the 15 games.

They were called the Florida Warriors during the summer of '69 and had a roster which included Coach Buddy Atkinson, Jr., Captain Judy Arnold, Vinnie Gandolfo, Erwin Miller, Otis Williams, E.G. Miller, and Sam Washington, along with Yolanda Trevino, Ginger Foley, Harlean Khien, Ann Leary, Lena McBride, and Yvonne Riggins. The Florida Warriors were successful enough to create the foundation for the Florida Jets, which were announced in October 1969, when the "Miami Jets" skated the T-Birds in two games; Sunday, October 26 at the Olympic, then again on Saturday, November 1, in San Bernardino.

The Florida Jets debuted in January 1970, with the following roster: Coach John Parker, Captain Adeline Hocker, Paul Rupert, Larry Lewis, Ann Leary, Ernie Lopez, Tom Whalen, George Crawford, and Jerry Reinhart. Louise Marziani, Dale Coblentz, Stephanie Walker, Gail Farrell, and Sandy Young. The Jets were unable to sustain the type of attendance the Florida Warriors had produced in '69 and lasted only six months until June, when they participated in the Eastern Regional Playoffs, finishing fourth behind the Warriors, NY Bombers, and Texas Outlaws.

In Miami they were broadcast on a UHF station; WAJA channel 23 weekly on Wednesday nights from 8 to 9 p.m. It was a good time slot ,but in 1970 not many people were tuning in to UHF channels. In Orlando they were on a VHF station, channel 9, weekly on Saturday afternoons at 3:30 p.m, which was not a great time slot.

The Florida Jets were never able to gain the type of primetime VHF television coverage that was afforded to the T-Birds in Los

Angeles and the Warriors in Philadelphia. Therefore, Roller Games lost money on the Florida operation and quickly vacated the area. Their green, white, and gold jerseys were used again at the start of 1972 for another startup, the Baltimore Cats. Later, John Hall obtained uniforms used by the Jets and Cats and converted them into the uniforms for the T-Birds. They replaced the original red, white and blue colors when John and Ralphie revamped the team following the closing of the NSD by Griffiths.

Chapter 21

Quarles with Lester (1971)

1971 THUNDERBIRDS

Jean Clark, Debbie Smith, Gwen Miller, Terri Lynch, Sally Vega, Joann Lamastus, Cathie Traylor, Jennifer Marshall, Colleen Murrell
Carmen Thompson, Ralph Valladares, John Johnson, Luther Matthews, Jim Terrigno, Danny Reilly, Greg Robertson, Bob Corbin, Ed Dresser

"The Los Angeles wheel is also operated adroitly and imaginatively. It is run by Bill Griffiths, a suave former adman, and he utilizes some of the same modern precepts of sports promotion that Seltzer does. Griffiths has also provided his constituency with a product that is flashier and more theatrical

> *than the Derby, and this seems to appeal more to the gaudier neon tastes of southern California."* – Frank DeFord, *Five Strides on the Banked Track*

1971 was the year Roller Games embraced the "general manager" position. Actually, it started in December '70, when the Warriors announced Coach Buddy Atkinson, Jr as the team's new G.M. Bob Lewis was already T-Birds' G.M., with the more visible, John Hall, as Assistant G.M. Lester Quarles was named G.M. of Chicago at the start of '71, then became Texas G.M., taking over the Outlaws from Coach Jim Trotter, who left for the Warriors. Hawks' Women's Captain Norma Rossner became the new Texas women's captain, wearing Hardman's old jersey, #17. Scoring was on the rise during this period, such as when the T-Birds beat Texas with a whopping score of 210-142 on Saturday, March 13.

As the '70s was coming into full swing, so were the "derby dramas" that often eclipsed the actual skating competition on the track. Nearly every game highlighted a storyline that was part of a larger, ongoing soap opera. Here is a brief outline of the 1971 storylines: Adeline Hocker became disgusted with the tactics of Judy Sowinski and quit the New York Bombers in April. She wanted to become a T-Bird. But she had to face Judy Sowinski in a series of match races in order for coach Ronnie Rains to release her contract. Hocker won races, but then Rains gave her contract to Leroy Gonzales and the Devils. A disgruntled Hocker then challenged Rains to four one-on-one match races with the stipulation that if she won just one race, she'd be released from her existing contract and could go to Los Angeles. Rains won the first three races but Hocker won the fourth to win the right to become a T-Bird, where she was a welcome addition to the team, as they no longer had the services of Sowinski or Liz Hernandez .

April also saw the return of Shirley Hardman, who after two years off, wanted her old job back with the Texas Outlaws. New Texas G.M. Lester Quarles didn't want her on the team and she could no longer skate full time due to serious back injuries. While she was in limbo without a team, she was named "Special Representative" of the Commission, and one of her first actions was suspending referee John "Gootch" Gautieri for a week.

A new controversy erupted at the end of April as Quarles announced that assistant G.M.s had to be barred from infield during games because of a Commission rule. This was aimed at trying to get John Hall off the track. Hall declared he would quit the team if he could no longer be effective in his role. On May 16, during the Sunday televised game, G.M. Bob Lewis read three letters to Quarles and fans. One stated that Hall was resigning as T-Birds Assistant G.M. The second stated Bob Lewis was resigning as T-Birds G.M. and was being moved to the Board of Directors. The third stated Hall was to become the new Thunderbirds G.M. Because Hall was then allowed on infield, Shirley Hardman stated Quarles had to meet Hall in a match race at the L.A. Sports Arena or be subjected to a lifetime suspension. Rains, Quarles, and Gonzales conspired with the NRL Commission to remove Shirley from her position as "Special Representative" effective May 23. After her job ended, Hardman's freelance contract was taken over by Ronnie Rains for the NY Bombers, which prevented her from skating and humiliated her. She reported to the Bombers and Rains assigned her to do menial chores on the infield. Soon after, she got into an argument with Sowinski and Judy slugged her. This gave her the loophole to quit the Bombers, as there was a rule in place in which coaches and captains could not physically abuse any of their skaters. She was immediately signed by John Hall to a T Birds contract. Hall challenged Ronnie Rains to a match race to avenge the mistreatment that Shirley suffered on the Bombers. At the match race, Hardman hit Referee Gautieri with a baseball bat and Gonzales then filed a grievance with the Commission to get her barred for life. Once again, John Hall stepped in and this time challenged Leroy to a series of three match races with the stipulation that if Hall won all three races, then Leroy would drop his charges and also Shirley would be free to race Sowinski at the President's Cup games. Hall won all three and saved Shirley. Hardman then proceeded to beat Sowinski in their match race during the President's Cup Finals at the Forum on June 26, as the T-Birds won the President's Cup game over the Devils, 118-97.

John Hall appointed Hardman as his Assistant G.M.; the first time a female had assumed a managerial role. In July, Hardman and Referee Gautieri were still feuding and Hardman challenged him to a series of three match races with the stipulation that if she won, then Gautieri would resign as a referee. She won all three races. After the races, Gautieri congratulated her and resigned on TV. Hardman saw how he had changed and decided to try and get him reinstated. Gautieri was named as a Special Representative of the Commission to look into the favoritism that Aussie Ref Darrigo gave to the Outlaws in their current series.

Later, Shirley Hardman and John Hall would challenge and defeat Judy Sowinski and Lester Quarles in two match races during the World Series Semi-Finals and Finals, culminating the Hall and Hardman storyline. It was a wild year and unless you tuned in to every broadcast, it wasn't easy to follow. Fans tuned in, in record numbers.

At various times during the season and especially as the Finals approached, Lester Quarles sought to beef up his Outlaws team by adding Australian skaters Elaine Everson and Larry Stone (husband and wife), Pat Summer and Pete Madden, Peter Kelly, Jim Baldock, Julie Carter, and Diane Hall, as well as an Aussie Referee, Jan Darrigo, who would reverse decisions to favor Texas in games. The T-Birds countered by adding Aussies Bob Murdoch, John Butta, Robin Hughes, and Sue "Little Orphan Annie" King, as well as Japanese skaters Kaz Kawano and Ken Mori, along with Miki Tsunoda and Yoko Sasaki.

In August, Jim Trotter petitioned the Commission to include the Warriors in the World Series and it was eventually approved. On August 28, Jim Terrigno debuted on the T-Birds and in his first game scored 55 points to set a men's rookie scoring record. In the same month, Adeline Hocker left the T-Birds and went to Australia to help restart the Australian league.

The 1971 World Series Semi-Final was a doubleheader hosted on Friday, September 3, at the San Diego Sports Arena. In the first match, the Texas Outlaws beat the Detroit Devils, 117 to 111. In the second match, the T-Birds defeated the Eastern Warriors 112 to 109. Both winning teams advanced to the final game, which was another doubleheader held the following night. For the Finals Championship, the T-Birds faced the Texas Outlaws led by Lester Quarles.

The '71 Texas Outlaws had G.M. Lester Quarles, John Parker, Ken Willis, Leon Jackson, Mike DeSantiago, Mike Adame, Dave Cox, E.G. Miller, Women's Captain Rossner, Baby Rocco, Toni Kadrmas, Sonja Sims, Barbara Jacobs, Georgeanna Daniel, Sandy Ford, Debbie Douglas, and Charlys Krouse, B.J. Peterson, Peter Kelly, Jim Baldock, Julie Carter, and Diane Hall, Frank Martinez, Elaine Everson, Larry Stone, Pat Summer, and Pete Madden. By the time the World Series rolled around, the roster had been refined to: Quarles (non-skating G.M.), Rossner, Parker, Jackson, Adame, Cox, Miller, Martinez, DeSantiago, Rocco, Kadrmas, Douglas, Sims, and Ford.

Over the course of 1971, the World Champion Thunderbirds were composed of General Manager Bob Lewis, Coach Ralph Valladares, General Manager John Hall, Assistant General Manager Shirley Hardman, Captain Terri Lynch, Sally Vega, Honey Sanchez, Gwen Miller, Colleen Murrell, Carmen Sugar Thompson, Betty Stone, Yoko Sasaki, Jean Clark, Diane Siegmond, Janet Parker, Carolyn Kruse, Carol Kruse, Jennifer Marshall, Adeline Hocker, JoAnn Lamastus, Cathie Traylor, Danny Reilly, Greg Robertson, Sam Washington, Jim Terrigno, Bob Corbin, George Fernandez, John Johnson, Miki Tsunoda, Billy Marshall, Bob Lockhart, Ed Dresser, Bob Rainer, Henry Sahagun, Luther Matthews, Ed Lockhard, Kaz Kawano, Ken Mori, and Kenny Brien. Hardman and Lynch, once bitter rivals, were now competing on the same team.

The 1971 Championship contest was held Saturday, September 4, as 15,250 fans showed up at the Fabulous Forum in Inglewood. This set a U.S. indoor attendance record for Roller Games. But the fans weren't only there to find out which team would be the '71 Champs; this was the culmination of an entire season of unprecedented high drama and excitement that was the trademark of Roller Games. Regardless of which team prevailed, the night would cap the league's best season ever.

In the consolation game that featured the teams that had lost the previous night, the Warriors beat the Devils 105 to 99. In the final game, the Los Angeles T-Birds defeated the Texas Outlaws, 161-134 to retain their crown of Roller Games World Champions.

Following the World Series, the T-Birds played a few exhibition series that the NSD All Star teams headed by various red-shirt team coaches, which concluded on September 25. In the Fall, they headed out on tour to the Midwest to cities in which TV ratings were high, in typical derby fashion.

The big media news for roller derby in 1971 was the publication of the book, *Five Strides on the Banked Track* by noted author Frank DeFord of Sport Illustrated fame.

While the article (and book) focused on the Bay Bombers and their stars Joan Weston, Ann Calvello, and Charlie O'Connell, it was really about the very sport of roller derby, whose popularity was undeniable during this period. He presented it as one of the purest endeavors solely devoted to fans rather than to profits like other professional sports. DeFord mentions Roller Games many times in the book and attended a T-Birds game at the Olympic. He commented on the T-Birds:

"All teams, except the Bombers and Thunderbirds, eventually are 'plagued by dissension.' The Bombers and Thunderbirds may, on the other hand, often be 'racked with injuries.' It is all wistfully delightful! The Los Angeles Games are, however, just as successful as the more subdued Bay Area original, and the frenzied crowds that show up at the dingy old Olympic Auditorium are never jarred by the predictable gambits that are dispensed at will. Thunderbirds fans at the Olympic, and at other home arenas in Anaheim, Long Beach, San Diego, San Bernardino, and the San Fernando Valley, are positively enthralled by it all."

Although *Five Strides* sold very few copies and went out of print not long after its release, it has become a sought-after classic and is now available once again in digital format as an e-book. Hardcover copies have sold for up to $100 on e-Bay! It is widely considered the best book ever written on the sport of roller derby.

With the recent release of *Five Strides*, the game's reputation, while never on par as compared to more conventional sports, was pretty good. Hollywood was fast at work preparing a blockbuster film on roller derby. 1971 was the prelude to the biggest season ever for Roller Games in 1972.

Chapter 22

KC Bomber (1972)

1972 *Los Angeles Thunderbirds*

Left to right: (seated) SHERRY JACKSON, YOKO SASAKI, COLLEEN MURRELL, DEBBIE SMITH, JENNIFER MARSHALL, GAIL BOWERS
(kneeling) KENNY BRIEN, LUTHER MATHEWS
(second row) SHIRLEY HARDMAN, JOAN LAMASTUS, LINDA ADAMS, TERRI LYNCH, CATHIE TRAYLOR, SALLY VEGA, RALPH VALLADARES
(third row) HENRY SAHAGUN, SAM WASHINGTON, ED DRESSER, JOHN JOHNSON, TOM CREWS, JIM TERRIGNO, MIKI TSUNODA

*"Roller Games is a microcosm of this country, the kind of thing
we create. The game is almost show business, it's a carnival
atmosphere, but I can understand its popularity. Most of the
spectators are basic people and there's something cathartic
about watching people get dumped. The yelling creates a*

certain kind of intensity. The type of violence draws you in, makes you involved. The skaters are tough but I think all women are tough. The skaters aren't any tougher than most of the women in the world, underneath. Skating is a batchy, sweaty, funky life. I don't want to do another film about it. I've done my number. But I enjoyed it." – Raquel Welch

1972 was the single most significant year ever for Roller Games. The same thing could be said for the entire sport of roller derby. At this point in its 11-year reign, Roller Games had never faced any serious challenges. Sure, not every step of the way was smooth but each year since 1961 had been successful, with each successive year building on the next. Of this period, 1968 to 1972 was the pinnacle with '72 being the absolute zenith, never to be repeated.

So many things had to come together to make a year like this possible. This was sports entertainment at its very best. The quality of the sport of skating was outstanding and the entertainment itself was reaching new heights with the scripts and the execution of the storylines. To top it off, one of the year's biggest feature films was about Roller Games and the sport of roller derby.

On August 2, 1972, *Kansas City Bomber*, starring Raquel Welch, was released on the big screen in the United States. It was the most significant film on roller derby since *The Fireball*, starring Mickey Rooney in 1950. It was a depiction of Roller Games in that very era, and NSD skaters were utilized as extras in the movie. The voice of the T-Birds, announcer Dick Lane, had a small speaking role.

"The film is an inside look at the world of Roller Games, then a popular league sport-entertainment, a more theatrical version of Roller Derby." – Excerpt from Wikipedia

The filming of the movie took place over a period of about 30 days in Portland, Oregon. John Hall supervised all 36 individuals that Roller Games provided to MGM and he worked directly with the star, Raquel Welch. John was not originally slated to skate in the film, but when Leon Jackson was delayed in getting to Portland, John took his place working in a jam with George Adams. Many skaters participated, but some of the most memorable action captured on film involved Richard Brown (Baltimore Cats) and Ronnie Rains (New York Bombers). Judy Arnold, women's captain of the Philadelphia Warriors Roller Games team, doubled for Welch in the skating scenes and had a minor speaking role in a dressing room scene. Other NSD star skaters who participated included Patti Cavin, who auditioned for the role of "Big Bertha" in the movie and played a significant role, along with Betty Brown and Judy Sowinski.

Welch was in her prime at the time and was a massive star, and roller derby was at the peak of its popularity. This combination brought out large numbers of moviegoers to theaters across the country. The film was one of MGM's most successful releases of 1972.

Raquel Welch is a Hollywood legend and *Playboy* ranked her number three on their "100 Sexiest Stars of the Twentieth Century" list. *Men's Health* ranked her number two in its "Hottest Women of All Time" list. *Life Magazine* called Welch the "hottest thing on wheels" in their comments on the film. She did many of the stunts for the movie until she broke her wrist. She was indeed the roller derby queen of 1972! Her role as a tough roller derby star and single mother, along with performing her stunts, made her a hero for feminists and brought newer female fans to roller derby. And like roller derby, Welch was a cultural icon of the 1960s and early '70s. It was an appropriate pairing, and although the film wasn't a critical success at the time, it was being discovered by the new young generation of female roller derby skaters who related to her perseverance and hardened attitude as they traversed a world still generally ruled by white males.

Although *Kansas City Bomber* was based on the Roller Games league, both major roller derby leagues (Roller Games and Roller Derby) saw attendance increases due to the popularity of the film. The popularity of roller derby, which had reached its apex in the early '70s, was one of the main reasons the film was made. In turn, KCB brought new legions of fans to the sport. The timing was perfect, and *Kansas City Bomber* was a smash hit.

Reviews of the film were mixed; the *New York Times* was highly critical yet there were also many positive reviews. "Welch [came] through with a characterization as unexpected as it [was] persuasive." The film was "...a well-observed slice of contemporary Americana," which "...[marked] Raquel Welch's coming of age as an actress and [was] a personal triumph for her after surviving more rotten movies than anyone would care to remember." – Kevin Thomas of *The Los Angeles Times*

Activist and topical songwriter, Phil Ochs, wrote a song called *Kansas City Bomber* as the title song for the film, but Metro-Goldwyn-Mayer rejected it. Ochs issued the song as a single on A&M Records anyway and hoped to publicly debut the song at the Olympic Auditorium during a Thunderbirds game. Bill Griffiths rejected the idea.

Actress Helena Kallianiotes was nominated for the Golden Globe Award for *Best Supporting Actress – Motion Picture* for her role as Jackie Burdette. T-Bird star Sally Vega doubled for Helena in the skating scenes. A young Jodie Foster also had a minor starring role in the film.

"Its reputation is about as inaccurate as a reputation can get, both in content and context. *Kansas City Bomber* is one of the better examples of the low-budget cinema of the early 1970s, surprisingly influential, ahead of its time and a really terrific film. *Kansas City Bomber* is not that many steps away from documentary. Roller derby was geared toward a working-class audience, people wanting to be entertained, pick sides and blow off steam, and *Kansas City Bomber* approaches that honestly and shows it as it happens." Edited Excerpts from the blog "*SheBloggedByNight*"

By 1972, roller derby had gained massive popularity, with some arenas selling over 50,000 tickets for a single game. Though the sport had been around since the 1930s, its time as a wildly popular sport was brief, from about 1969 until the gas shortage crisis of 1973. *Kansas City Bomber* is, to date, the most significant and widely viewed film on roller derby ever released.

Another movie about roller derby was also released in 1972, simply titled *Derby* as starring members of the Bay Bombers and other Roller Derby skaters, played themselves. It featured some worthy footage of Charlie O'Connell and Ann Calvello, and received good reviews from the likes of Roger Ebert and the *New York Times*. But the low-budget film, which was directed by Robert Kaylor and commissioned by Jerry Seltzer himself, had little impact at the time as it had limited distribution and was seen by very few. But it was one more positive for roller derby in 1972 and eventually became somewhat of a time capsule of a classic, bygone era.

Capacity in Chicago

It's no coincidence that just six weeks after the release of the blockbuster hit *Kansas City Bomber*, roller derby broke all previous attendance records with 51,118 showing up in Chicago at White Sox Park for an interleague contest featuring the top teams of both Roller Derby and Roller Games. It's also no coincidence that this attendance record occurred during an interleague game that combined the popularity and marketing reach of both major league roller derby outfits. This wasn't the first attempt at interleague play. Some co-operative interleague games started in 1966 and continued through 1973.

Roller Derby had a team in Chicago, the Midwest Pioneers. They had a huge following and skated weekly in many of the area's arenas. Television broadcasts of the L.A. T-Birds games were being shown in the same areas and especially Chicago. It was a natural progression for the two teams to meet in a Midwest game. Eventually, they did so and on September 15, 1972, the Chicago Pioneers and the Los Angeles Thunderbirds skated at White Sox Park (Comiskey Park) and the game was completely sold-out! On the first day the game was announced, 21,000 tickets were sold. It was reported that over 6,000 fans were turned away. This was the largest attendance ever for a banked track event, and the record still stands today. The 51,118 nearly doubled the previous Roller Derby attendance record set on July 4, 1970, when 28,314 showed up to a Bay Bombers game at the Oakland Coliseum.

Jerry Hill worked well with Jerry Seltzer and had been at the forefront of the California interleague games featuring teams from "Derby" and "Games." But for this record-breaking game at White Sox Park, it was Bill Griffiths who handled the negotiations with Seltzer. Griffiths convinced Seltzer to give the baseball park a try.

Despite the attendance record, Jerry Seltzer stated that he only made $8,000 from the game. It was also the beginning of a gasoline shortage in the USA; a shortage that affected the fortunes of both leagues. Roller Derby folded up its tent just 15 months following this record-setting game.

Dave Pound

Roller Games of 1972 will be remembered for many things. *Kansas City Bomber*, 51,000 fans in Chicago, John and Ralphie, Shirley Hardman as a T-Bird, and so on. But there were two figures and two promotions that undoubtedly drew more fans to Roller Games then at any other time in its history: Dave Pound and Danny Reilly. The storylines that they were involved with overshadowed anything else from the 1972 season, even, for the first time, the skating itself. This wasn't due to the fact that the skating talent had declined; to the contrary, it was as good as ever. It was merely because both Reilly and Pound executed their promotions with such passion and precision that it drove fans crazy and led to record TV ratings and game attendance.

David Pound is a member of the National Roller Derby Hall of Fame. He is one of the greatest skaters ever to grace the banked track. Some very prominent skaters have told me that Pound was the best male skater of all time, even better than O'Connell. That's how good he was. But he was even better as an actor. In his role as Thunderbird G.M. and V.P., he was often perceived as siding with the opposition. He was rough with his T-Bird skaters and especially cruel to some of the ladies. Fans were outraged.

In the 1972 President's Cup game, a Roller Games mid-season

tradition, Pound defeated Ronnie Rains of the New York Bombers in a well-publicized match race to decide the cup winner. Following this, a match race was scheduled between Pound and John Hall to be held at halftime during a game at the Fabulous Forum in Los Angeles. The contest was a complete sell-out. The match race featured two battle-scarred derby veterans, both who had sustained career-ending injuries in the past: Hall, with a broken neck, and Pound, with a broken back. Cheering John on in the infield was Shirley Hardman, who had also broken her back. The match race was won by John Hall, and Dave Pound was forced out of town. The long-lasting promotion of 1972 had turned almost every event into a sell-out. After leaving Los Angeles, Pound took his promotion to other cities including Philadelphia, where sold-out games would follow.

Reilly's Renegades

Danny Reilly was so popular as a Thunderbird defensive skater and enforcer that management decided to reward him with a team of his own, Reilly's Renegades. On the East Coast, they were called the Western Renegades. Danny was a big guy. His girth alone could make it difficult for a jammer to pass him. But while he may be remembered for his size and red hair, Danny was an excellent skater and extremely agile. He was well conditioned in his prime. Like Pound, he was also a great showman. His Renegades and the promotion that led to his departure from the T-Birds was another ticket bonanza for Roller Games. Reilly was one of the first homegrown stars of Roller Games.

His Renegades went to the Championship in that fateful 1972 season, losing to the perennial champs as forecast. His team had some talented skaters, but it was more noteworthy for its leader. Never before had a team been so identified with one skater.

Lynch Retires

The summer of '72 saw the retirement of one of the greatest skaters ever to grace the track for the Los Angeles Thunderbirds, as an exhausted Terri Lynch decided it was time to hang up her skates. Although they tried, it was nearly impossible to fill the void left by her departure.

Cleveland Bucks

In 1972, at the height of Roller Games popularity, the league set out to further expand their reach by establishing teams in Cleveland and Baltimore. The Cleveland Bucks (also known as the Tri-City Bucks) were officially formed in January 1972. Although, a home team based in Cleveland Ohio, they skated not only in Cleveland, but also in Detroit and eventually in Cincinnati. This new venture started in October 1971, as the Los Angeles Thunderbirds began skating back East with headquarters in Cleveland, Ohio, which eventually lead to the creation of the Tri-City Bucks at the start of '72. A Pittsburg Executive and friend of Bill Griffiths, Jack Lease, was the unit manager. A league office was set up. Ed Darian, Warriors house announcer, was the TV voice of the Bucks, but used his real name, Setrak Egdaharian. Tom Post was the Trackside Announcer.

The T-Birds opened the Cleveland series against the Texas Outlaws and then skated the Northern Hawks, (no longer from Chicago as not to confuse local fans). T-Bird games were shown on TV stations in Cleveland, Detroit, Toledo, and Canton, as well as other cities in Ohio and Michigan. On the Cleveland trip, the T-Birds featured G.M. John Hall, Assistant G.M. Shirley Hardman, Coach Danny Reilly, Sally Vega, Greg Robertson, Sam Washington, Bob Corbin, Kenny Adams, Al Ruiz, Don Michaels, Peggy Fowler, Carmen Thompson, Sue Warren, Gwen Miller, Lynn Congleton, and Donna Siegmund. Terri Lynch skated a few weeks in Cleveland in the Fall, too, before heading back to L.A. The Fall series was focused on establishing Peggy Fowler as the top female star. Lester Quarles claimed her for Texas, then was beaten in three match races by Hardman, losing rights to her contract. Danny Reilly would be maligned, setting him up to be the male star of the new Bucks. This T-Birds series in Cleveland was all about establishing the Bucks and made fans sympathetic to the team with one controversy after another about skaters being signed from the T-Birds to the newly-formed Bucks, while opponents tried to stop it. Herb Roberts did house announcing for games.

With television always such an integral part of the success of any home team operation, league officials designated the Akron Armory as the venue where games would be taped. Akron is about 45 miles from Cleveland. The Armory was a small venue with a capacity of 2,500 if the balcony area was used and 1,500 if the lower level was used exclusively. Attendance averaged between 1,200 and 1,500 fans, so the upper balcony was rarely used. The TV cameras panned only towards the lower level. The team performed at major arenas in the area including the Cleveland Arena, Detroit Olympia Stadium (capacity 12,000 with attendance generally above 6,000), Canton Memorial Auditorium, Toledo Sports Arena (3500 seats), Akron Armory, Pittsburgh Civic Arena, and others. Later in the Fall, the team held games at the Cincinnati Gardens (12,000-seats) after Derby dropped the Ohio Jolters.

The Tri-City Bucks officially debuted January 4, 1972, and skated against the Brooklyn Devils (no longer Detroit) at the Cleveland Arena for a two-week series. A few weeks later, it was announced that John Hall was leaving the T-Birds as G.M. in order to become Bucks G.M.

The Bucks debuted with G.M. John Hall, Coach Danny Reilly, Captain Peggy Fowler, Greg Robertson, Bob Corbin, Sam Washington, Al Ruiz, Don Michaels, Billy Marshall, Gwen Miller, Carmen Thompson, Lynn Congleton, Sue Warren, and Donna Seigmund. After the first month, Sam Washington was gone and at the end of February '72, Sue Thomas, Mike Taylor, and Larry Petrasek were added to the team. Curt Furber joined the team in

April and at the end of May '72, Sherry Jakowski (Jackson) joined the team. By June, Reilly was gone and given his own team (the Renegades), and veterans Dave Cox and Jim Nolan joined the team to make up for the loss. Jim Terrigno joined the team in July and at the end of July, Peggy Fowler was gone. Sherry Jakowski was the top female star of the team and in the Fall of '72, Lynda Chaney and Gail Hawkins were with the team. Greg Quinn, Patti Reed, Donna Fox, and Diana Vickers were added in October. In November '72, with things falling apart quickly, Greg Robertson was named men's coach and Jennifer Marshall, Sam Washington, and Ralph Valladares came and skated for the Bucks.

In April '72, the Bucks did a mini-manager promotion when John "Gootch" Cautieri was announced as the Special Consultant for the Bucks. John Hall disappeared for a bit and Gootch went about trying to destroy the team from within. Like most teams in 1972, the Bucks would skate two-week series. They squared off against the Brooklyn Devils, Northern Hawks, New York Bombers, Australian Kangaroos, Texas Outlaws, and Baltimore-Washington Cats. The summer season ended at the beginning of August '72. They also skated some interleague doubleheaders against IRDL (Roller Derby) teams.

The team was popular with a small core fan base that was slowly expanding, but the support was not enough for the league to continue the Tri-City operation. One year was hardly enough time to build a proper following and judge the potential of a new startup. The advent of the U.S. gas shortage, combined with the added expenses of housing skaters from out of town, along with the mediocre fan support, was too much for the Tri-City Bucks, who were disbanded at the end of 1972.

Baltimore Cats

The Baltimore Cats were a home (white shirt) team formed by the National Skating Derby in 1972 and skated until '74. In their first week, they temporarily donned the jerseys used by the old Florida Jets;

the same jerseys that would eventually be used by the Thunderbirds in their rebirth period. The new, official "Cats" jerseys were brown and-gold on white with jersey numbers in the single digits. The team debuted in January of '72, about the same time as the Cleveland Bucks.

The home venue for the Cats was the legendary Baltimore Civic Center (the Baltimore Arena) with a capacity of 8,000. It's located about a block away from the Baltimore Convention Center on the corner of Baltimore Street and Hopkins Place. The NBA's Baltimore Bullets were tenants from 1963 until 1973 when they relocated to Washington, DC. Acts such as the Beatles, Elvis, Jim Hendrix, and Led Zeppelin performed there. The arena operates today under the name Royal Farms Arena. On weekends, Roller Games typically pulled in a healthy 6,000 or more seats. The Cats games were broadcast on WBFF, Channel 45 in Baltimore on Sunday at 2 p.m. and on WDCA, Channel 20 in Washington, DC, which aired at 8:30 p.m. on prime time. Both of these were UHF stations, which at the time were not as popular as VHF stations, and the signal was often not nearly as strong. Several other cities also carried the Cats broadcasts. The geography of Baltimore, Cleveland, Philly, and Montreal was good for the league, as teams rotating from the West Coast would have several major cities that could facilitate a six to ten-week tour for opposing red-shirt teams. In '72, opposing teams would often skate a two-week series in Philly, move onto Baltimore-Washington for another two weeks, then to Cleveland for two weeks, then to L.A. for another two weeks, and sometimes to Canada for a final two-week series.

These teams would often be scheduled for an additional two to three weeks in Canada. When Roller Games lost the local TV deal, attendance began dropping and the Cats were merged with the Philadelphia Warriors (a.k.a. Eastern Warriors in mid 1974 and rebranded as the "War-Cats.")

The team was created by combining star skaters from the Philadelphia Warriors and other teams that had skated in Philadelphia, as well as stars from Warrior games that were skated in Baltimore. There were also a few former Roller Derby skaters on the Cats team including Jerry Cattell and Bill Hill, as well as some former Bucks skaters. Former Warriors, Coach Vinnie Gandolfo and Captain Ruberta Mitchell led the team. Sonja Sims was a rising star on the Cats. She was a former red-shirt opposition skater that the fans loved when she became a member of the home team and continued to skate in her red-shirt style (mean and dirty) for the Cats. During their three year tenure, many Roller Games stars wore the Cats jersey, including: Richard Brown, Yolanda Trevino, Erwin Miller, Peggy Fowler, Lois Decker, Sherry Jackson, Peter Kelly and his wife, Marti Zinni, Ed Dresser, Sam Washington, Leon Jackson, Lynn Congleton, Jan Vallow, Gail Berndt, Cal Stephens, Greg Quinn, John Early, Bill Hill, and many more.

Parting Ways

Bill Griffiths and Jerry Hill had just overseen an extraordinarily prosperous and successful ten-year period with Roller Games. What had started out as one of many "outlaw" leagues, now featured a team that was a household name in America and that was every bit as successful as the original Roller Derby. The T-Birds were selling out most of their games and TV ratings were soaring. And Roller Games had not one but two successful operations as both Los Angeles and Philadelphia were booming. The release of the 1972 blockbuster film *Kansas City Bomber*, which featured skaters from Roller Games, brought with it a whole new crop of fans. Teams were loaded with stellar skaters including named veterans and up- and-coming stars. These were the best of times for Roller Games.

There was just one problem: Jerry Hill decided he wanted out. By all accounts, Jerry was an integral ingredient in the success of Roller Games, despite the fact he kept a low profile. At the time, Hill was the managing director of the National Skating Derby. He was also the publisher and editor of the *Roller Games Annual* and *Roller Games Gazette*. He was the head supervisor of track construction. Other vital roles included director of ticket sales, booking arena dates for games, and the coordinator of coaches, players, and referees.

In the weeks following the release of the box office smash *Kansas City Bomber*, the record-breaking sell-out in Chicago, and a future that looked brighter than ever before, Hill and Griffiths dissolved their partnership. Jerry Hill took $3 million with him, which depleted the league's cash reserves at a time when they were already spread way too thin.

Skaters and others who were on the scene during this period commented that Jerry felt Griffiths no longer appreciated him. The breaking point may have been the game at White Sox Park as Hill received little credit for his efforts.

John Hall was in Cleveland when he heard that Jerry had left. He stated, "We were all very dejected. Jerry was well liked and well respected by so many of us. We felt that we had lost a friend."

In 1972, we were kept on the edge of our seats by the likes of Shirley Hardman, John Hall, Ralphie Valladares, Skinny Minnie Miller, "747" Earlene Brown, Sam the Man, Danny Reilly, and Dave Pound. 1972 proved to the world just how popular roller derby could become if the right ingredients were present.

Chapter 23

One Man Band (1973)

1973 Los Angeles Thunderbirds

CARMEN THOMPSON, COLLEEN MURRELL, CAROL PHILLIPS, HONEY SANCHEZ, EARLENE BROWN, SALLY VEGA, GWEN MILLER, JEAN CLARK, VICKIE McEWEN
SHIRLEY HARDMAN, RALPH VALLADARES
JIM TERRIGNO, SAM WASHINGTON, LEON JACKSON, RONNIE RAINS, JOHN JOHNSON, ED DRESSER, GREG ROBERTSON, MIKE GOCHNAUR, HENRY SAHAGUN

"No one looks at the Derby very carefully below the surface, for its fans embrace it emotionally without question, and its skeptics dismiss it just as quickly as fraudulent and savage." –
Frank DeFord, *Five Strides on the Banked Track*

In 1973, Bill Griffiths proceeded onward without Jerry Hill as part of the Roller Games equation. There were great opportunities and potential pitfalls ahead. Bill was now flying solo. His first challenge was rebuilding capital reserves. Over $3 million dollars left the coffers of Roller Games and went straight into the hands of Jerry Hill when he departed. Griffiths had hoped Hill would take a two to three-year payout, but Hill insisted on a one-time payment, despite knowing the potential impact it would have on the league and its skaters. This left the league on thin ice and was one of the primary reasons things didn't go as planned. Looking back now, it is quite likely that had Jerry Hill remained, Roller Games would not have been forced to close operations just two years after he departed. At the beginning of 1973, when Bill set out alone, he had no idea that later in the year there would be a severe oil shortage that would affect his enterprise and many others in the U.S. and abroad. Griffiths started 1973 with tremendous optimism: And why not with Roller Games coming off its best year after a 10-year winning streak? If this trend continued, Bill stood to rake in significant profits now that he no longer had to split the earnings. He also no longer needed to consult with anyone else on decisions—large or small. But with all this potential came more significant responsibilities and pressure. It is important to note that at the time Hill departed, Roller Games was already spreading itself thin by entering more markets than they had qualified management personnel to handle. In addition to Los Angeles (So Cal), they also had ongoing operations in Philadelphia (successful), Cleveland (struggling), Baltimore (struggling), and Canada (struggling). Furthermore, not only were there no partners or co-owners to share the burden, there were no franchises whatsoever. Only one man was trying to run several operations, and it was challenging to say the least. But Bill made it through much of his first year at the helm, until world politics abruptly changed the course of events for Roller Games and Roller Derby up North as well.

Amidst the turmoil, the 1973 World Series featured the Texas Outlaws and Thunderbirds. The Outlaws were led by Judy Sowinski, Vicky Steppe, Vicki McEwen, Lester Quarles, and Jim Trotter. The

Thunderbirds were missing Ralphie and Reilly, who were on other assignments, but still had a cast of stars, including Julie Patrick, Gwen Miller, Peggy Fowler, Sally Vega, Colleen Murrell, Carmen Thompson, Honey Sanchez, Earlene Brown, Carol Phillips, Jean Clark, Denise Todd, Richard Brown, Sam Washington, Greg Robertson, Ronnie Rains, Jim Terrigno, John Hall, John Johnson, Ed Dresser, Eddie Williams, Henry Sahagun, Mike Gochnaur, and Leon Jackson.

The Thunderbirds prevailed once again. 1973 was a terrific year, but it was anti-climactic compared to 1972, and the game continued to devolve in the years to come. There would never be another 1972.

Canadian National Roller League

Roller Games held several experimental games in Montreal, Canada in 1971 and 1972, which turned out to be financially successful. Then Roller Games and Roller Derby formed a joint venture league backed by Canadian businessman, Norman Olson, under the title Canadian National Roller League (CNRL).

With little fanfare, the Detroit Devils, now called the 'Brooklyn' Devils once the Bucks came along in 1972, began skating North of the Border as a home team, now known as the Quebec Fleur de Lys or Ontario Monarchs, depending on where they would skate. Led by Coach Paul Rupert, Larry Smith, and jammer Frankie Macedo, the All-Stars had an outstanding team. Captain Diane Syverson led the women. She was assisted by Francine Cochu—a former Roller Derby skater and Canadian, with former Bucks jammers Gwen Miller and Donna Fox. The Fleur de Lys also had G.M. Buddy Atkinson Jr., Michele Peloquin, Sue Thomas, Andre Rochon, Lenny Silverman, Frankie Macedo, Sam Washington, Jack Hess, and Erwin Miller.

Plans were announced to open a training school in Canada. By March, Roller Games could be seen on 33 television stations across Canada from Vancouver to Halifax, and by June, four more stations had been added. Barry Dale did the announcing while Bob Sirois did the play-by-play.

In 1973, the Fleur de Lys skated a couple of series against the visiting L.A. Thunderbirds and lost the series. The Thunderbirds returned after the Jolters faced the Canadian team. The Thunderbirds were led by Women's Captain Sally Vega and Men's Coach Greg Robertson. Skating for the Thunderbirds was Denise Todd, Jo Wolfgang, Roger McLeod, Bessie Gonzales, and Tony Nichols.

A heavy schedule of four to five games a week was maintained. The main buildings in Montreal and Toronto had a capacity of 10,000. Teams averaged 6,000 on weekends and slightly less during the week. There were also games in smaller arenas between Toronto and Montreal that took place on weekdays, which averaged about 2,000. Travel happened by car and sometimes by a charter bus for long distances. A tour was booked with games scheduled across Canada from east to west and back in medium-sized arenas. There was sporadic television coverage in these smaller cities, which was neither consistent nor highly rated. The road games went across Canada to medium-sized arenas. Vancouver, Ottawa, Winnipeg, and many other cities were visited. The morale and outlook of the skaters was high. However, there were financial problems despite solid fan support, due in part to the travel expenses. The fans liked the action, but never responded the way they did in Los Angeles or Philadelphia. They loved hockey, and it was tough to convert them from ice blades to wheels. Another factor was that Roller Games was spread very thin in terms of management, with so many active operations. These expansions happened faster than Roller Games could hire qualified staff to manage.

With the start of the ISC later in 1974, Team Canada looked strong with Ken Monte (G.M.), Paul Rupert (Men's Coach), Diane Syverson (Women's Captain), Frankie Macedo, Francine Cochu, Larry Smith, Peter Kelly, Gwen Miller, Sue Thomas, Donna Fox, Louise Marziani, Otto Jones, and Jack Hess. Warriors great, Harry Morgan, was in Philadelphia for the opening of the season, but did not skate for Canada against the Warriors. During their second week on TV in Philadelphia, the promise of Team Canada was shattered when Ken Monte quit the team.

In Canada, in the Spring of 1974, the Fleur de Lys—as they were still called North of the Border—were facing the Baltimore-Washington Cats, from March 16 through April 28. Later in 1974, the Canadian team was renamed the Canadian Braves and skated as late as December of 1974.

During the time Roller Games was involved in the Canadian market, its Canadian team went by several names, including Fleur de Lys, Canadian All-Stars, Team Canada, and Canadian Braves. The CNRL closed shop at the end of 1974, six months prior to the closing of the International Skating Conference.

Seltzer's Exit

The oil embargo started in October of 1973 and lasted six months up until the spring of 1974. There was no planning for something like this, but it hit Griffiths and Roller Games extremely hard as Bill had little in the way of reserves to compensate for the potential lost revenue. But by the end of 1973, Bill was still standing. Battered, but not beaten—yet.

However, up North in the Bay Area, Jerry Seltzer's once proud original Roller Derby league was facing a myriad of difficulties. The successful way the league had always operated, with Bay Bombers games being shown across a vast syndicated television market and promoting a phenomenally successful national tour, was turned on its head in the Fall of 1971 when three new "home" teams were added to the IRDL as the legendary Bay Bombers became a visiting red-shirt road team. Charlie O'Connell's New York Chiefs began the summer season in Northern California as the "Bay Area Chiefs," skating home games to the consternation and anger of longtime fans. With O'Connell, the Bay Bombers were soon back, but fans in the East and Midwest were now witnessing their home teams skating 'red' against the Bay Bombers on the syndicated network.

The tried-and-true "morality play" elements of the Derby no longer worked since fans in NYC saw their Chiefs skate dirty in the Bay Area. A two-day player strike in the Fall of 1972 deeply hurt Seltzer, who had always depended upon the loyalty of skaters with his family-run business. The Jolters would no longer be a "home team" in Ohio, and more regular appearances by the Derby in certain cities began taking their toll on attendance. The old saying, "familiarity breeds contempt" became true with the beloved Derby. The IRDL was down to four teams, with longtime veterans still carrying the race with new upcoming stars in short abundance. Seltzer tried to duplicate the success of the Comiskey Park record-breaking attendance with a playoff tripleheader at New York City's Shea Stadium over Memorial Day weekend in 1973. But Ticketron, the company responsible for selling tickets to the event, had a glitch with their system that stopped them from working for several days, which they never shared with the Derby. Seltzer was stunned by Ticketron's failure to notify him, but Mother Nature would have the last laugh when a rainy weekend in the New York metropolitan area put a damper on the event. Over 27,000 fans showed up for the "Gold Cup Championship" at Shea Stadium—certainly an impressive number—but it left Jerry Seltzer demoralized and disheartened, and the idea of closing the entire operation was now becoming a reality. Not even the great Charlie O'Connell could block this opponent. The original Roller Derby organization that had been operating as a professional sport since 1942 and had seen great success in the Bay Area in recent years was now gone. It was indeed a sad day for roller derby, and the game would never be the same. On December 8, 1973, the original Derby skated its final game at the Long Island Arena.

Ironically, there was one more interleague contest that took place on December 9, 1973, the day after the IRDL (Roller Derby) had skated their final game in Long Island. This final Roller Derby vs Roller Games Interleague contest was a doubleheader held at Madison Square Garden and featured the Philadelphia Warriors vs. the Midwest Pioneers, followed by the Los Angeles Thunderbirds vs. the New York Chiefs. The games went ahead as scheduled even as the

IRDL had officially closed shop the night before. What had originally been scheduled as a holiday doubleheader featuring the four IRDL teams at Madison Square Garden in New York City on Sunday, December 9, became the last time fans ever saw the Midwest Pioneers and New York Chiefs, or the "Derby." Buddy Atkinson Sr.'s Midwest Pioneers, with the addition of Charlie O'Connell, faced Buddy Atkinson Jr.'s Philadelphia Warriors in the first game. O'Connell had been skating with the Pioneers during the final weeks of the IRDL. He and Buddy Sr., who were long time antagonists, tussled with each other during the game, with Atkinson finally quitting the Pioneers and cheering the Warriors onto victory. Roller Games veteran, Candi Mitchell, led the Pioneer women, since Derby's biggest female star, Joan Weston, skated with the L.A. Thunderbirds in the second game of the doubleheader against the Chiefs. Judy Sowinski and Danny Reilly also joined the Thunderbirds for the game in another preview of what was to come the following year when the Los Angeles team would be packed with stars, including O'Connell. Few people knew of the IRDL demise the night before. Over the next few weeks, rumors that both leagues had merged gave fans a glimmer of hope, but no one knew what the future held.

International Skating Conference

Chapter 24

Charlie Thunder (1974)

1974 *Thunderbirds*

JULIE PATRICK, VICKIE COOPER, JOAN WESTON, JUDY SOWINSKI, DENISE TODD, VICKY McEWEN, JENNIFER MARSHALL
RONNIE RAINS, RONNIE ROBINSON, HAROLD JACKSON, ROBERT McDONNELL, JIM TERRIGNO, EDDIE WILLIAMS, CHARLIE O'CONNELL

"Charlie brought a rugged sports mentality to the Derby, which relied much more on finesse prior to that time. A bigger than life (6'2", 200 pounds) skater who towered over most of the others. And he played the game as he played football and hockey; skate fast, hit hard, and never back down. The pivot

> position – the player who could block, jam, and quarterback
> the pack, was really created for him. The recalcitrant hero,
> didn't like interviews, autographs, was gruff, but adored by fans
> everywhere. He and Joan Weston signified the Bay Bombers
> for years to the millions who watched on television and in
> person." – Jerry Seltzer, *Roller Derby Jesus*

Now Griffiths was all alone. He wasn't just the leader of his kingdom, he was the sole ruler of the roller derby sport itself. Within the span of one year, he had seen both his business partner and his chief competitor leave the game. It may have been a bit lonely and undoubtedly daunting as Bill was the last man standing. The opportunity was enormous of course as at that point, the Thunderbirds had no rivals. Griffiths had all the skaters and television markets all to himself. If one's occupation was a professional roller derby skater and they wanted to continue this livelihood, Roller Games was the only option. And skaters from Derby came knocking. Fortunately, despite their roles as competitors and to their credit, Bill Griffiths and Jerry Seltzer had maintained a working relationship over the years. This continued even to a greater extent following the closure of Derby. There was mutual cooperation, as Seltzer introduced Griffiths to some arena managers and Bill agreed to maintain the current salaries of the former Derby that he wanted. Jerry sold the promotional rights to the term "roller derby", which allowed him to continue using the name "International Roller Derby League" used by Roller Derby. Griffiths began to use the term roller derby freely but did not elect to keep the IRDL. He disbanded both the IRDL and his own National Roller League (NRL) and formed the International Skating Conference (ISC) dba Roller Games. But all of this was inconsequential to the average fan as Roller Games, as always, continued as Roller Games.

The first official ISC game was on Thursday January 3, 1974 at the Baltimore Civic Center and featured the Baltimore-Washington Cats versus the Western Renegades.

In 1974, the list of active teams in Roller Games included the status quo of the Thunderbirds, Outlaws, Devils, Bombers, and Hawks, as well as the Renegades, Tokyo Bombers, Latin Liberators, Canada All-Stars, and New York Chiefs. There were now ten teams instead of just five. But while a few squads were very active, some skated as little as one series.

Seltzer had asked Griffiths to employ some of his "stars". Griffiths' executives advised him not to, as it would put a further strain on company resources. Griffiths, however, rejected the idea, as he wanted to help Seltzer out with gainful employment for his elites. Seltzer informed his stars to call Griffiths, and many did. Yet there weren't enough positions available for all of the Derby skaters who inquired, and Griffiths couldn't take on all the skaters, dates, and venues that would have been needed to keep everyone employed.

But even the skaters he brought over were not necessarily content. The closing of the Derby was not their choice, and many were angry with Seltzer. And they were left with only one option, and that was to skate with the so-called "other outfit." Throughout much of the 1960s, skaters had routinely gone back and forth between the two leagues and skated just as hard for either one. There wasn't a conclusive favorite amongst the skaters during this time. Before 1961, pro skaters either skated with Derby or didn't skate. Many were pleased to have an option, and this provided some leverage to ask for higher salaries. Some star skaters held out their services to the highest bidder. But in the latter part of the '60s when profit sharing was introduced, skaters tended to stay put and there wasn't as much shuffling around. So, for this recent five-year period before the Roller Derby closed its doors, Derby skaters had mostly remained in the Bay Area, skating their style of game and Roller Games skaters were in Southern California skating an increasingly more theatrical version of roller derby. These were good times with both leagues doing exceptionally well. For the most part, the skaters were content. But suddenly all of that changed for Derby skaters. Their lives and livelihoods transformed overnight. The closing of Derby wasn't a gradual decline where it was known ahead of time; it happened suddenly and unexpectedly. Whether one liked it or not, Roller Games was the only option. Some of the star Derby skaters had never skated with Roller Games, such as Weston and O'Connell. Others, such as Calvello, had spent quite a bit of time with the SoCal based league. The transition didn't go smoothly for most Derby skaters.

The 1974 T-Birds roster was often in-flux, but due to the influx of Derby skaters, it was one of the most interesting and talented rosters in the history of the sport. It included ten future Hall of Fame inductees!

The 1974 Los Angeles T-Birds roster included G.M. John Hall (HOF), Coaches Ralph Valladares (HOF) and Dave Pound (HOF), Men: Charlie O'Connell (HOF), Ronnie Rains (HOF), Tony Roman (HOF), Danny Reilly, Ronnie Robinson (HOF), Jim Terrigno, John Johnson, Bernie Jackson, Harold Jackson, Greg Quinn, Eddie Williams, Bobby Campbell, Robert McDonnell, Richard Anderson, and Sam Evans. The Women's team included: Joan Weston (HOF), Jennifer Marshall, Julie Patrick (HOF), Sally Vega, Rita Williams, Denise Todd, Lois Decker, Debbie Cho, Patti Cavin, Earlene Brown, Stephanie Williams, Vicki Cooper, and Margie Laszlo (HOF).

The view of Charlie O'Connell wearing a Thunderbirds jersey was something no roller derby expert ever imagined. He was as loyal to Seltzer and Roller Derby as Ralph Valladares was to the Griffiths and Roller Games. When many Derby skaters jumped ship hoping the grass was greener on the other side, Charlie never crossed the line. So it was only by virtue of having no other options that O'Connell became a T-Bird. It didn't last long, but for Thunderbirds fans that were still tuned-in, it was a magical moment. The pride of San Francisco was now the pride of Los Angeles, for a short time. He was the Babe Ruth of his sport. And speaking of baseball, National League teams and American League teams didn't compete head to head until 2002. Prior to that, fans of one league wouldn't get to witness star players of the other league in action (unless they traveled outside their cities). This situation was very similar in Roller Derby and Roller Games. Each league had their own markets and rarely trod into the territory of the other. That meant Bay Bombers fans rarely had access to the Thunderbirds and vice-versa. In 1974, that suddenly changed and Roller Games fans were treated to the best of both worlds. For the first time, they witnessed the likes of O'Connell, Weston, and other future Hall of Famers.

Derby Dissention

There was dissension and resentment on both sides. Many Roller Derby skaters refused to skate in the more theatrical Hollywood version that Roller Games was known for; or they just went through the motions. John Hall stated, "The big exceptions were Charlie O'Connell and Joan Weston. They skated hard and sold as well. Some others followed Charlie and Joan's lead, and the Roller Games skaters did not resent them. When the NBA and ABA merged, the mixture did not sit well at first with all participants, but eventually, they realized that it was the game that mattered. Charlie, Joan, and some others knew that."

Despite the initial hope and optimism, 1974 was not going as planned. Some Roller Games skaters felt slighted when they learned that some Derby skaters made more money than them due to Seltzer and Griffiths' agreement that kept existing Derby salaries in place. The most glaring example was when Charlie O'Connell took home at least $400 more per week than any skater in Roller Games, including Ralph Valladares. The highest paid Derby female skater, Joan Weston, was on a pay scale similar to Roller Games' highest paid female, Shirley Hardman. It was not a good start for the newly formed ISC and certainly not what Bill Griffiths had hoped for.

The steady increases in attendance and revenues from 1968 to 1972, began to show the first signs of decline. Griffiths faced several looming problems, such as the oil crisis that reduced league revenue and the internal strife amongst skaters that was negatively impacting the game. To make matters worse, he was over-extended, and his operation did not have the staffing and capacity to handle it all proficiently. But this one-person show continued forward, often unaware of what the various wings of his establishment were doing.

Too many things were happening all at once. It is of course easy to look back at history and proclaim that things should have been done differently, although it is not possible to know all the outcomes in the moment. Based on what we now know, it seems that Roller Games would have been better off not bringing in skaters from Roller Derby.

When the ISC (Roller Games) skated in established Roller Games cities, fans who were accustomed to the elaborate storylines and drama did not approve of the more straight-forward game, and attendance suffered. And when games were held in areas formerly occupied by Roller Derby, fans were not keen on the hyped-up promotions and storylines typical of Roller Games. Even the T-Birds, with Charlie O'Connell and Joan Weston, were not always a big draw.

John Hall said, "In my opinion, the ISC helped Roller Games become a side-show in the eyes of the fans, in Roller Derby areas. In Roller Games areas, it became an unattractive event as the former stars were gone. The games staffed with a majority of ex-Roller Derby skaters were not entertaining or well attended."

During this period, Roller Games continued to skate the typical schedule in Los Angeles: Tuesday was a TV game at the Olympic, Wednesday was Santa Barbara or Santa Monica Thursday was San Bernardino, Friday was the Long Beach Sports Arena or San Diego Sports Arena, and weekend games were held both Saturday night and Sunday afternoon at the Olympic. This accumulated to a total of five or six games a week. In the Philly area, the Eastern Warriors were also continuing to skate a full schedule of games with five to six games every week. Bill Griffiths wanted the teams to have at least five games, as the skater's salaries were set and based on a five-game week.

Not only were the T-Birds and the Warriors skating a packed schedule, but John Hall was heading a full-blown T-Birds home team operation in Chicago, with games held at the 9,000-capacity Chicago Amphitheatre. The T-Birds wore blue uniforms and had an average attendance of 6,000 to 7,000 fans for the Saturday games in the windy city, and 2,500 for the mid-week contest in smaller arenas of 3,000 to 4,000 capacity. In Chicago, the T-Birds' tapes were still on the air and featured many of the hottest T-Bird stars, such as Danny

Reilly, Margie Laszlo, and John Hall as infield manager. Splitting the popular home team Thunderbirds allowed for more games and thus more work for skaters. Attendance was stronger when a Roller Games team came in as opposed to squads with primarily former Derby skaters.

In the summer of 1974, Bill arranged for an all-girls team to tour in 30 Midwest cities at County Fairs. The culture of Midwestern county fairs was full Americana, as was roller derby. But the two were not destined to match. Many sports have done well in outdoor settings such as baseball and football, but others like basketball and hockey have historically not fared as well when scheduled in outdoor venues. Roller derby, with a few exceptions, has been better suited for indoor arenas. When outdoors, the classic noise from the wheels on the banked track or the cheers from a crowd noise are diminished, whereas these are both amplified indoors. Constant exposure to the elements, such as sun, wind, rain, dirt, or dust is not good for the longevity of the track or its metal components. But Griffiths was willing to try anything, so he scheduled the first of its kind: an all-girls contest at county fairs. The teams were the T-Birds (who wore white uniforms) and the Bombers (in orange and black Hawks colors).

The only men were two referees, one truck driver, and John Hall. The men also served as the track construction crew. Fortunately, each fair provided extra labor for the track setup and removal. It was unlikely that the men would have chosen to do a similar outdoor tour, as it was highly labor intensive and often done in sweltering conditions during the daytime set-up. The entourage traveled in five motorhomes and covered fairs from Kentucky to Pennsylvania, crisscrossing the country in a grueling and poorly planned routing. Roller Games was paid a flat fee for each fair, which was much different from typical arena games where ticket sales were involved. With fairs, there was no effort needed to sell tickets as attendance was built into the arrangement. If proper accounting was undertaken beforehand and the budget adhered to, a profit was a virtual certainty. That "built-in" crowd could have easily walked away from the game while it was in progress to make their way to other numerous fair attractions. And often it did. It wasn't something the skaters were used to, since paying customers weren't known to walk out in the middle of a game. Roller Games was paid $4,500 for each fair appearance. John collected the agreed upon amount from each fair and then, after drawing money for payroll and expenses, wired the remaining funds to Griffiths in L.A. Fair dates made some profit, but it likely wasn't good for the game long-term. "It was an adventure that I prefer never to do again," said John Hall.

Other things also weren't going in the right direction for Griffiths and Roller Games. Cleveland was struggling and would fold-up later in the year, as did Canada. The Australian Kangaroos had initial attraction, which quickly faded. The Philadelphia area was hurting quite badly as well.

Roller Games, at the organization level, was suffering. Bill Griffiths could only be in one place at one time and he hadn't designated nearly enough managerial staff to handle the various operations. John Hall was doing as much as he possibly could to assist Bill, but they were understaffed. Many of the other management associates had recently departed, mostly due to salary reductions based on dwindling revenue. "Roller Games was ebbing out as Roller Derby had done. Roller Games-East (the Warriors) eventually did so as well," said John Hall.

The final World Series that took place in this first phase of Roller Games featured the New York Chiefs and the Philadelphia Warriors (known as the Eastern Warriors or War-Cats at that time).

The Warriors were stacked with great talent with most of the skaters based in Philadelphia. Here was the roster: G.M. Buddy Atkinson Jr. (HOF), Coach Jess Adams. Men: Jim Trotter, Richard Brown (HOF), Billy Joe Hill, Jerry Cattell, Bob McDonald, and Otis Williams. Women: Judy Sowinski (HOF), Judy Arnold (HOF), Ruberta Mitchell (HOF), Lynn Congleton, Dru Scott, Yvonne Riggins, Sonja Sims, and Cindy Ogbin.

The Warriors tenure in Philadelphia was on a downward spiral similar to the plight of the T-Birds in L.A. Both operations soon dissolved. But for this series, the big guns of Philadelphia were on display and the Warriors were led by Richard Brown, as well as Buddy

Atkinson Jr., who had spent the better part of his roller derby career in Philadelphia. Longtime Warrior, Jim Trotter joined them, along with Judy Sowinski and the quartet, which made winning the title very difficult for the Chiefs.

On August 4, 1974, the first ISC World Championship playoff finals was held in New York City at Madison Square Garden. The preliminary game to decide who would face the hometown N.Y. Chiefs, went into double overtime. The Philadelphia Warriors (the War-Cats) defeated the Thunderbirds when future Hall of Famer and former T-Bird, Richard Brown scored the winning point. This was the last time the T-Birds skated at the Gardens until 1983. There were close to 9,800 people in attendance. Roller Games held several games there during the ISC period and typically drew over 12,000 fans. But MSG was a Derby stronghold with substantial support for the Chiefs. In the final evening at the Garden, tensions from the skaters boiled over and several made this their last game, not returning to Roller Games. Mike Gammon of the New York Chiefs took his shirt off and threw it to the fans as he skated off in disgust, quitting Roller Games on the spot. Derby skaters didn't approve of the Roller Games style of play and elevated storylines in comparison to Derby. Later that same evening, in the Championship game between the Chiefs and Warriors, Richard Brown again scored the winning points on the final jam, as the Warriors won the Championship by a score of 83-80. Chiefs fans left the Garden shocked and disappointed.

It was the first time that the Thunderbirds did not reach the Finals. It was also only the second time that the T-Birds did not prevail to take the Championship, and it was also the last time. In 1968, Leroy Gonzales had single-handedly stolen the series, which was completely off-script.

Back in L.A., the remnants of the T-Birds team were hard pressed to maintain large crowds at the Olympic Auditorium. Shirley Hardman had drowned in a pool accident and Terri Lynch had retired. Ronnie Rains and Judy Sowinski were the only well-known red shirt skaters. The only big star remaining for the T-Birds was Ralph Valladares.

Griffiths lost the TV syndication at the conclusion of the 1974 season. He was not satisfied with the rights fees that syndicators were offering. Television broadcasts were vital to the success of roller derby. Thus, at the end of the 1974 season, National Skating Derby Inc. and its International Skating Conference ceased to exist. Roller Games joined Roller Derby in closing its doors, at least temporarily.

This ends this very compelling chapter in the history of Roller Games that followed the demise of Roller Derby. Numerous factors came into play, and it's possible that if one or two of these hadn't occurred, Roller Games could have continued on with only a few track burns and bruises. The final blow likely could have been averted if Griffiths had been willing to compromise on the TV syndication deal. Love him or hate him, those who were close to Bill would testify he was a hard-bargainer and not afraid to walk away from the table if he felt slighted. It had happened previously and happened again in the 1980s with ESPN. "After Jerry Hill left, the style of the games changed as Bill Griffiths desperately needed income to meet demands after paying out such a large sum to Hill. He needed to sustain large crowds and an intense schedule of games in all areas. Unfortunately, not all areas were successful, and attendance was declining overall," said John Hall.

Some T-Bird fans and historians consider this moment to have been the official end of Roller Games. But that isn't accurate, as there was a new beginning very shortly thereafter featuring many of the same key players leading the new venture. And this revitalized league was still using Roller Games as its dba. But it can be said that things were never quite the same after 1974. Roller Games bounced back and experienced highs and lows, but the highs would never reach the zenith of 1961-1974. The best example of this is the fact that never again were any seats sold in the upper deck of the Thunderbirds home base, the Olympic Auditorium. Roller Games eventually got back on its feet and forged ahead. That period is discussed at length in the following sections. A more detailed analysis on the death of Roller Games during this and other periods is featured later in this book.

Chapter 25

Roller Void (1975)

1975 Thunderbirds

Colleen Murrell, Gwen Miller, Vickie McEwen, Earlene Brown, Julie Patrick, Margie Laszlo
Ralph Valladares, Eddie Williams, Sam Washington, Harold Jackson, Danny Izzard, Carlos Marquez, Ronnie Rains

"Rollerball *was a landmark movie of the 1970s, igniting
controversy and record box office attendance. Norman Jewison,
the director of* Rollerball, *described the film as a warning
against public bloodlust that seemed to be demanding ever*

> *rising levels of conflict within major sports like prize fighting,*
> *football, and pro wrestling. The film is all the more interesting*
> *because that warning holds even more meaning today, with*
> *sports like Ultimate Fighting, Toughman and no hold barred*
> *combat sports taking up so much TV time. The fact that the*
> *violence of Rollerball seems tame compared to an hour of*
> *WWF wrestling proves his point and firmly establishes the*
> *movie as one of the most forward looking science fiction tales of*
> *the '70s."* – Rick Sanchez, *IGN Movies*

Roller Games and its International Skating Conference (ISC) hobbled into 1975 with game attendance on the decline as the league had lost most of its TV coverage. Nevertheless, the faltering league still managed to put together a World Series contest. But rather than hold the series in the Thunderbirds' home city of Los Angeles, where attendance had crashed and the league had lost its TV contracts, it was held on the East Coast. Rather than calling themselves the "Los Angeles Thunderbirds", this 1975 series was really a matchup of the "Chicago Thunderbirds," otherwise known as the "Traveling Thunderbirds" and the Eastern Warriors.

Game 1 of the 1975 World Series opened in Chicago on May 30th with the Thunderbirds winning the match. Game 2 was held at the Philadelphia Arena with the Thunderbirds again coming out on top, this time in Warriors territory. Game 3 was held at the Centrum Arena in Cherry Hill, New Jersey, as the home team Warriors took their first game. The fourth game occurred on June 6 in Baltimore, Maryland, as the Thunderbirds won yet another time, taking a 3-1 series lead in the best of seven. The following night, on June 7, the two teams returned to the Philly Arena for the fifth game. The Thunderbirds won, by a score of 80-79 after a five-minute overtime period, claiming the series 4 games to 1. This June 7 Championship Final would be the last game for the ISC, as Roller Games closed shop immediately thereafter and Seltzer's Roller Derby followed suit less than two years later. The second half of 1975 began without a professional roller derby league operating in the United States, an occurrence that had not been seen since the 1940s.

Ironically, just three weeks following the closing of the ISC, a major motion picture was released that depicted—at least to some extent—the banked track sport. On June 25, the film *Rollerball* was released in theaters across North America. The movie starred actor James Caan and depicted an ultra-violent quasi-version of roller derby. William Harrison wrote it, and it was directed and produced by the legendary Norman Jewison, whose work often addressed important social and political issues. Other films he directed include: *In the Heat of the Night* (1967), *Fiddler on the Roof* (1971), *Jesus Christ Superstar* (1973), *A Soldier's Story* (1984), *Agnes of God* (1985), *Moonstruck* (1987), *Other People's Money* (1991), and *The Statement* (2003).

Rollerball was set in the future when corporations ruled the world. With our current state of affairs, one might argue that Jewison was a visionary—in fact, many have. Bill Griffiths was allegedly contacted about using skaters from Roller Games for the skating scenes in the movie, as they had done in *Kansas City Bomber*. Unfortunately, a deal was not reached and no skaters were used from Roller Games. Ironically, *Rollerball* was the first major Hollywood film to give screen credit to its stunt performers.

Rollerball was a smash hit in the box office and made over 30 million dollars for United Artists. The movie featured a banked track with participants on roller skaters battling one another in a highly competitive sport like roller derby, but one that was much more violent. No doubt it stimulated further intrigue for Roller Derby. Unfortunately, both leagues were unable to capitalize immediately on this opportunity as there were very few games skated in 1975 and almost nothing televised other than a few re-runs of games from previous years.

The film caused such a stir that Howard Cosell interviewed Norman Jewison and James Caan on ABC's Wide World of Sports. There was even discussion about forming rollerball leagues. *Rollerball*, with its dramatic use of classical music and murderous violence, was unforgettable. It likely had a small but helpful impact on Roller Games as the league attempted to resurrect itself in the following years.

Despite the renewed interest and intrigue from *Rollerball*, there was no clear path forward for Roller Games in 1975. Bill Griffiths wasn't penniless, but those who knew him said his lifestyle had changed drastically. He staged some local games at the Olympic Auditorium in San Bernardino and a few other smaller arenas under a figurehead corporation named *Roller Games of California*, Inc. with John Hall as its President, Ken Monte as V.P., Jess Adams as Secretary, and Peter Brascia as Treasurer. The games were marketed as "Roller Games Presents the L.A. Thunderbirds." None of the games were profitable. The skaters and personnel were paid, but at highly reduced rates based on a pro-rated per game formula rather than the previous weekly rate based on five games per week. As John Hall put it, "The good old days were gone."

While Bill was in Los Angeles attempting to revive his beloved Thunderbirds, John Hall remained in Philadelphia trying to do the same with the once mighty Warriors. Games were still being held in the Philadelphia Arena, but attendance was averaging only 2,500 and dwindling fast without TV coverage. There were insufficient funds available for advertising. Many would-be attendees didn't know when a game was scheduled. Captains Buddy Atkinson, Jr. and Judy Arnold had left the team after TV coverage was lost at the end of 1974. However, the Warriors still had a few recognizable skaters. Although the Philadelphia area struggled and despite the large load John had to carry, the Warriors were still meeting expenses and even outdrawing the Thunderbirds while skating three games per week. At one point, Bill couldn't make payroll in Los Angeles and asked John for help and to wire funds. John did so, and Bill repaid him with funds from games that had better grosses. However, without TV coverage, attendance continued to suffer both in L.A. and Philadelphia. John stated, "Our fan base was getting smaller. I saw that if I continued this way—barely meeting expenses, and not drawing any salary—I would be doing it all for nothing. We closed the Philadelphia areas, placed the tracks and uniforms in storage and prepaid the storage rent for the remainder of 1975. I left Philadelphia with enough funds to get an apartment in L.A. and find a job somewhere."

While 1975 marked the lowest point in the history of Roller Games then, there was a notable change made to the basic rules on how points were scored. During a road trip to Puerto Rico by the Eastern Warriors and their opposing teams, John was concerned that the fans in Puerto Rico—and elsewhere— might be confused by the concept of two jammers per team. This was further complicated by the second jammers staying visibly in the pack even when they were not adequately blocked and had an easy way forward. The two jammers concept didn't sit well with John. He felt it created suspicion and confusion among fans so he lobbied Ralphie Valladares to support him in presenting a rule change to Bill that would limit teams to one jammer each. Ralphie agreed. Most skaters on the Warriors and Thunderbirds were for the move, while all other squads opposed it. But John and Ralph convinced Bill, and the rest is history. Thus, from that point onward, Roller Games teams had only one jammer each. Although conservative Roller Derby purists have argued this to be an unnecessary change, Roller Games experienced a period of growth in the following years to come.

Furthermore, the voices of Roller Games changed drastically following the shut down in the middle of the year. New announcers Dick Holway and Jim McInerney were brought in to call the games, and the two remained with Roller Games throughout the rest of its existence. Holway took over Dick Lane's role—although Lane called a few games occasionally—and McInerney took over most of Hoppy's position as a co-announcer, while also conducting trackside interviews. Elmer Anderson did some games during this period as well, coming over from Philadelphia when it shut down. What was next was anyone's guess.

Roller Superstars

Chapter 26

Rollerdrome (1976)

OCTOBER 23, 1976

DEBBIE HELDON · DONNA YOUNG · GAIL RICKABAUGH · CAROL MEYERS · GWEN MILLER · PATSY DELGADO
JERRY MARRS · SAM WASHINGTON · DANNY IZZARD · BRYAN STEVENS · DANNY REILLY · CARLOS MARQUEZ

"As compared to any other pro sport, roller derby had to nurture its own or face extinction." – Frank DeFord

The second generation of Roller Games can be framed as 1976 through 1989 and included many highs and lows. Like the glory years of the first phase, it lasted about 15 years, and there were many similarities. In both periods, Bill Griffiths was at the helm, and the primary venue was always the Olympic Auditorium. Many skaters overlapped and there was good television coverage for most of these years. In both phases, Roller Games was either the top drawing league in existence or in a dead heat for that honor.

But in this second phase, Roller Games was undoubtedly the most successful league in existence. There were many upstart leagues in this period – most notably those featuring skaters from Seltzer's Roller Derby league – but none came close to the popularity and longevity of Roller Games after 1975. Jerry Hill also tried to put a league together to compete against Griffiths, but it was short-lived.

Many of the game's historians have overlooked this period and written it off as a time when the sport had ceased to exist. While it's accurate to state that the game and both major leagues reached their peak from about 1968 to 1973, Roller Games rose up from the dead and continued onward following its short-lived demise. Bill Griffiths (with help from John Hall and Ralphie Valladares) quickly reestablished the sport of roller derby complete with televised games, sold-out arenas, and international tours.

Despite the valiant efforts of Griffith, Hall, Valladares, and their flock of skaters, it must be said that all aspects of the game paled in comparison to the first 15 years of Roller Games. That includes the number of games, attendance per game, skater salaries, television audience, and overall quality of skating.

The only thing that saw an increase in this period was the level of fraudulent antics, which increasingly tarnished the reputation of the sport. In a somewhat desperate attempt to recoup lost income and fan support, Bill Griffiths gradually added more and more monkey business to the game. In the short term, these promotions increased attendance, but from a long-term standpoint, it may have been detrimental to Roller Games and to the sport from where it came.

This was a time in which Roller Games desperately needed a

boost. The prominent G.M.s from this period included John Hall (Thunderbirds), Georgia Hase (Devils), Ana Anaya (Outlaws), E.G. Miller (Bombers), Roberto "El Fabuloso" Juarez, and John "Guru" Drew (Hawks). Others who worked the infield for shorter durations included Bill Gatchell, Dee Booher, Leroy Gonzales, Jess Adams, and Bob Marten. All of these colorful actors played their roles well, but Juarez and Hase stood out and drew packed houses on a consistent basis.

I've covered the first period; that glorious time in which Thunderbird skaters were household names. Now let's look at the following period, which despite its short comings, might be an even more interesting historical topic than the first 15 years were.

By 1976, things had dried up and even many of the skaters who had hung on through a dismal year in 1975 were busy looking for other work. Some skaters hadn't worked in any other occupation during their adult lives. Two of these skaters were John Hall and Raphie Valladares. Fortunately for roller derby fans, John and Raphie didn't have much luck finding new jobs, so they began to contemplate how to get Roller Games back on (the banked) track.

Through most of the rebuilding year of 1976, only about one game was being held per month at the Olympic, and no other venues or cities were utilized. All other operations were closed; the last to go was the Warriors in Philadelphia. Roller Games was starting over, and the focus was plainly on Los Angeles, where it had all been launched.

Most casual roller derby fans didn't even know the extent of the decline of the sport in the mid 1970s. There weren't many new stories on the subject and back then there were no blogs, web pages, or fan sites. Some fans may have noticed a decline in the number of televised games or were confused when Roller Derby or Roller Games telecasts featured contests from the past rather than current games. UHF stations were carrying a mix of current and past games randomly at various odd time slots. In 1976, the Thunderbird games were either not televised or aired by a small UHF station, KBSC-TV, Channel 52. Major VHF stations like KTLA-5 in Los Angeles no longer carried the Thunderbirds. All but the most hardcore fans were likely quite confused and didn't have a clue the sport had (unintentionally) gone "underground". These were strange times indeed. This was the final year that Roller Games featured Hall of Fame announcer Dick Lane. Once KTLA was no longer broadcasting Thunderbirds contests, he did a few select games as a freelancer until he retired when he and Bill Griffiths parted ways, unable to agree on compensation. Roller Games lost one of its best assets when Lane departed.

John Hall returned to Los Angeles in early 1976 with just enough left in his pocket to rent an apartment. Ralph Valladares, who was in a similar position financially, mentioned to John that he knew of a roller rink in Pico Rivera that was going out of business. The owner of the building was knowledgeable of the Thunderbirds and knew who Ralph and John were from watching them on game broadcasts. John Hall noted, "This gave us an advantage in negotiations." An agreement was hammered out for John and Ralph to lease the building annually, as partners, for a set monthly rate. In late 1976, the Thunderbird Rollerdrome was established and opened for business.

Taking on a new business venture is never easy. To complicate things, John and Ralph were both nearly broke. John Hall remembered, "With the limited funds that Ralph and I had, we estimated that we could maintain the rink for about nine months and then we had to start showing a profit; or we would go under."

The term "drome" (not to be confused with "drone" or "dome") refers to an aerodrome, which is a small airport or airfield. Roller skating rinks have been using the term since at least the 1940s to describe their venues. "Roller" in the place of aero. In the case of the Thunderbird Rollerdrome, this is the place where many careers "took-off" skyward.

Bill Griffiths assisted with funding to place banked tracks into the Rollerdrome to train skaters for his rebooted Roller Games. The banked track had to be specially fitted to a shorter size to fit inside the space of the Rollerdrome, compared to what was being used at the Olympic. Bill also made John and Ralph ten percent partners each in the new venture, as well being paid as game participants on a per game basis.

With the Rollerdrome now in the hands of John and Raphie, and the refurbished track in place, the rebirth of Roller Games began in the heart of Los Angeles, not too far from the Olympic Auditorium. Pico Rivera was a working class, mostly Hispanic city, 11 miles southeast of downtown Los Angeles. The location was convenient and easily accessible for most Los Angeles area residents. It was a tough neighborhood with its share of gangs and crime. In many ways, it was a perfect location to recruit and develop talent for Roller Games. The Thunderbirds were well known and loved in this community as they were in all of the Los Angeles inner cities. The building itself, and its surroundings, had a gritty feeling similar to the Olympic Auditorium. Roller Games was part of the fabric and culture of L.A., and this place just fit. The Rollerdrome drew its share of the nearby Hollywood crowd, especially as roller skaters in the form of roller disco became the trend of the late 1970s. Judy Norton-Taylor (*The Waltons*) was a regular trainee at John and Ralphie's rink and was a great fan of Roller Games.

During this rebuilding period and forward, John Hall worked very closely with Bill. John's tasks included scheduling of skaters, insurance matters, overseeing track construction, and much more. Both Ralphie and John derived the bulk of their income from the Rollerdrome business, so they had to focus much of their energies there. During this period, the goal was running the rink efficiently to stay well ahead of overhead. Ralph handled business with the skate company, public relations for various schools in the area, in addition to other tasks. He also "set" the jams for each upcoming game. The two worked together on training new talent and assigning skaters to teams.

John and Ralph were not receiving any income from their ten percent partnership with Bill at this time, but with the success of their rink and game pay, they were making ends meet. Bill had a production company, VIP Video, that handled the money transactions for building rentals, track set-up, insurance, and advertising.

Slowly but surely, the crowds and popularity of the games grew, and Bill hired his son, Bill Jr., (through VIP Video), who handled many of the tedious and time-consuming details that John had been previously responsible for. This allowed John to focus more on the aspects of running the roller rink in Pico Rivera and business grew accordingly. The roller rink was also supportive for Bill and Roller Games as John and Ralphie were developing a new breed of young skating talent that the league so desperately needed.

Being skaters themselves and having witnessed the results of overused promotions, John and Ralphie both lobbied Griffiths to rebuild Roller Games, primarily with fast, exciting, and hard-hitting skating. Griffiths listened and sometimes implemented their suggestions, but often it was difficult to persuade him to change. John Hall commented, "It was a delicate road to travel for us, but we managed." There was pressure to get things rolling again quickly as margins were thin and all of them were struggling financially. In the past, they had witnessed how quickly a good promotion could fill arenas. The most popular and profitable period for Roller Games had been 1968 to 1972 when promotions had been ramped up a bit. But those teams were loaded with talent and experience and could sell the craziest of scripts to an audience and make it believable. This was a completely different era. With only a smattering of games and skater fees lower than ever, many stars and experienced skaters discontinued their careers in roller derby. Pulling off elaborate scripts was entirely more complicated and difficult than merely skating a hard, fast game.

Even back in the glory days of the Thunderbirds (1968-1972), there was a widespread discussion among veteran skaters that early Roller Games (and Roller Derby) used to feature a much higher percentage of top skaters. And this was at a time where there were almost no "filler skaters." Then some rookie skaters were hired at low rates to fill out team rosters, skate primarily in the pack, and take occasional "kill jams." Kill jams are pre-determined jams in which the jammer (usually from the home team) is repeatedly taken down by blockers, often brutally, with no points scored. And although any skater could be called upon to take the punishment of a kill jam, it was most often younger skaters, or filler skaters of any age, who were given these assignments. In the 1950s and 1960s, there were few of these lesser talented skaters on team rosters. But in 1976, this new era with tighter budgets, almost every Roller Games team had at least two or three skaters who absolutely could not have qualified to skate professionally in the 1950s or 1960s. If these hard working, dedicated (but less gifted) skaters weren't asked to do too much, they were hardly noticed and did little harm. But when pressed into more complicated tasks such as key jamming and blocking tasks on scripted jams or involvement in altercations, they often didn't have either the skills or experience to "sell the jam" and fans saw this. The decisions made to involve these inexperienced skaters on complex jams hurt the potential growth of this revival period.

One of the recurring themes of this rebirth era was the frequent failed attempts at recreating the same scripts that had worked so flawlessly in better times. Not to say there weren't some successful promotions. It was those well-written, well-executed promotions that led to the best attended games of this period, culminating with five solid years from 1978 through 1982. It didn't come close to the past, but it was an exciting period.

Another sign of the times for roller derby was the gradual slowing of the pack. That is to say, the speed at which skaters circled the banked track. While there isn't a definitive way to prove my next point, most of those whose skating careers spanned several decades would attest to the fact that the game has slowed down since the 1950s. Speed was the essence of the sport in the 1950s and skaters were in top shape by participating in several games every week. In the 1960s, the skating remained nearly as fast. But following the crashes in 1973 (Derby) and 1975 (Games), when the game got rolling again, it didn't roll as quickly as before. The main reason simply came down to conditioning or lack thereof. With only one game per month being held at the lowest period (1976), skaters got out of shape quickly. The home team Thunderbirds skaters skated monthly, but the opposition (red-shirt) teams skated even less. Skaters in general had never been known to be fitness fanatics, so you weren't likely to find many skaters hitting the jogging trails or swimming laps at local community pools. The most likely place to find a professional roller derby skater was at a card table or casino with an adult beverage in one hand and a cigarette in the other. The pack slowed down to allow jammers (who had to skate two to three times faster than the pack) time to get around to the rear of the skater's pack and still have enough energy left to score points. Most skaters and front office representatives knew that a faster game was more exciting, but the slowdown was mostly out of necessity. Yet it wasn't only out of shape skaters that slowed the pace. The professional skating population was aging. Veteran skaters stuck around longer and longer and with fewer young twenty-somethings on the track, it also slowed the pacing. The problem of veteran skaters hanging on too long became an even bigger issue later in the 1980s and further on. Also, many veteran skaters who hung up their skates after 1975, slowly began to trickle back into the game once it was back on TV and growing again. These skaters were usually far from being in top shape. It was certainly exciting for fans and young skaters to see these named veterans making their comebacks, but they rarely skated at the same level as they did in their prime. The slowing down of Roller Games hurt the game and its potential growth. The slower pack speed impacted all aspects of the game and more deliberate action meant it was easier for fans to see through some of the façades.

I started training at the Rollerdrome the same year it went into operation, but I had no idea the state Roller Games was in. All I knew was that inside the Rollerdrome were legendary skaters that I had grown up watching on television, and I was on the banked track with them. For the next five years, Roller Games and this fantastic training facility would be a big part of my life. The Rollerdrome was very successful from 1977 to 1985, and many skaters started their careers in this building. "We got lucky," said John Hall on the success of the Rollerdrome. John is naturally humble and sometimes understated in his comments when referring to his career and accomplishments. I am familiar with the work ethic of both John and Ralphie and personally witnessed them working tirelessly at their rink and know that "luck" had little to do with their success.

My first encounter with John Hall was in 1976 at the Rollerdrome. I had seen John leading the Thunderbirds over the years from the infield of the Olympic Auditorium, although I never attended a game in person. John was a large, handsome, strapping man in excellent condition and just about to turn 50. He looked much younger than his age (and still does today at 90). It did seem John was a magnet for young, beautiful females. He was dating beautiful skater Debbie Heldon, who was less than half his age at the time. John spoke clearly and forcefully and had an air of confidence that some might have misinterpreted as arrogant. He commanded authority and went about with the spirit of a man who had started in this sport in the late 1950s and who know every aspect of the game. He was a wealth of knowledge. I regularly trained in 1976, 1977, and 1978 and John was the most frequent trainer during this period. I still recall him yelling, "Go Scotty!" during drills in his loud, commanding voice. When John said go, you went! He trained skaters hard but was always fair. We all learned a lot from both John and Ralphie, and they molded us into decent skaters, despite our frequent failures. It indeed required a lot of patience to take skaters from scratch and turn them into pros. John and Ralph had a fair amount of patience, but were also quick and sometimes unmerciful, dishing out criticism when trainees were not putting in enough effort. Yet they were always impartial and commanded the respect of everyone on the track.

To take a training class, it only cost three dollars per session (up from one dollar back in the 1960s). Classes were typically taught either by legendary Thunderbirds Ralphie Valladares or John Hall. Both men are now in the Hall of Fame. Other skaters sometimes taught or assisted classes as well. The rink was open daily, and the banked track was available for potential skaters to train on their own almost any time. Formal classes were held every Thursday night from 7 to 9 p.m. and there were sometimes classes on Saturday mornings from 10:30 a.m. to 12:30 p.m. Many of the Saturday trainees would stay for the regular skating session, which started at 1 p.m.

The training was hard, well-organized, and often fun. There were sessions for beginners, intermediate, and advanced (pro) skaters. The beginner's classes focused on fundamental skating skills and didn't involve blocking, falling, or simulated game scrimmages.

These classes helped skaters develop their agility with drills, involving stopping, running, maneuvering, and most importantly learning the classic "five-strides" method of skating on a banked track. Once a trainee graduated to the intermediate level of training, he or she began to get a taste of the physical side of roller derby. Departing from a session without bumps and bruises was rare.

It was in the intermediate classes where the fun started. Trainees were taught how to throw a legal block: fall correctly without breaking a wrist. They also learned to take (and give) a whip. Receiving a whip had to be one of the most fun and exciting things about participating in roller derby. The "whip" is unique to roller derby and not found in any other sports. It's something you must experience to understand the level of adrenaline it provides. You can practice whipping on a flat surface, but nothing compares to the sensation that comes from receiving a well-executed whip at the precise time of coming out of the high part of a banked track. For the skater on the receiving end, it provides a tremendous rush, both in terms of speed and exhilaration. It can send the skater up to speeds above 30 m.p.h. The banked track allows for higher speeds due to the incline, which is better than a flat surface for keeping skates from sliding out. Giving a whip requires proper training to execute this technique properly and provide a fast yet controlled boost to the receiving jammer (skater). Just as important is the jammer's skill in knowing exactly how and when to pull forward and when to release the hold. In game situations, whips are not only exciting to the audience, but often can be the difference between scoring and not scoring. All pro skaters need to be well-conditioned to keep up the fast pace of the moving pack, while at the same time blocking, maneuvering, and whipping out the jammers. But jammers need to be in extraordinary physical condition, as they are required to work their way through the pack and then lap these skaters. Aside from good conditioning, these skaters must possess great speed. They are essentially sprinting a long distance to get to the back of the pack. Once they are successful at lapping the already swiftly-moving pack, they now need to maneuver their way past opposing skaters to score points. This part of the jam is often the most demanding and grueling. Providing a whip to your jammers helps them conserve energy, so they still have enough strength to score. Whips most often occur just after the start of a jam when teams try to assist their jammer out of the pack. If a jammer is lucky, he or she might receive two or three whips while trying to escape the pack. Once free from the chaos of the pack, sometimes a teammate might skate out of the pack with the jammer at full speed and give that skater an additional furious whip to provide an advantage to them over the opposing jammer (if the opposition jammer had also escaped the pack). And finally, once reaching the rear of the pack, key teammates often try to "drop-back" to the rear of the pack to assist the jammer in getting past the opposition blockers. Sometimes this may involve the use of a whip. This one technique, learned early in training and practiced often, has tangible benefits in game situations. Everything taught in training classes has applications in game circumstances.

In these intermediate and pro level classes, young hopefuls would rub shoulders with professional skaters whom they were often familiar with from game telecasts. You never knew who might show up to the pro sessions. Sometimes even the larger than life superstars of the sport would turn up. Most of the pros were very giving of their time and talents and would take time to pass along their knowledge of techniques learned throughout their careers. Remember, roller derby was not a sports option in high school and there were almost no "how-to" manuals or books available on proper techniques. The only option was to make the drive to Pico Rivera in Los Angeles and take classes. Anyone who was attending their first class was totally "green." It didn't matter if you had experience skating on flat surfaces in roller rinks or outdoors during your youth (although it helped). Roller skating on a banked track was a different animal. Many would-be skaters would show up for one class never to return. But a small percentage of those who tried it quickly became addicted. Once you get the knack of the banked track and become familiar with her curves, rough edges, and personality, it's easy to fall in love. And once hooked, it's likely to last a lifetime. If you've followed the old-school version of the sport in recent years, you may have noticed more than a few grey-beards on the track in professional games. For better or worse, many hooked skaters cannot resist the urge to get back on a banked track and perform, no matter how old they are. Legendary Ann Calvello skated into her 70s! There are hardly any banked tracks to train on recreationally. So one practically has to compete professionally these days to experience that banked track they've become so attached to.

When star pro skaters attended classes, there was a certain excitement in the building that is hard to put into words. It was subtle yet powerful and boosted the attention of everyone at the Rollerdrome. One might think that rubbing elbows with these stars and seeing them in their street clothes (or workout attire) might rub off some of the "stardust", but it was just the opposite. It was at these training sessions that one learned just how talented pro-level skaters were in this period. This was realized much more in training even than in games. The disparity between the trainees and pros was enormous. All of us knew we had a long way to go before we performed at even close to the level of these pros. Some of us who had the necessary tenacity and dedication ultimately did become pros, but most never reached the level of these pre-1974 pros. A few (but not many) became stars.

Roller Games majority owner Bill Griffiths never skated on one of his banked tracks (neither did Roller Derby owner Jerry Seltzer). Had Griffiths trained with his skaters, it might have influenced his thinking on the game and resulted in more focus on athletics rather than theater. He had enormous skating talent in his organization. And this was even after he lost about half of that talent due to the pay decreases and tighter budgets of this rebirth period. Quality skaters that had in-depth knowledge of how to skate on the banked track and the intricacies of this unique game were genuinely commodities and a rare breed.

The Thunderbirds had a lot of "pure-skaters." That is to say, those skaters who had the prodigious athletic ability, but were not inclined to participate in the theatrics of the game. A good example might be Sam Washington. Sam and skaters like him sold the game with their extraordinary abilities on skates. Frankie Macedo was another such skater. These pure skaters were the glue that held Roller Games together. Their actions never detracted from the sport and never alienated fans. And while it could be argued that those who possessed acting skills may have sometimes dramatically increased ticket sales and revenues, they were the icing on the cake. It was the talented skating that was the foundation of the sport, whether it was Roller Derby or Roller Games. Without these true pros, there was nothing to work from; there was no game and no competition. And when there weren't enough of these skaters on the track at any given time, the game could quickly devolve into a fiasco that drove fans away much faster than well-worked scripts might have excited them. It was training centers, like the Rollerdrome and the Olympic before that, which were the nucleus for the development of the skating talent that made Roller Games famous worldwide.

Many future Thunderbirds began their career at the Rollerdrome. A few of the homegrown skaters included Debbie Garvey, Darlene Langlois, Patsy Delgado, Pattie Frazier, Ray Robles, Mike Flaningam, Bren Futura, and Raymond Rose. The most well-known red-shirt skaters were Ted Marolf and Stephanic Garcia. Many other pro skaters trained here, but this list only contains those that started at the Rollerdrome.

The talent developed during this period pales in comparison to what was produced in the 1960s and early 1970s at the Olympic Auditorium, in both quantity and quality. These skaters helped sustain the league as it moved forward, but it was still veteran skaters who were the leaders. One fact that stands out is that not one future Hall of Fame skater was developed in the ten years the Rollerdrome was in operation. Many factors exist, but the main one was that the game just wasn't as popular then as it had been in the past. There was usually only one game per week, so all skaters had to carry regular jobs. In the better years, many skaters were full-time. There was much more incentive to become a pro skater. In the second phase of Roller Games, participants did it purely for the joy and excitement inherent in banked track skating. All skaters were paid, but the money was not commensurate with the effort and time it took to be a pro skater. These skaters had a love affair with the game and many of them continue this dedication today as they give back to the sport in various ways.

Training centers were the "holy grail" of the sport. Jerry Seltzer stated, "The Derby must produce its own natural resources. Otherwise, no matter how popular or how successful, the game will die as the breed peters out." Every successful roller derby league always had a training facility. Those that discontinued their training centers for budgetary reasons fell slowly and painfully to their eventual demise. The Rollerdrome was in operation until 1985.

The rebuilding year of 1976 featured very few games and no championship for the first time. Many never returned to the renewed Roller Games, but those who were dedicated enough to come back, faced fewer games and less in skating fees. In the early period of the rebound, 1976 and 1977, very few older veteran skaters returned. Five notable exceptions were Ronnie Rains, Danny Reilly, Jennifer Richards, Frankie Macedo, and Honey Sanchez. The majority of the skaters who returned were younger skaters who emerged in the early 1970s, still just entering their athletic prime. A few examples were Gwen Miller, Sam Washington, John Johnson, Vicki McEwen, Donna Young, Greg Quinn, Greg Robertson, Vicky Steppe, and Peggy Fowler. To fill the holes, there were many newcomers fresh from the training center in Pico Rivera. Those rookies included Debbie Heldon, Patsy Delgado, Carlos Marquez, Stevie Santillian, Jennifer Richards, and Joy Smith.

Ralphie continued to skate regularly, and John Hall did so when needed, which was frequently when funds were tight. The pair were engaged in every aspect of the business, from training the skaters, coordinating rosters and personnel for games, and everything else needed to run a new business.

Chapter 27

KCOP (1977)

1977 Thunderbirds

Gwen Miller, Gail Rickabaugh, Carol Meyers, Patsy Delgado, Betty Brown, Dee Wilson
Greg Quinn, Sam Washington, Danny Izzard, Greg Robertson, Carlos Marquez, Danny Reilly

"We all fall down at some point. It's what you do when you get up that matters!" – Helen Wheels, #67, Denver Roller Derby

In 1977, owner Bill Griffiths moved from his small office on Santa Monica Blvd near West Hollywood to a second-floor, three-room office in Burbank. There he conducted business for VIP Video, Roller Games, made deals with TV shows, and so on. He and his wife Doris and son Bill Jr. occupied this new office. Griffiths consulted with Hall and Valladares on a daily basis on topics regarding Roller Games. Now that things were getting better, Bill began to discuss the possibility of having road games again. John and Ralphie arranged the skaters for these trips, and Bill set their pay rates. John Hall said, "Bill stated, if a person can't or won't go for the designated pay, find a replacement. We didn't always agree with that, but we allowed Bill to do as he wanted. We knew that we could find the needed skaters for any games or trips."

By the start of 1977, things were looking up. Bill's VIP Video was able to secure TV coverage for the 1977 season games on KCOP CH-13, a prominent VHF station in Los Angeles. The deal came about due to VIP Video locking up major sponsors that included McPeek Chrysler Plymouth of Orange County. Their spokesperson, Ralph George, was a frequent guest on Roller Games broadcasts, and he turned out to be a popular addition. Games were broadcast on Saturday mornings in the 9 a.m. time slot. The new station called this show *Roller Superstars*. With Channel 9 onboard, attendance increased at the Olympic, as did the number of games scheduled. Hope was in the air as every aspect of Roller Games saw some improvement. The Thunderbirds began to venture out of the haven of the Olympic Auditorium and hit the road. In cities like San Diego, where games were again being regularly shown, the Thunderbirds were drawing capacity crowds of up to 16,000.

In the history of Roller Games, it seemed that if games were regularly broadcast in a decent time slot, the Thunderbirds would draw large and steady crowds. There were no geographical boundaries where this didn't occur. Success was nearly 100% if all the proper necessities were in place; TV was the most important. This was highly evident when Roller Games was back on TV in a reasonable time slot.

The Thunderbirds had a strong team in this era. The women's team featured Gwen "Skinny-Minnie" Miller, who was in her prime and a fan favorite. With the departure years ago of legendary Thunderbirds female stars such as Terri Lynch and Shirley Hardman, Gwen was the top star for the Thunderbirds women's squad. Other key skaters included Donna Young, Debbie Heldon, and young Pasty Delgado. On the men's team Sam Washington, Danny Reilly, Ronnie Rains, Frankie Macedo, Ralphie Valladares, and others led the way. With powerful KCOP filling the role formerly played by KTLA, fans, both old and new, began to make their way to the Olympic Auditorium once again. There were no playoffs or championship games in 1976 or 1977, but the Los Angeles Thunderbirds were back. Many casual fans didn't even realize they were ever gone.

In October of 1977, the popular ABC science fiction action series *The Six Million Dollar Man* did an episode in which star Steve Austin (Lee Majors) goes undercover as a Roller Derby skater with the Chicago Hawks. It aired in prime time on October 30, 1977. The show also starred future rock star Rick Springfield as Niles, who was featured as one of the Thunderbirds. This installment was entitled *Rollback,* and the skating scenes were filmed from the Olympic Auditorium and featured current Thunderbirds and Chicago Hawks skaters. Lee Majors starts out as a Hawk and then is hired by the Thunderbirds. He wore both uniforms in the episode, including the red, white, and blue of the Thunderbirds. 1977 was the last season these uniforms were used and they weren't in the best of shape. In 1977, roller skating was again all the rage with roller disco starting its rise to factitious fame, peaking the following year. There are close-ups of Sam Washington and Ralphie Valladares, and John Hall did some of the skating stunts.

1977 saw the return of Dave Pound, who was brought on as G.M. of the New York Bombers, a post he remained in until 1980. Pound helped make the Bombers into a reliable draw for Roller Games once again.

Chapter 28

Green and Gold (1978)

1978 World Champion Thunderbirds

DEBBIE HELDON · SUE DELAPA · PATSY DELGADO · DONNA YOUNG · COLLEEN MURRELL · GWEN MILLER · JUANITA RICARDO
RALPH VALLADARES · SAM WASHINGTON · CARLOS MARQUEZ · FRANK MACEDO · RONNIE RAINS · DANNY REILLY

"The roar of the crowd has always been the sweetest music. It's intoxicating." – Vin Scully

hile the years 1976 and 1977 had been difficult, there was still progress made and by 1978, Roller Games was back on solid ground. The league was staffing teams with seven members each on both the men's and women's teams. Growing attendance was a sign of the times. But Bill Griffiths was still cautious with expenses, and John Hall and Ralphie Valladares—who were past their skating prime—were often pressed into action. While they received extra pay when skating, they nevertheless carried a large load for Bill both on and off the track.

The most significant and visible change in 1978 was the new Thunderbirds uniform. Gone was the red, white, and blue that had been imprinted into the minds of Thunderbirds fans everywhere. These previous uniforms had seen better days. They featured numerous battle scars, which were repaired time and time again, and the once pristine colors were fading. The new uniforms highlighted the shades of green and gold, and nearly everyone commented how sharp they looked. Green pants with a gold stripe replaced the traditional navy blue pants. The tops featured the Thunderbirds logo in a similar, memorable script but were slightly thinner and more defined. The classic Roller Derby shoulder stripes were now green and gold rather than red and blue. Numbers were now green instead of red. This change ushered in a new path for the Thunderbirds – one paved with green and gold.

In 1978, Harold and Bernie Jackson—otherwise known as the Jackson Brothers—were tearing up those new uniforms and the Thunderbirds skaters who donned them, leading the Chicago Hawks to an undefeated regular season. It wasn't a good start for the green and gold Thunderbirds and some long-time fans undoubtedly longed for the winning charm of the red, white, and blue uniform.

Harold Jackson was an athletic and aggressive—even acrobatic—skater and fast becoming one of the league's top draws. The fans loved to hate "Mr. Mean," and Hawks games against the Thunderbirds were pulling in large crowds. Burnett Jackson, or Bernie, was Harold's much larger brother and very tough for opposing jammers to get around. He was extraordinarily agile and athletic for someone his size. Other than them being teammates on the Hawks and biological brothers, the two were opposites in many respects. Harold was relatively short, loud, fast-talking, and aggressive while Bernie was tall, quiet, and humble. They were a formidable duo and hurt the Thunderbirds. On the subject of pain, no skater in the league hit harder and skated better than Harold. Mr. Mean was a fearless, gifted athlete who ought to have been paid extra for the dangerous stunts he began to pull off in 1978 and onward. It is believed that some people have a much higher pain threshold than others; if that is the case, Harold must have one of the highest thresholds of all time. It often seemed he was numb to pain. His signature move was breathtaking but extremely dangerous. At the end of a close game, there was often a scripted jam called the "blow-off." This jam typically involved star skaters and was designed to create high drama and excitement for a big finish. Harold's "blow-off" finishes were legendary and jaw-dropping. In the final seconds of the closing jam, he often took a substantial hit from a Thunderbirds jammer or blocker and flew headfirst towards the top railing of the banked track. But Harold didn't just smack the railing or spin over and around it while clinging to the guardrail. He soared up and over the top and was airborne, landing on the hard concrete below. His body never touched the handrail. He sometimes even flew over the highest part of the track. And while he likely calculated where he might land at the end of his stunt, there were many times when he crashed hard into the seats. I witnessed these stunts firsthand multiple times in 1978, as I was then his teammate in the Hawks and later his opponent in 1980 when I was a Thunderbird. I never understood how he could manage to get up and walk to the locker room thereafter. Unfortunately, the TV camera often didn't capture these moments of highlight due to the problematic angles involved. There are a few tapes that exist which feature Harold going over the rail, but rarely any footage of the inevitable crash that ensued at the end of his stunt. Many fans in the arenas were also unable to see his landing. It is doubtful this stunt had ever been executed before or after Harold's time in Roller Derby, and most certainly he was the only skater of his era to pull it off successfully. If such a stunt was attempted today and captured fully on video, it would likely be all over social media, with many in disbelief.

Roller Games skaters were featured in an NBC mini-series produced by director James Komack called *The Roller Girls*, which debuted April 24, 1978. Four episodes aired before the show was canceled. The plot centered around team owner and manager Don Mitchell and his Pittsburgh Pitts, an all-girl roller derby team. The Pitts team was aptly named and featured a group of sexy but often inept skaters. The scheming Mitchell was continuously looking for ways to make a buck and save his investment. Such a plot could lead one to wonder if director Komack had been following the story of the Thunderbirds during that time. After all, Bill Griffiths had begun to recruit attractive female skaters for the Thunderbirds home team, often without much regards to their skating ability. The similarity between the show's premise and the real-life Thunderbirds team was a bit uncanny. Of course, that is not to imply that there weren't some talented Thunderbirds women during this period. Donna Young was featured in the opening credits of *The Roller Girls*, and she was a very talented skater. It should be noted that early Roller Derby often used "cheesecake" images of their female players to sell tickets, and there was an award for the "Roller Derby Queen" who was thought to be the prettiest amongst the league's female skaters. However, there is one important difference: nearly all who were awarded the title of "Roller Derby Queen" were excellent skaters. The Thunderbirds female squads of the late 1970s and early 1980s Thunderbirds featured a mixed bag in terms of ability. A seven-member Thunderbirds women's team might typically have two bonafide stars, three ordinary pros, and two skaters that had no business on a banked track, but were extraordinarily pretty.

The Roller Girls, a 1978 sitcom, should not be confused with *Rollergirls*, a 2006 A&E Network reality show about the Lonestar Rollergirls roller derby league in Austin, Texas. Ann Calvello was featured in the 2006 show, and despite its short three-month run, it had a significant impact on the growth of female roller derby leagues in the USA and worldwide.

Despite its short-run of just four episodes, *The Roller Girls* was shown across the entire country on NBC and likely gave the league a nice raise as things continued to build.

Later in the same year, another primetime hit TV show featured a Roller Derby segment. It was ABC's hit *Fantasy Island*, starring Ricardo Montalban. The episode, entitled "The War Games/Queen of the Boston Bruisers," aired October 28. The very brief Roller Derby scene included footage from a Devils vs. Outlaws game.

In addition to the new uniforms, 1978 marked the first year Roller Games held a World Series since 1975.

The Chicago Hawks had been a Roller Games team since the league's inception. The Hawks were one of only two teams in Roller Games history that had never tried to build a home team. The other was the New York Bombers. These two teams had always been red-shirt opposition teams. The Hawks were also the only long-running opposition team that had never once participated in the World Series. The Devils, Outlaws, and Bombers had each been involved a minimum of five times.

The year 1978 would change all that. The Hawks had dominated the league in the regular season. Led by their superstar Harold Jackson and flamboyant field manager Roberto "El Fabuloso" Juarez, the Hawks strolled into the World Championship series having not lost a single game. The women's team was led by veterans Candi Mitchell and Peggy Fowler, with rising star Stephanie Garcia. Aside from the Jackson brothers, the men's squad featured a mix of talented skaters in their prime, such as speedster Kenny Saunders, Neal Chambers, and Victor Redmond. The Hawks also had three hard-hitting youngsters, Ted Marolf, Tony Trujillo, and Stevie Santillian, who all later spent many years in Roller Derby. In 1978, these three were still learning the game but were on their way to becoming solid pros. It is my belief that if you asked any of the Hawks men's skaters what their favorite year as a pro skater was, many would likely answer 1978 as they were a part of a tough, talented, and exciting Hawks team. In 1978, I rode the bench much of the time, but I certainly could feel the chemistry of this gifted Hawks team.

The 1978 Thunderbirds women were led by veteran speedsters Gwen Miller, Donna Young, and the ever-tough Jennifer Richards. Debbie Heldon and Patsy Delgado looked splendid in the new green and gold, but they were more than just eye candy, as they took skating seriously. Colleen Murrell, the Australian skater who married Ronnie Rains and emigrated to the United States, occasionally skated for the home team. The men's team featured veteran stars such as Sam "The Man" Washington, Danny Reilly, Ronnie "Psycho" Rains (HOF), and the ageless Frankie Macedo (HOF). Jerry Reis was a young skater from the Rollerdrome Training Center who played a limited role on this team, but later developed into a highly featured skater. Both John Hall (HOF) and Ralphie Valladares (HOF) skated on the 1978 team as needed.

As the story goes, the Hawks would eventually lose a close World Series to the reigning Champion Thunderbirds, but it was an excellent ride for the skaters and fans alike. The lower section of the Olympic Auditorium was sold out for many Hawks-Thunderbirds games, including the World Series. Harold and company set the stage for even bigger events in the future.

Chapter 29

Harold's Hawks (1979)

1979 LOS ANGELES THUNDERBIRDS
DEBBIE HELDON, DONNA YOUNG, PATSY DELGADO, DEBBIE GARVEY, GWEN MILLER,
JENNIFER RICHARDS, JULIE HALLIWELL
JOHN HALL, DAVE MARTINEZ, SAM WASHINGTON, RAY ROBLES, FRANK MACEDO, RONNIE RAINS,
DANNY REILLY, RALPH VALLADARES

*"Without humor, a sports fan is a religious
fanatic."* – Keith Olbermann, journalist and former sportscaster

979 was the year of *Roller Boogie,* the now cult-classic film set in Venice Beach at the height of the roller-skating fad of the late 1970s; the masses were skating in large numbers, cruising around on eight wheels was in vogue. *Skatetown,* Patrick Swayze's first leading role, and other movies featuring skating were released during this period.

The T-Birds of 1979 were much the same as in 1978 with a few exceptions. Young Ray Robles and David Martinez were added to the men's team and brought youth and enthusiasm. Both skaters were still in the process of learning their craft and were often assigned to "kill jams" and were thrashed about by opposition skaters. The ritual of "schooling" rookie skaters, or any younger white shirt skaters, had been practiced since the early days of roller derby. This vetting process typically weeded out skaters who were not cut out for the rough and tumble of the sport. Both David and Ray were fearless and quickly earned the respect of their opposition. Due to their persistent dedication, they became solid skaters within a few years and both had lengthy careers over 30 years. In 1979, they were green and took the standard rookie poundings in stride.

David and Ray were prime examples of the new breed of banked track skaters who started their careers at a time when you could no longer make a living skating in roller derby. These skaters had other jobs and although they were paid professional skaters, they did it for the love of the game. It's important to clarify that I'm referring to traditionally paid roller derby skaters and not the newer, mostly female, flat track skaters whose sport was strictly on an amateur level. This crop of skaters started their careers in the late 1970s or 1980s. The Davids and Rays of this period grew up at a time when Roller Games (and Roller Derby) were still extremely popular. They had a love and respect for the game and watched their skating heroes on Channel 5, 13 or 9 in Los Angeles in their youth. They worked hard in training to have the chance to skate pro with Roller Games. Once they made the team, they were skating beside many of the heroes of their youth. David and Ray were part of the last generation that witnessed good pro roller derby growing up. They were the final generation to be trained by former pros who had retired and could still move skillfully around a track. The generation that followed grew up in an era where there was no quality roller derby on television or debacles that featured alligators and aging skaters in games that should have been classified as old-timers' exhibitions at best. In 1979, wide-eyed David and Ray were the sixth and seventh men on a strong Thunderbirds team.

The Thunderbirds had several tough opponents in 1979, as the league was growing stronger year by year and veteran talent was re-entering the expanding league. Harold Jackson's Hawks, who had dominated the 1978 season, were still drawing large crowds to the Olympic Auditorium with Roberto Juarez (aka El Fabuloso) leading the promotional side of things. But the unstoppable Jackson Brothers were split up with big brother Burnett going to the Outlaws, who also had a formidable team. The New York Bombers, led by Greg Quinn and Brenda DeShields, were another strong opponent and fielded a deep men's team with the exciting Ken Saunders and George Fernandez. In addition to veteran DeShields, the women's squad featured up and coming stars Stephanie Garcia and Debbie Heldon. I spent the 1979 season with the Bombers. In 1979, long-time rival Detroit Devils were one of the biggest draws with future Hall of Famer, Larry Lewis leading them. Larry was the league's most talented skater and arguably the greatest homegrown talent that Roller Games ever produced. But the Hawks became the most prominent "red-shirt" draw for Roller Games and they earned the right to face the T-Birds in the 1979 championship series. The reason for the big crowds at the Olympic and other venues can be attributed to El Fabulso. The T-Birds took the exciting World Series in the final game on September 1 at the Olympic to remain the champions, as per the script, but Harold and the Hawks made it fun. In the final championship game, there was a match race with E.G. Miller and El Fabuloso Roberto Juarez teaming up and beating Ronnie Rains in what was known as a "handicap" race. But in the second half of the game, Rains got revenge and dominated the men's final skating period to lead the T-Birds to a lopsided victory.

The T-Birds always had their share of rivals and adversity, but an insidious devil was lurking in 1979 with roller derby its eventual victim. The first in-line skates were being tested in Minneapolis to be used for training purposes when ice wasn't available. These new skates didn't come into prominence until 1986, and it wasn't a coincidence that as the popularity of "rollerblading" increased, the popularity of the sport rooted by quad skates soon decreased.

The tumultuous 1970s ended on a high note for Roller Games and enthusiasm was high. Attendance had continued to rise every year from 1976 to 1979, and the training center in Pico Rivera was going strong and regularly pumping out new and talented skaters. The future once again looked bright as the 1980s were approaching.

Chapter 30

Glamour, Glitz, and Georgia (1980)

L.A. T-Birds – Super Champs

BACK ROW—(Mascot) T-Bird Chicken, Sam Washington, Jerry Ruiz, Big John Johnson, James Scott, Billy Marshall, Ralph Valladares, John Hall

FRONT—Debbie Heldon, Donna Young, Patty Delgado, Debbie Garvey, Gwen Millar, Rena Lamaestra, Darlene Langlois de la Chapelle, Lori Gregory

Roller derby was anything but conventional. It was dark, violent, and underground. It was non-conformist: hip

*and authentic. It welcomed all races, genders, and sexual
orientations. It was a "people's sport" with low salaries and
low admission fees, revered by the inner-city working class. It
was a combination of Rock and Roll, Funk, Goth, and Punk
and was edgier than all of them. It was a traveling circus; a
dysfunctional but happy band of gypsies including some of the
most colorful characters the sports world had ever seen. This is
why I love it!* -The Author

In 1980, Bill Griffiths purchased the master lease to the Olympic
Auditorium. John Hall, Ralphie Valladares, and Debbie Heldon
(who was John's girlfriend at the time) pitched in some funds as well.
Bill planned to book a variety of events at the Olympic, with Roller
Games having priority and convinced John, Ralph, and Debbie that
this move would be great for the league.

1980 was the peak of the roller disco craze, and it seemed everyone
was all dressed up in neo-late 1970's fashion and hanging out at the
local skating rink. The Rollerdrome was doing good business and
Roller Games was in the midst of one of the best years of its comeback
phase and certainly the best up to this point in time (1976-1980). The
Thunderbirds skated a total of 65 games in 1980, including 40 regular
season games, a five-game World Series, and 20 exhibition contests.
These were the most games held in a single season since 1974 and
more than in any years that followed. The team skated almost every
Saturday night at the Olympic Auditorium, drawing bigger crowds
than any years during their comeback period. And with the popularity
of Roller Games expanding, the Thunderbirds ventured into larger
sports arenas including four games at the Los Angeles Sports Arena,
one at the San Bernardino Swing Auditorium, and two at the Fabulous
Forum for the President's Cup series. The Thunderbirds traveled to
San Diego six times in 1980, where the games at the San Diego Sports
Arena were sold out or near capacity every time. San Diego became
an unofficial second home for the Thunderbirds and they held game
three of the 1980 World Series there.

Part of the storyline for 1980 was a lengthy winning streak, and the Thunderbirds came out of the gate hot taking 39 straight games before finally dropping a contest six months into the season to the Texas Outlaws in July. Winning had become an obsession.

Reality TV was in its infancy at this time, and one of the first shows was *Real People,* an NBC series that aired Wednesdays at 8-9 p.m. from 1979 to 1984. In the spring of 1980, the show did a segment that featured host Sarah Purcell training with the Thunderbirds women's team at the Rollerdrome. This culminated with her appearance during halftime at a Thunderbirds vs. Bombers contest on March 22 at the Los Angeles Sports Arena. Sarah laced up a pair of skates and was filmed skating as a guest member of the Thunderbirds women's team. A decent crowd of 5,500 had shown up for the game, which the Thunderbirds eventually won 80-78. At the time, *Real People* was NBC's most popular series.

These *Real People* episodes can be seen on YouTube in their entirety, exposing the lack of skating skills of some the newer Thunderbirds girls. Some of the game's highlights featured Thunderbirds women stars such as Gwen Miller and Donna Young, whose skating stood out and salvaged what was otherwise a mess. This old footage contains rare footage inside the Thunderbirds' Rollerdrome training center, including Ralphie Valladares training the skaters on camera. Despite the show's clichéd and corny bits, its vast following attracted new fans to Roller Games and kept the momentum rolling forward. One could only wonder how many more fans would have tuned in to future Roller Games broadcasts had this and other shows with a large reach featured top skaters and more legitimate skating action. The cheesecake element was pitifully overplayed during this era and many of the Thunderbirds girls were just not ready for prime time.

A couple months later, another NBC prime time series again featured female skaters from Roller Games, *The Misadventures of Sheriff Lobo.* It aired Tuesday nights, at 8 p.m from 1979 to 1981, but despite the similar time slot, it did not achieve high ratings like *Real People* did. In fact, in 2002 the series was ranked #36 on *TV Guide's* "50 Worst TV Shows of All Time." This episode featured thirteen

Roller Games women wearing red and white Detroit Devils uniforms and took place on April 15 at the Olympic Auditorium. The episode was titled "Orly's Hot Skates" and aired nationally on May 6, bringing additional exposure to Roller Games.

Just two days earlier on May 4, the Olympic Auditorium made rock history, hosting its first punk rock show as Public Image, LTD, featuring John Lydon, aka Johnny Rotten, formerly of the Sex Pistols, took the stage for a legendary appearance that is still talked about today. Punk rock promoter, David Ferguson booked the UK singer and this concert commenced the Olympic Auditorium's reputation for being a notorious punk rock venue that set off a wave of nearly weekly punk shows including acts such as The Exploited, SIN 34, Suicidal Tendencies, Circle Jerks, The Dickies, Wasted Youth, Dead Kennedys, The Vandals, D.O.A., and Bad Religion amongst others. Bill Griffiths was part of punk rock history from the early 1980s as he held the lease to the Olympic and worked with music promoters to make these shows possible.

The Olympic Auditorium had rightfully earned the badge of an underground, anti-establishment people's venue. It's location in a rough part of Los Angeles and its long history of being associated with violent, unconventional sports (wrestling, boxing and roller derby) made it a natural choice for the anarchists and rebels of punk.

The Olympic was all the rage to the hip, alternative crowd and Roller Games had contributed to that reputation. During this time, attending a Thunderbirds game was en-vogue for members of the Los Angeles underground. The Thunderbirds were so popular at this time that Debbie Harry and Nigel Harrison of the New York new wave-pop-punk band Blondie wrote a song about them. It was simply called Thunderbirds and released in November on their *Autoamerican* LP. This hard-earned reputation had been earned back in the days of hard, fast, and exciting skating by the likes of Shirley Hardman, Terri Lynch, and Danny Reilly, and sustained by the likes of Gwen Miller, Donna Young, and Sam Washington. However, the ongoing attempt at marketing the Thunderbirds women as sex symbols was rapidly diminishing this hard-earned reputation.

Hollywood has always adored the Olympic and many major motion pictures were filmed there, including: *The Manchurian Candidate* (1962), *Requiem for a Heavyweight* (1962), *California Split* (1974), *Rocky* (1976), *The Champ* (1979), *The Main Event* (1979), *The Sting II* (1983), *Virtuosity* (1995), *Ready To Rumble* (2000), and *Charlie's Angels: Full Throttle* (2003).

The glamorous 1980 Thunderbirds women's team shined more off the track than on it. Bill Griffiths assembled one of the most physically attractive women's sports team in history. Roller derby was one of the first co-ed professional sports with locker rooms separated by gender rather than by opposing teams. At the Olympic Auditorium, the two lockers rooms were adjacent to each other. Following each game, the girls showered and often put on full makeup to go out on the town. I was 20 years old and in my third year in the league, the first with the Thunderbirds. I recall being mesmerized by the beauties coming out of that locker room, making their way to the parking lot. They were often accompanied by their boyfriends or husbands. There was pretty Patsy Delgado, a former Miss L.A. Latino; tall, long-legged Penn State Coed Debbie Heldon, who was John Hall's girlfriend; gorgeous girl-next-door Debbie Garvey, who was the wife of skater Ted Marolf; another girl-next-door type, young Lori Gregory; and frosted hair glam girl Darlene Langlois. Griffiths heavily promoted Darlene as the "star attraction" of the Thunderbirds. Ironically just a year later, Darlene would be part of the musical act *Chain Reaction* that featured one of the guitarists I was working with in my band Electric Warrior, Michael Vangerov, who would eventually become a mainstay for Liquid Blue. But the one Thunderbirds skater whose beauty stood out above all in my eyes was the sweet and reserved Rena Lamaestra. Rena, like Patsy, was a Latin beauty and I, like several other male skaters, had a big crush on her. We had a few things in common: we were both mostly pack skaters, both wore number seven, and were both Thunderbirds. Before the start of each game, the members of each team were announced with the corresponding numbers of the male and female team skating a lap together, often hand in hand. This was one of the highlights of the game for me, and it is likely Rena had to work to remove her hand from mine. She was married to a police officer. They've since divorced, and although we are still good friends, our romance never manifested.

Despite the Thunderbirds women's team looking great on camera, Gwen "Skinny Minnie" Miller and Donna Young carried the load on the track and were two of the most talented female skaters in roller derby history, taking most of the critical jams. Debbie Heldon and Patsy Delgado also contributed solid blocking and jamming. At the very least, this was an exciting team to witness and lots of folks came to the Olympic and other venues to see these ladies up close.

The Thunderbirds men's team was a bit more well-balanced and featured a solid squad of veteran skaters (including four Hall of Fame members), with a couple of younger skaters in the mix. The team was led by speedsters Sam "The Man" Washington and Billy "Hot Wheels" Marshall. Both were still in their prime having come up together as rookies in 1969. Frankie Macedo (Hall of Fame) skated much of 1980 before breaking his ankle and Big John Johnson was in the process of a comeback. Ralphie Valladares (Hall of Fame) continued his long career skating in almost all 65 games. Ronnie Rains (HOF) and Danny Reilly skated much of the 1980 season and John Hall (HOF) occasionally skated when needed. Jerry Reis and I were the team's newest and youngest skaters and had trained together at the Thunderbirds Rollerdrome. Jerry made skating his priority and progressed much faster than I did. He quickly became an integral part of the team, even being called upon for some match races. I was in the pack much of the time, but as the season progressed, I was called upon to jam more often. I have reason to believe Griffiths, Hall, and Valladares may have been grooming me for a larger future role on the team. I was asked to do television interviews during two of the five World Series games, including game one and the fifth and final game. Although I loved the game and being a Thunderbird, much of my time was devoted to other pursuits including my band, whose performance dates often collided with the Thunderbirds' schedule. I also questioned whether or not I had enough natural skating talent to take it to the next level. My biggest struggle was properly executing my role on "set jams." My knowledge and understanding of the game was still limited and I often had difficulty recalling all of the instructions for highly scripted jams. In addition to my frequent "brain-freeze", I skated much of the 1980 season with cracked ribs, which adversely affected my performance. This occurred on February 10 in just my fourth game as we went up against the Hawks for the second straight night. While I went on a "kill jam" and was being held by one opposing skater, Harold Jackson skated in the opposite direction and drop kicked me in the ribs. They would eventually take months to fully heal and I didn't disclose the pain I was experiencing to any members of management for fear of losing my position on the team. I don't believe Harold intended to injure me. He executed every move with the highest intensity and his high tolerance for pain likely influenced the force of his hits. During the months that followed after the injury, my skating was defensive and sub-par. It hurt to breathe deeply, to fall, and of course to take an elbow to the ribs. I made it through the 1980 season and enjoyed every moment of the experience, but never skated up to par until mid-summer. The other T-Bird newcomer, Jerry Reis, went on to become a terrific skater and continued his career until the demise of Roller Games. I left the game to pursue music in early 1981.

On June 7 the President's Cup tournament was held at the Fabulous Forum and featured the Harold's Hawks and Georgia's Devils going up against the Thunderbirds. The doubleheader event drew a decent crowd with the Thunderbirds winning both games. John Drew played his role as the maniac G.M. of the Hawks and fans despised him as they did Georgia while leading the Devils. The President's Cup saw the return of Dave Pound who became G.M. of the Thunderbirds as he reworked his classic role made famous in 1972 where he went "red" against his own Thunderbirds team. He was eventually kicked off the Thunderbirds and John Hall returned as G.M. Pound then became infield G.M. of the New York Bombers and assisted Georgia Hase in the 1980 World Series.

A month later, the Thunderbirds and Bombers traveled out of the country to skate six regular season games in four days at the 21,000 seat Palacio De Deportes in Mexico City. This was the first time Roller Games had visited Mexico since the highly successful tour of 1970. The fans still remembered and loved the Thunderbirds. Games were scheduled Thursday through Sunday with two games each on Saturday and Sunday. All the evening games drew capacity crowds and the afternoon games were about 75% full. The ever-present Harold Jackson led the Bombers challenge, but the Thunderbirds took all six contests. By Sunday, the skaters were exhausted but the large crowds lifted their spirits. The Mexico City trip had been a great success and Griffiths put dates on hold in the Fall for what would be an even bigger tour.

When the Thunderbirds returned to California, we skated four games in three weeks- winning two and finally losing the final two games of the season going into the World Series. The long winning streak had been promoted throughout the 1980 season with fans encouraged to come out to witness whether or not the Thunderbirds could extend the streak. Losing the final two games helped set up more drama for the World Series.

The former NSD champion Detroit Devils came back again to challenge the Thunderbirds for the Roller Games World Series crown. The Devils were led by the ever-present Georgia Hase, whom fans loved to hate. The best three out of five series opened on August 2 at the Olympic in front of a loud audience. However, the crowd went home disappointed as the Devils won the game 113 to 110, as well as the next one, leading the series 2-0 as the teams headed to the San Diego Sports Arena for the third game.

With timing that coincided with the Roller Games World Series, the musical fantasy motion picture *Xanadu*, starring Olivia Newton-John, opened to audiences across the USA on August 8 and featured several roller-skating scenes including one backed by the number one hit song, *Magic*. The film's soundtrack garnered five Top-20 hits, and three of them featured skating in the movie. The other two were *All Over the World* by Electric Light Orchestra (No. 13), and *Suddenly* by Olivia Newton-John and Cliff Richard (No. 20). It all seemed so appropriate as the Xanadu Thunderbirds women's team fit the glam theme of the movie perfectly. The "Thunder-Girls" had several pretty blonde skaters with similar hairstyles to the Aussie star of *Xanadu*. To discerning eyes, *Xanadu* was a cheese factory with a side dish of corn but if you sat in the back of the theater and didn't pay too close attention or take it too seriously, it was a fun fantasy ride for all ages. So analogous to the 1980 Xanadu T-Girls.

The Devils were in a good position where one more win would bring them their second Roller Games Championship. No Roller Games "red-shirt" team had ever won more than one title, but as par for the course, the Friday night capacity crowd in San Diego witnessed the Thunderbirds win their first game of the series. The teams headed back to Los Angeles for the forth game the following night with the Thunderbirds evening things up with their second victory. The next week on August 23, the Thunderbirds would take an exciting fifth and final game at the Olympic by a score of 107 to 104.

The Thunderbirds were once again the de facto world champions despite the Devils' best efforts. During the series, the petite Hase was knocked to the infield concrete quite hard by fast incoming Thunderbirds skaters, much to the crowd's enjoyment. I wondered how long she could take the punishment. This was the last time the Devils were involved in a Roller Games championship series. Georgia would continue her schtick for a few years to come, but in 1979 and 1980 she was at the zenith of her fame. In the 1980 World Series, with both Pound and Hase on the infield, fans were treated to quite a drama, in addition to the skating action.

In September, Chinese film star Jackie Chan made his American film debut in the *The Big Brawl*, his first English-speaking role, which was released in both the United States and Hong Kong on September 10. Chan was already an 18-year veteran of Asian Kung Fu movies before this role. There was a skating scene in the film featuring seven Thunderbirds, including John Hall, who were hired as stunt persons to engage in rough-house skating.

In September, Roller Games returned to Mexico City as Bill Griffiths scheduled a three-city exhibition series featuring the "World Famous, World-Champion" Thunderbirds and Texas Outlaws. It started in Mexico City with five games in four days, and again the arena was at near capacity for all the contests. There were only paid TV and newspaper ads for the games, and no televised games were shown locally leading up to the events. Despite this, turnout was excellent, and this was a profitable venture. But once again, Griffiths did not return, and this was the last time the team performed in Mexico City.

The Thunderbirds returned home to the Olympic Auditorium on September 27 to take part in the All-Star Game before heading to the second and third legs of the tour held in Guadalajara and Tijuana.

The games in Guadalajara had good crowds, but the Tijuana games drew poorly. Each series consisted of four games over three days (Friday through Sunday) with two games on Saturday. Skaters had Monday to Thursday off, and, as always, they partied hard on the off days. The weekend games in Tijuana were held in a bullring near the Mexico-U.S. border. Sparse crowds and the smell of bullshit made for a sour ending to the overall successful Fall road trip.

Six more games were scheduled in Los Angeles in November and December, including a second All-Star contest that concluded the season on December 14. In Roller Games, All-Star teams competed against the League Champions, which, not coincidentally, were most often the home team Thunderbirds. These games showcased the league's elite skaters and usually presented the very best quality skating that would be witnessed the entire season. Typically, these All-Star contests featured pure skating with little or no fighting nor scripted drama. For avid fans of unadulterated roller derby skating, it didn't get any better. The only drawback was that the Thunderbirds won most of these contests, including both of the 1980 games despite the skating talent on the All-Stars often exceeding that of the champion Thunderbirds. However, this being roller derby, it was expected, and the simple fact that the home team was victorious didn't taint the great skating witnessed by fans.

Love em' or hate em', the glamour and glitz Thunderbirds had a big year in 1980.

Chapter 31

Return Down Under (1981)

1981 Thunderbirds

Raymond Rose, Freddie Lucero, Ray Robles, Mike Flaningham, Danny Reilly, Ralph Valladares
Debbie Helson, Kim Becker, Julie Griffiths, Gwen Miller, Sara Sparks, Darlene Langlois

"We can't always guarantee the game is going to be good; but we can guarantee the fan will have fun." – Bill Veeck, owner, Chicago White Sox

In early winter 1980, there was a Christmas party held at the home of Bill Griffiths. John, Ralph and other key people were invited. Everyone in attendance was excited about the future now coming off a big year in 1980 with Bill now the leaseholder of the New Olympic Auditorium. After some minor renovations, Bill had renamed it "The Grand Olympic Auditorium."

The big plan for 1981 was for the Thunderbirds to return to Australia and re-establish Roller Games in the land down under. With his league now on solid footing, Bill felt confident things were finally in place for a triumphant return. Everyone involved with Australia in the 1960s had fond memories of this expansive, beautiful country and its people that had learned to love Roller Games and had treated the participants with great warmth. Many felt RGI had left much too soon.

Griffiths booked a three-week late Summer/Fall tour of Perth, Sydney, and Brisbane (summer is Australia's winter in the Northern Hemisphere). John and Ralphie assembled the skaters to fill the rosters of the Thunderbirds and Texas Outlaws. Keep in mind that in 1981, unlike in 1967, all skaters had other jobs, so not all the regular Thunderbirds and Outlaws were available for the trip. I was requested for the trip but declined due to an already scheduled tour with my band Electric Warrior in Canada. My last game was March 21.

Australian fans were accustomed to the Thunderbirds of the 1960s when the skaters were in terrific shape and almost all young and in their athletic prime. Ralphie Valladares was the biggest marquee star from that era and would return for this trip. But the aging Valladares of the 1980s was a completely different skater than the Guatemalan Flyer of the 1960s. Veteran John Parker was men's captain and star of the Texas Outlaws. Both Valladares and Parker had started their derby careers in the 1950s. Debbie Heldon led the Thunderbird women and Peggy Fowler led the Outlaw ladies.

The tour started with four games in Perth. Attendance was mediocre from 2,000 to 3,000 in a 6,000-seat arena. There was a week of games scheduled in Sydney. Advance sales were just average, but then an ill-timed airlines strike stranded the teams in Perth the entire week and all games in Australia's largest city were scraped. Quantas and all the major airlines had gone on strike, unfortunate timing for Roller Games. For the skaters, Perth was a great place to be confined to for a week, but for Bill Griffiths and Roller Games, it made for a financial loss. Sadly, this spelled the end of Roller Games in Australia.

The two teams spent a week in Perth with pay and by all accounts everyone, except Bill, had a great time.

"Bill wasn't in a good mood, but he managed to stay level-headed, and we all looked ahead to the final week in Brisbane, if we were able to get there," said John Hall

Bill planned for a charter bus to get to Brisbane. The cross-country trip took two days, the distance from Los Angeles to Boston, but fortunately, the strike ended just in time for the teams to make their previously scheduled flight to Brisbane. Once there, more bad news arrived. Advance ticket sales were abysmal, despite the fact Griffiths had billed the Brisbane games as the 1981 World Series. The airstrike had created havoc and panic, and there were cancellations galore. To make matters worse, Bill had been counting on the income from Sydney to generate much-needed funds for a blitz advertising campaign to try to fill the 4,500 seat Festival Hall Arena. Without any funds from Sydney, the desperately needed advertising didn't happen. Many Roller Games fans didn't get the word that the Thunderbirds had returned. Of the four games in Brisbane, the highest attendance was just 1,800 for the Saturday night contest. The total tickets sold for these games was approximately 6,000. Griffiths didn't have enough funds to cover all the hotel bills. Debbie Heldon, at the request of John Hall, used her American Express credit card to pay the amounts that Bill wasn't able to cover. He repaid her once back in the USA.

In 1981, the Thunderbirds landed Tory Christopher, a promising new rookie who was invited to the tour in Australia. He was a good athlete who would later become an ice-hockey competitor in the Pacific Coast Hockey League (PCHL). He also became known in the Sci-Fi world from his role in *Star Trek: Deep Space 9* as science officer Paxton Reese. Tory skated four years with Roller Games. He is also an award-winning independent feature film writer/director and partner at Eleven Eleven Pictures. The new Thunderbirds rookie scored the winning points in the final game of the series for the victory in Brisbane. The last jam was supposed to go to Ralphie, but time ran out.

During the period in which John and Ralph were in Australia, they enlisted trusted associate Steve Schwartz to oversee their rink operations and training school. The rink did very well under Steve's care. Steve had started his career with Roller Games back in 1963 as a scorekeeper when the regular scorekeeper could not make a game. Steve did such a good job, he was hired as the official scorekeeper for Roller Games. Steve was detail-oriented and Bill Haupt (Hoppy) appreciated his attention to detail as it gave him more information to use in the *Roller Games Gazette*, which he produced. Steve was well-liked by everyone, including the skaters, and was also in charge of taking team photos. Steve was one of the many unheralded, behind the scenes associates that helped make Roller Games possible.

After the trip to Australia, Bill resumed Roller Games mainly in Los Angeles. He went back to skating more games at the Olympic, but it never returned to the weekly schedule of the previous year (1980). There were usually one to three games per month scheduled at the Olympic in 1981. Attendance was roughly the same per game as 1980 had been, but fewer games meant less revenue.

One of the darkest moments of 1981 occurred when Ralph Valladares sent Roberto Juarez "El Fabuloso" to the hospital with badly broken ribs and a broken nose in an altercation that occurred in the dressing room of the Olympic. Roberto had questioned Ralph's manhood publically while on the track and laughed aloud at Ralph in what was most likely an acting bit for the fans; Valladares didn't perceive it that way. Later in the dressing room downstairs at the Olympic, Ralphie let loose a fury of rage on Roberto. Blood was everywhere. "El Fabuloso", whose large legion of detractors despised his every move, was one of the biggest attendance draws for Roller Games, second only to Georgia Hase. Could it be that Roberto's acting was so believable that even Ralphie misinterpreted his actions?

The Thunderbirds returned to Mexico in April of 1981, heading back to Mexico City, Tijuana, and adding Mexicali and a few other cities. The crowds were good in Mexico City, but not compared to 1980. Mexicali and Tijuana did poorly. On the tour of Mexico, the Thunderbirds were outfitted in unfamiliar gold uniforms. The team had a few top veteran skaters such as Vicki McEwen, Colleen Murrell, Ronnie Rains, George Adams, and young Raymond Rose, but most of the faces were unrecognizable. The crowds were sparse and this was the last time Roller Games ventured into the territory of our neighbor to the south.

The Thunderbirds of 1981 did mini tours to midwestern cities such as Minneapolis, St.Louis, Chicago, and others. None of the road games sold out but attendance was good, and many of the younger skaters enjoyed the chance to work and travel the country.

The Thunderbirds of 1981 featured Coach Ralph Valladares and G.M. John Hall, a women's team of Debbie Heldon, Patsy Delgado, Debbie Garvey, Gwen Miller, Rena Lamaestra, Darlene Langlois, Kim Becker, Julie Griffiths, Sara Sparks, Colleen Murrell, Vicki McEwen, Linda Campbell, and Cheryl Lynch, and a men's team of Raymond Rose, Sam Washington, Fred Lucero, Ray Robles, Frankie Macedo, Mike Flaningam, Ronnie Rains, Danny Reilly, John Johnson, Scott Stephens, Carlos Marquez, Victor Redmond, George Adams, Jerry Reis, and Billy Marshall. There was no official World Series held in 1981.

After such a great year in 1980, 1981 was certainly a disappointment. The roller coaster decade of the 1980s would continue to bring highs and lows.

Chapter 32

Hell On Wheels (1982)

1982 Thunderbirds
Pattie Frazier, Donna Young, Lyle Morse, Gina Gonzales, Terry Appleton
Nancy Grand, Kelly O'Hara, Darlene Langlois, Debbie Garvey, Ralphie Valladares
Bren Futura, Ray Robles, Raymond Rose, Tony Trujillo, Mike Flaningam

"The skaters become properly enraged at any suggestion that their game is less than real. In defense of authenticity they invariably cite the physical injuries incurred. Of course, this is not germane. It is their own obviously fraudulent antics that solicit legitimate doubts." – Frank DeFord, *Five Strides on the Banked Track*

In 1982, following the disappointments in Australia and Mexico, Griffiths hunkered back down in Los Angeles with most of the games at the Olympic. Crowds were fair and the announcers were Dick Holway joined by Harry Magidson with Jim McInerney at trackside. Hoppy was used very rarely as his health was poor and his game fee was more than Griffiths was willing to part with.

The Thunderbirds Rollerdrome was developing some solid talent to help fill the rosters of the early 1980s, courtesy of trainers John Hall and Ralph Valladares. This included Gina Gonzales, Nancy Grand, and Debbie McCorkell for the women, and Darryle Davis, Raymond Rose, Mike Flaningam, Adam Gonzales, Bren Futura, Tony Trujillo, Fred Lucero, Jerry Reis, Ray Robles, and others for the men. In addition to the new skaters, many veterans joined either regularly or on a per game basis. This included big Danny Reilly who was no longer living up to his nickname. Reilly who was always larger than life in both physical stature and personality was on a diet and shrinking fast. Coach Ralphie Valladares was almost always present. Ronnie Rains, Sam Washington, and Billy Marshall were familiar faces from the 1960s and 1970s who appeared occasionally and whose veteran skills were much needed. Rarely did more than two of these five veterans appear in the same game in the 1980s. Veteran women included Gwen Miller, Donna Young, Pasty Delgado, and Debbie Heldon, all of whom skated sporadically. The Thunderbirds were on a much-needed youth movement and with the Rollerdrome in full swing, there was always hope that the development of the next Hall of Fame skater was just around the corner; however, this never materialized. Other than infrequent tours, local contests were held about two to three times a month. Despite the well-intentioned youth movement, the quality of the game was still in slow decline.

In this period of the league, even Thunderbirds skaters who performed on a fairly regular basis could not rely on their limited income from Roller Games to get by. But one thing they could depend on was a litany of injuries. The game of roller derby was a rough contact sport despite parts being scripted. As an example, here is a list of the injuries sustained in the career of veteran Thunderbirds skater Mike Flaningam (the California Kid), who skated in nearly every game in the 1980s and until the very end of Roller Games.

Mike Flaningam's injuries (courtesy of Mike Flaningam):

- Concussions (several)
- Broken nose (1)
- Whiplash (several)
- Fractured neck (3 vertebrae)
- Dislocated both shoulders (several times)
- Broken ribs (multiple times)
- Ruptured spleen (with other internal injuries)
- Groin pulls, quad strains
- Hyperextended knees
- Damaged shins
- Broken toes (many)

Most skaters can attest to a similar list of injuries and scars as permanent memories of their battles in roller derby.

Four years after doing the initial roller derby installment, *Fantasy Island* once again utilized Roller Games skaters for a second show that aired December 4, 1982. The episode was titled "Roller Derby Dolls/Thanks a Million." John Hall was the stunt coordinator and was on many TV shows and movies that featured Roller Games.

Just four days following the airing of *Fantasy Island*, another prime-time television show featured Roller Games skaters, *The Fall Guy* starring Lee Majors and Heather Thomas. This episode entitled "Hell On Wheels" was aired December 8 and featured lots of skating action, more than any previous television programs. Filming was shot at the Thunderbirds Rollerdrome and a game at the San Diego Sports Arena featuring the Thunderbirds and Devils. The Thunderbirds name was used several times but the Devils were called the "Titans." There were some decent shots of San Diego circa 1982 and the Sports Arena. The conclusion of the show featured an "anything goes" grudge match with all skaters, men and women, on the track at the same time. The crowded bank track is the scene of some great hitting during this segment, but there were lots of misplaced blocks and clumsy skating. Long-time roller derby fans would have to wonder what this episode would have looked like if the 1950s New York Chiefs had been the featured team, or the Bay Bombers and L.A. Thunderbirds of the 1960s. However, this was Roller Games of the 1980s and by this time, it almost seemed like most people had forgotten what good skating looked like. This video is available to view on YouTube and Roller Games fans will be able to recognize many of the skaters from this era.

The 1982 Los Angeles Thunderbirds featured Coach Ralph Valladares, G.M. John Hall, a men's team of Raymond Rose, Bren Futura, Ray Robles, Mike Flaningam, Danny Reilly, Tony Trujillo, and Billy Marshall, and a women's team of Donna Young, Gina Gonzales, Darlene Langlois, Debbie Garvey, Pattie Frazier, Lyle Morse, Nancy Grand, and Kelly O'Hara.

On August 21, 1982, the final and deciding game was held, with the Thunderbirds defeating the New York Bombers in the World Series.

Chapter 33

Garden Party (1983)

Thunderbirds - July 29, 1983
Darlene Langlois, Julie Griffith, Nancy Grand, Debbie Garvey, Rena Lamaestra, Donna Young
Ralph Valladares, Billy Marshall, Bruce Schaefer, Victor Redmond, Adam Gonzales, Bren Futura, Mike Flaningham

*"Griffiths' teams alienated fans by tipping the
delicate balance between genuine sport and carnival
sideshow." –Newsweek, 1983.*

n 1983, Roller Games was once again ready to head out on tour as there were enough cash reserves from the past few years to bankroll the trip. Games were scheduled in St.Louis, Chicago, Washington, DC, and Philadelphia, then up to New England to Boston and some smaller cities, enroute to Madison Square Garden for the finale on February 27.

Roller Games hadn't visited most of these cities since before 1975, so everyone was curious about the turnout numbers. The actual results varied from city to city. St. Louis and Washington, DC drew poorly. Chicago was strong with 4,500 coming out. Philadelphia, which was a mainstay area for Roller Games with the Warriors team, was a bit disappointing with a turnout of only 4,000.

The highlight of the tour was the triumphant return to Madison Square Garden in New York City. This was the first appearance for the Thunderbirds at the Garden since 1974, when the New York Chiefs and Los Angeles Thunderbirds drew 9,500 fans and Mike Gammon famously walked off and threw his jersey at the crowd in disapproval of the style of game being presented. Now, nearly ten years later, the crowd topped 11,000 for the contest featuring the Thunderbirds and Georgia Hase's Detroit Devils.

The game featured several stars well past their prime, including hefty John Parker, who for the first time was wearing a Thunderbirds uniform and skating for the good guys. This would be Parker's last game as a pro skater. Another great who was winding down a long career in roller derby was Leroy Gonzales. Yes, the same Leroy who had stolen the 1968 World Series for the Detroit Devils, was back at his "bad boy" best and creating havoc on the track. Vicky Steppe was the women's captain. She and the Thunderbirds' Debbie Heldon went head-to-head on several jams. Heldon, who was now based on the East Coast, hadn't skated in a professional contest for over two years.

The Thunderbirds prevailed in this contest with their legendary captain, Ralphie Valladares, scoring the final points on the last jam for a 101-99 victory over the Devils. It was a great finish, capping a successful tour.

With optimism running high, Griffiths booked a Caribbean tour that would include stops in Puerto Rico and Trinidad in the Summer of 1983. The games in Trinidad were co-promotional between Roller Games and the Trinidad Civic Association. All costs, except skaters' pay and transportation, were covered by the association. The outdoor arena held 6,000 people, but in the four games there were less than 2,000 fans in total. However, due to the co-promotion, Roller Games didn't lose any money despite the sparse attendance, and it was onto the next stop in Puerto Rico where things turned out much better.

The 5,500 seat Guaynabo Mets Pavilion (now Mario Morales Coliseum) had just opened, and roller derby would be one of its first events. The Thunderbirds drew well with an average of 3,000 fans in attendance over a four game series. The final contest on Saturday night featured a women's match race and attracted an audience of 4,200 to conclude another 1983 road trip with positive results.

While the Caribbean tour was happening, Roller Games had scheduled a series of games in Mexico City, which overlapped. Consequently, a second Thunderbirds unit, led by Ronnie Rains and Sally Vega, made the trip to Mexico to go up against the Texas Outlaws, who were led by Harold Jackson. Griffiths sent Lester Kirch, one of his game managers from the Olympic Auditorium, to manage the tour and oversee the teams. Kirch was experienced in handling travel, hotels, and financial details but not in leading skaters. He had no knowledge of the game and didn't know the skaters.

Reports which circulated to Bill, John, and Ralph described the game as a "three-ring circus." There was a glaring lack of leadership and the games got entirely out of hand. Attendance was mediocre, but fortunately Griffiths had arranged a financial guarantee on the three-game series that still gave Roller Games a small profit. Following the final game, Mr. Kirch inquired about booking future dates but was informed that the building had a full schedule and that he should have Bill Griffith communicate with them. When Bill called, he was told they had no interest in future dates. This was the final trip to Mexico.

The Thunderbirds returned to Los Angeles for weekly games at the Olympic. Crowds were good, especially when successful promotions ran or when there was a big match race scheduled. Georgia Hase was still busy stirring up the fans as manager of the Detroit Devils. Ted Marolf was the Devils' Coach, and he and Ralphie had some exciting promotions and match races that drew very well.

At the conclusion of the regular season, there was a four-team league championship that included the Hawks, Devils, Bombers, and Thunderbirds. The World Series playoffs were conducted in St. Louis at the Checkerdome and in Chicago at the International Amphitheatre. The Checkerdome seated 18,000 and was renamed the St. Louis Arena just a year later. It was home to the St. Louis Blues of the NHL, among other franchises, and closed in 1999. The International Amphitheatre in Chicago was a historic arena holding 9,000, and was the scene of numerous national political conventions since its birth in 1934. The Beatles opened their final tour there in 1966. Like the Checkerdome, it closed in 1999. Both were 20th century icons. The same can be said for the Thunderbirds. In these two buildings, the Thunderbirds eliminated the Devils in the Semifinals, then took on Leroy Gonzales and the New York Bombers in the Finals, which were held in the last week of September. To no one's surprise, the 1983 Championship was won by the Thunderbirds.

The 1983 Los Angeles Thunderbirds featured John Hall (G.M.) and Ralph Valladares as the coach. The women included Debbie Heldon, Cindy Phillips, Patsy Delgado, Julie Griffiths, Donna Young, Gwen Miller, Beatrice Solis, Rena Lamaestra, Darlene Langlois, Debbie Garvey, and Nancy Grand, while the men included Billy Marshall, Bren Futura, Adam Gonzales, Darryle Davis, Victor Redmond, Mike Flaningham, Danny Reilly, John Parker, and Bruce Schaefer.

Chapter 34

The Last Champions (1984)

LOS ANGELES THUNDERBIRDS - November 10, 1984
Left to right: Daryle Davis, Tony Swatton, Mike Flaningam, Dave Moore, Gwen Miller, Cindy Phillips, Beatrice Solis, Gina Gojnzales (holding poster), Stephanie Garcia, Ralph Valladares, Sam Washington, Sam Washngton, Bill Griffiths, Sr., Debbie McCorkell, John Hall

"Most people gave Mr. G a bum rap. Everything is always wrong. Rarely, and I do mean rarely, was his ability to keep the business going, even when his family suggested it was time to stop and hang on to the money, recognized. He put every penny back into Games to keep it going. His legacy became large, while his pocketbook became small. I've never forgotten that." – Bill Griffiths Jr.

The year 1984 was slightly anti-climactic compared to the years prior and just before the ESPN bonanza of 1985. The Thunderbirds stuck close to home in 1984, except for a southern tour that included New Orleans and Houston. Bill Griffiths worked hard to make another deal with the Tropicana Hotel in Vegas that didn't pan out, but the Showboat Casino was courting Bill and Roller Games, which came to fruition in 1985.

Up to this point, the partnership that John Hall and Ralph Valladares had with Griffiths had yet to net them any income. Increasing or unexpected expenses were typically cited as the reason there were no profits to share. At the time, the Thunderbirds Rollerdrome was sustaining them, so they didn't vocalize their disappointment with the lack of partnership earning. Neither John nor Ralph was privy to the inner-workings of the business side of Roller Games, which included Bill's VIP Video company. They were often left to wonder and had to take Bill at his word, but the truth was, things weren't all that rosy and profits were thin at best. In addition, Bill was not having great success with his lease of the Olympic Auditorium. The Auditorium was leased out for enough events to pay expenses, but with little left over. Bill's best tenant was Roller Games, and its attendance was up and down. Roller Games had to pay for their Saturday morning slot on Channel 9, and in 1984, the station increased the cost of the telecast. Bill didn't want to spend the added fees and sought other alternatives. He eventually left the contract with KHJ (9) during 1984, and the *Roller SuperStars* program ceased to exist. It wasn't long before this impacted game attendance. Bill continued his standard routine of mailing out over 2,000 postcards to fan club members, as well as small advertisements in the L.A. Sentinel and La Opinion, which helped generate some decent attendance.

The *L.A. Sentinel* is one of the oldest and most widely read African-American newspapers in the United States. Its largest circulation is in South Los Angeles, Inglewood, and Compton. The Thunderbirds were long-time supporters and vice versa. Black Thunderbirds athletes had long been household names and heroes in these inner-cities, including Gwen Miller, John Hall, Big John Johnson, Billy Marshall, Sam Washington, Donna Young, Raymond Rose, and others. Likewise, in Spanish neighborhoods, *La Opinion* is widely read, influential, and the largest Spanish language newspaper in the United States. Only the *L.A. Times* can claim a larger circulation in Los Angeles. Hispanic fans idolized the Thunderbirds stars such as Ralphie Valladares, Honey Sanchez, and Sally Vega in the early days, and skaters such as Patsy Delgado, Jerry Reis, Ray Robles, David Martinez, Gina Gonzales, Tony Trujillo, Adam Gonzales, and others in the '70s and '80s. Ads in these papers were inexpensive and paid significant dividends in terms of increased attendance. When the Thunderbirds lost their television contract with KHJ (9), it was these local newspapers that allowed the games to continue. Griffiths harnessed the power of these papers wisely and consistently. The minority communities of Los Angeles sustained the Thunderbirds since their inception—in good times and bad. In late 1984, the team relied heavily on these fans, even more so than usual.

The Louisiana Superdome was the scene of a Thunderbirds game in 1984. The team had become popular once again due to TV syndication of recent games. Over 10,000 advance tickets were sold before the contest, but on game day, New Orleans was hit by a torrential rainstorm that crippled travel in and around the city. Only 6,000 fans showed up to the 70,000-seat home of the New Orleans Saints.

Back at the Olympic Auditorium, the 1984 World Series featured the Thunderbirds and Texas Outlaws. The Thunderbirds featured a team like that of 1983, with one notable exception: the addition of tough Stephanie Garcia. The Outlaws were led by Ana Anaya, Leroy Gonzales, Harold Jackson, and Bernie Jackson. In addition, the men's team featured, E.G. Miller, Bill Hukriede, Fred Lucero, Jerry Teel, Keith Hildreth, and Juan Molano. The women's team featured Tammy Contreras, Julie Martinez, Vicki McEwen, Arlene Sanders, Linda Campbell, Tammi Villalobos, Lolly Waterman, Lory Weikel, and Peggy Fowler.

The Outlaws fought hard in a tight series, but no matter how hard they tried, they weren't going to defeat the Thunderbirds, who hadn't lost their title since way back in 1975. In the Roller Superstars era and beyond, the Thunderbirds were billed as "The World-Champion Los Angeles Thunderbirds," and that was something that didn't change. The Harlem Globetrotters of roller derby weren't allowed to lose their crown. But this was the final season in which a championship series was held. The Thunderbirds flew the 1984 Championship banner for a few more years to come.

International Roller Derby League

Chapter 35

Showboating in Vegas (1985)

WORLD CHAMPION
Los Angeles Thunderbirds
MAY 18, 1985

GWEN MILLER, DEBBIE McCORKELL, RANDI WHITMAN, CINDY PHILLIPS, DARLENE LANGLOIS, DEBBIE GARVEY
BREN FUTURA, MIKE FLANINGAM, RAY ROBLES, SAM WASHNGTON, RALPH VALLADARES, DARRYLE DAVIS

*"The rock 'em, sock 'em skaters are back on television, too.
There is a new contract with ESPN, a nationwide sports*

cable network. Every Tuesday at 6:30 p.m., just after big-time wrestling, ESPN shows the roller derby game of the week. Slam 'n' Jam, ESPN calls it. The ratings have been good: ESPN considers a 2.0 rating excellent and roller derby has brought in a 1.7 for the first 14 weeks. That means 630,000 households each and every Tuesday night." – Los Angeles Times, 1985

In the second half of the 1980s, Roller Games presented games under the league name "International Roller Derby League", or IRDL. This period is noteworthy for the two major national television deals involving Roller Games in 1985 and 1989, which led to the Thunderbirds getting national coverage equal to that of the early years when syndication brought Roller Games into homes throughout America.

1985 began with a winter series in the Northeast featuring the Thunderbirds vs. New York Chiefs in January and then a follow-up tour in March. Both drew good crowds. The Thunderbirds skated single games at the Olympic Auditorium in February and March against the Outlaws and Hawks, and in April against the Renegades in Anaheim. However, negotiations were going on behind the scenes that would change everything. Bill Griffiths frequently used the term "halcyon days" as he harkened back to the "good old days." This new deal provided hope that those days might come around again soon.

ESPN is a cable and satellite network featuring sports-related programming, including live and pre-taped events. Roller derby is "sports-related" and usually pre-taped. This fledgling network that kicked off in 1979, began broadcasting NBA games in 1982. They also carried the USFL, starting in 1983. However, by 1985, both of those leagues had left ESPN, and the network—while still on the upswing—was looking for programming and decided to give roller derby a try.

In the 1980s, Roller Games was the most viable roller derby option and the only stable league in operation. The timing was right as Bill Griffiths had not renewed with KHJ Channel 9 in Los Angeles and was looking for a way to get the Thunderbirds back on television.

Without TV, attendance was starting to show signs of decline. Then, along came ESPN. Griffiths signed on for the 1985-1986 season, and his Thunderbirds were back on television. But this new station wasn't solely based in the Los Angeles market like KTLA (5), KCOP (13) or KHJ (9). This station didn't require syndication to reach markets outside of Southern California. The new Thunderbirds TV station was national international!

The first roller derby game of the week was shown on August 27th, 1985 and continued every Tuesday evening at 6:30 p.m., following Big-Time Wrestling. Initially, the program duo was called AWA Championship Wrestling and Championship Roller Derby. ESPN appropriately coined the pairing "Slam & Jam." Ratings were very good at 1.7, where 2.0 is considered excellent, and over 600,000 households were tuning into the Thunderbirds games every week. It should be noted that even with 600,000 homes viewing Roller Games on a weekly national broadcast, the exposure was still not as high as it was in the heyday of Roller Games when it was on in over 100 markets nationwide. Nevertheless, this arrangement was much more straightforward; one network and all the markets covered! Griffiths, Hall, and Valladares had come a long way since the initial days of their partnership when the Thunderbirds games were aired on a tiny UHF station—KBSC-TV, channel 52, and only shown in Los Angeles.

The ESPN games were broadcast from the Showboat Casino in Las Vegas. It was built in 1954 and it was the first casino tourists would see upon coming into the city of Las Vegas. It saw its heyday in the 1960s just as Roller Games did. By the 1980s, it was losing the battle to compete with the many brand-new casinos going up all along the strip. It would eventually close in 2004. However, in the early 1980s, large unused space on the second floor was converted into the Showboat Sports Pavilion. From there, boxing, wrestling, and roller derby events were held regularly.

The Showboat became a second home for the Thunderbirds in 1985 and early in 1986. Jim McInerney was the trackside announcer, and former skaters Jess Adams and Ted Marolf were the announcers.

Once the ESPN games started in mid-summer, they were held every other week for TV taping. During this period, the Thunderbirds rotated between the Olympic Auditorium and the Showboat.

Bill Griffiths, the crafty former television pitchman, had negotiated a sweet deal for his league. In addition to nationwide TV coverage, his newly formed International Roller Derby League (Roller Games) would get 70% of the paid attendance. Rooms at the casino were comped to all skaters and Roller Games staff, including his VIP Video crew. ESPN did not pay a fee to Roller Games to air the contests but provided free advertising spots, which Griffiths could sell or use to promote the games. The Showboat Sports Pavilion could hold up to 3,000 spectators, and the Thunderbirds were drawing about half that. VIP Video produced the shows to be aired by ESPN and did an excellent job of framing the action, so the 1,500 attendees looked like a packed house. Once aired, the tapes became the property of ESPN. This would have a future impact as ESPN began rebroadcasting the games from time to time in the 1990s, as well as using them for lampooning Roller Games in some episodes of the "Cheap Seats" series broadcast in the 2000s.

The ESPN-era Thunderbirds included Bren Futura, Mike Flaningam, Darryle Davis, Ray Robles, Sam Washington, and Ralphie Valladares for the men, and Gwen Miller, Debbie McCorkell, Randi Whitman, Cindy Phillips, Darlene Langlois De La Chappelle, and Debbie Garvey for the women. Opposition team names and regions were changed in 1985. The red-shirts included the Northern Devils, Hollywood Hawks, Eastern War-Chiefs, and Southern Renegades. There was no World Series held in 1985.

While there were still some standout skaters, this was overall the weakest group Roller Games had ever fielded up to this date in the league's 25-year history. What is more, this talent—or lack thereof—was on display for all of America to see.

Once the ESPN contract was underway, there were no games skated at the Olympic. However, in October and November, games were held and taped for TV from the San Diego Sports Arena. A new team, the War-Chiefs, made their debut in a fall tour back to the

Northeast that featured an ESPN taping in Hartford, Connecticut with large turnouts. The War-Cats was a combination of the Philadelphia Warriors and Baltimore Cats in the hopes of enhancing attendance for the tour in these nearby areas. The War-Cats featured skaters such as Richard Brown, Lynn Congleton, Bessie Gonzales, and others who were well known in the eastern cities.

The Thunderbirds were back in the mainstream on a national level and were once again, America's team. Except, it didn't last long. Just as ESPN was showcasing Roller Games like never before, the foundation underneath was crumbling.

The Thunderbirds Rollerdrome closed in 1985. The reasons for the closure were related to an economic downturn in the immediate area as two major car companies closed their plants nearby. Both the Ford Plant in Pico Rivera and the GM plant in Southgate shut down. After these closures, rink attendance dropped almost immediately and significantly. In desperation, John and Ralphie rented the rink space to any takers, which included dance band parties and even punk rock concerts. The fees received for these events were healthy and sustained the rink until the Pico Rivera City Board paid a visit to John and Ralph and informed them they did not have the proper license for these events. The duo objected and presented their case at a meeting at City Hall, where they were told their case would be reviewed. However, soon city building inspectors and the local fire department conducted a complete inspection of the building and placed an occupancy limit of 55 people on the Rollerdrome, which put John and Ralphie out of business. They had to give up their lease.

The closing of the Rollerdrome spelled doom for Roller Games, just like its opening in 1976 was the stimulus for the eventual success during the rebirth period. After that, there was still occasional training held at the Olympic on game days, but those games occurred less frequently now. Consistent weekly training was now a thing of the past. Most of this post-Rollerdrome training was conducted by Ralphie Valladares as John Hall left Roller Games not long after the closing.

Chapter 36

Hall Departs (1986)

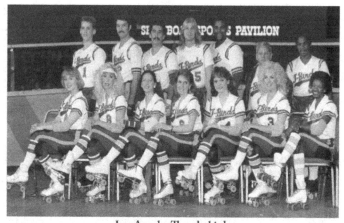

Los Angeles Thunderbirds
February 1, 1986
Debbie Garvey, Darlene Langlois, Valerie Vega, Pattie Frazier, Randi Whitman, Debbie McCorkell, Gwen Miller
Fred Barr, Bren Futura, Ray Robles, Mike Flaningam, Robert Smith, Ralph Valladares, Darryle Davis

*"My departure was due to creative differences with Bill Griffiths
in the operations and structures of the Roller Games." –* John
Hall

SPN's Roller Derby Game of the Week show was doing well, and Griffiths wanted a bigger slice of the pie. With the Nielsen ratings showing bigger audiences for Roller Games, Bill wanted to sweeten his deal and asked the folks at ESPN to help cover the production costs. He requested that they either pay for the cost of production or share a portion of these expenses. The cost of producing a television-ready roller derby event was expensive, and the existing contract made ESPN the owner of these videotapes once they were aired. Airing old roller derby games had never been a common thing, so it's unlikely Bill worried about this aspect of the deal. However, just a few years later, ESPN ran these past games regularly and profitably.

Both parties had profited from the initial arrangement, and there were already discussions about the future. One idea was to hold a big playoff tournament involving all the Roller Games teams to be taped by ESPN from the Olympic Auditorium. The Finals would be held at the Fabulous Forum in Los Angeles or the San Diego Sports Arena. This was to be followed by a national tour billed as the 'Ralphie Valladares Farewell Tour', to highlight the prolific career of one of the all-time great Thunderbirds. However, this never happened.

ESPN wanted Griffiths to pay $3,000 a week to air the Roller Games broadcasts. They were gambling that Griffiths needed them more than they needed him. There was no way Griffiths could justify the expense ESPN wanted. So, Bill told them that he would sign a contract for another 52 shows, but only if they agreed to reduce this cost, which they said was to cover the cost of production. ESPN said no. They wanted to re-sign Roller Games, but only under their own terms. "Bill told Ralph and I that he would make them worry and wait until the deadline and hopefully by then, they might change their offer," said John Hall. Neither John Hall or ESPN waited. In a matter of just a couple of months, both had moved on.

John Hall has been one of the most loyal subjects any company owner could have ever dreamed of. He and Ralph Valladares marched lock-step to every directive of their trusted leader. Many skaters likely thought their loyalty went too far. By 1986, John Hall felt that way himself. John had stuck it out through the good times and bad. On several occasions, Bill Griffiths had come through with the goods as promised. But by 1986, John had finally seen enough unfulfilled promises that he began to consider a life away from the game and the league he so dearly loved.

This could not have been an easy or quick decision. For one, John had no place to go. He had been employed by Roller Games since 1961 (25 years) and had been working in the sport of roller derby since he was 16. He had given his life to the game and now, well into his 50s, he had little to show for it except his memories. His so-called partnership with Griffiths hadn't netted him a dime. He had witnessed almost every deal or creation made by Griffiths eventually falter or be discontinued. He had usually kept quiet even when he disagreed with Griffiths, but this time was different. The possible loss of ESPN was a significant factor in John's decision. It was just before ESPN that Roller Games had lost their Los Angeles TV station (KHJ-9). Roller Games almost never left a market or failed due to lack of fan support. It was nearly always due to disagreements between Griffiths and those he was negotiating with. Just a year earlier, Griffiths had also lost the lease on the Olympic Auditorium. He had not paid John, Ralphie, or Debbie Heldon the money they had loaned him to acquire the contract initially. Before ESPN, John had always given Griffiths the benefit of the doubt—to a fault. John and Ralphie had also just lost the roller rink, which had been sustaining them through the down cycles of Roller Games. Now, with that income gone, John was left to rely on Bill and Roller Games for his livelihood. John told Bill he was taking a sabbatical, but never returned. By this time, the two had developed irreconcilable differences. It was a mutual parting. They didn't speak again for 24 years.

Ralphie Valladares was also down and out, but the Thunderbirds legend told John that while he understood why he was leaving, he still wanted to "keep on trying." Ralph did some work for friends and patiently waited for the next Roller Games opportunity to materialize. John was hired to help construct some new editing rooms at a post-production facility in Hollywood. He eventually went full-time with this company, The Post Group, and stayed for many years.

Ed Koch describes John's departure in his book *Roller Derby Requiem*: "Hall did not see his former boss until 24 years later when Griffiths, in 2009, was inducted into the National Roller Derby Hall of Fame's executive wing. Ironically, Griffiths' former partner, Jerry Hill, had been enshrined two years before Griffiths. Hall, who would be enshrined in the hall in 2014, was in attendance for the ceremony honoring Griffiths and greeted Bill, his wife and son Bill Jr. with polite handshakes and wishes of congratulations. When Griffiths went to hug Hall, Hall rebuffed him." They would never see each other again.

ESPN couldn't convince Griffiths to pay and now didn't have their highly rated Thunderbirds, so they went to Bay Area promoter, David Lipschlitz. Lipschlitz was running the IRSL revival league up North with the Bay Bombers as the headline team and rosters filled with former Roller Derby skaters. They signed a temporary, 13-week deal to test the waters with the intention of extending to 52 weeks for the full 1986-87 season, and possibly beyond. Bill was out, and Roller Games now had no television. The Bay Bombers were now front and center for the first time since 1973. Furthermore, for the first time, skaters wore their names on their backs, just like in most major sports. It seemed that the Thunderbirds loss was the dawn of a new age for the IRSL.

When ESPN signed on with David and his four-team league, they assumed that the game would be very similar to that of Roller Games. But the Bay Area game lacked the same showmanship that Roller Games brought, and ratings were lower. There was disagreement between the skaters and Lipschlitz as to the amount of theatrics that should be incorporated into the games. Most of the skaters had come up the ranks with Jerry Seltzer's Roller Derby. There were a few former Thunderbirds skaters, but most of them also frowned on the excessive mayhem. The list of past Thunderbirds included Frankie Macedo and Sally Vega of the Eastern Express, Ann Calvello and Diane Syverson of the Southern Stars, and Larry Lewis, Ed Dresser, and Joan Weston of the Bay Bombers. The skating itself was fundamentally sound, but the skaters were old—very old. For the most part, this was the Bay Bombers of the late '60s, who were between the ages of 40 to late 50s. The first Rollermania game was broadcast in November of 1986 and it lasted only 11 weeks. In February, ESPN pulled the plug on IRSL roller derby and never looked back.

What is truly ironic and unfortunate about this is that roller derby had finally made its way back to the mainstream, with a national television audience looking on. For most viewers, it was their first experience seeing roller derby, since an entirely new generation was watching, compared to those who watched 10 or more years earlier when the sport was at its peak. Throughout 1985 and 1986, ESPN viewers witnessed (in name only) America's teams; the L.A. Thunderbirds and the Bay Bombers. Unfortunately, both teams and leagues were just a shadow of their former selves.

What's even more tragic is that tapes of these games are still in circulation, and many of today's younger skaters look to these games to gain historical insight on their sport.

Later, it got even worse. In the years that followed, the various incarnations of roller derby displayed even further deterioration. Worst of all, very few tapes remain from the game's heyday. Both leagues destroyed their game tapes, unaware of the demand for classic roller derby years later. In doing so, they demolished their own history.

Simply put, 1980s roller derby, especially involving Roller Games, was not an accurate representation of classic roller derby. It also did not embody the will of most skaters, who had little say in the matter and had to choose between skating in a soap opera or not skating at all.

With both ESPN and local TV gone, we enter the second of three "dark ages" of Roller Games. The first was in 1975, the second was from 1986 to 1988, and the third was from 1991 to 1992.

There was no longer any banked track skating on television. The Thunderbirds skated a few sporadic games, and skaters were paid at a reduced rate. Those that remained did it for the joy of skating. There was no longer any fame or fortune to be had.

Chapter 37

Underground (1987)

1987 THUNDERBIRDS

Left to right: Mike Flaningam, Debbie McCorkell, Lyle Morse, Yumiko, Bren Futura, Pattie Frazier, Gwen Miller, Ralph Valladares, Ray Robles, Harold Caldwell, Unidentified, Robert Smith, Darlene Langlois

"The modern game is still trying to wash itself of its seedy past—a past that was effectively created by Bill Griffiths and his one-ring circus act." – Steven "WindyMan" Rodriguez, *RollerDerbyNotes.com*

In 1987, without a TV affiliate in Los Angeles, Roller Games essentially went "underground" as Bill Griffiths tried to salvage his operation and capitalize on the Thunderbirds recent national popularity generated by ESPN in 1985 and 1986. In February, the Thunderbirds kicked off their 1987 season in Hawaii at the Neil S. Blaisdell Arena in downtown Honolulu against the IRDL. All-Star Super Stars. The Thunderbirds drew a big crowd in their return to Hawaii.

The next game wasn't for three months when the Thunderbirds went to Albuquerque, New Mexico and skated at the 11,000-seat Tingley Coliseum on May 17 against the Northern Devils. Then in July, the Thunderbirds went up to Northern California to the San Jose Civic Auditorium, which held 2,800 spectators. Once again, the opponents were the Northern Devils. A few weeks later, the team was back in Southern California at the San Bernardino County Fairgrounds in Victorville to face the Northern Devils on August 9, one more time. The Devils were the most well-known opposition team from the ESPN games, which is why they skated in all but two of the scheduled games of the very thin 1987 season. A week later, the same two teams battled again, this time in Ventura County.

August was the busiest month of 1987 and it ended with another road trip. The Thunderbirds returned to Canada to skate two games in the capital city of Ottawa on the 29th and 30th, this time against the Western Outlaws who made their first and only appearance of the year. But regardless of the team's names, many of the prominent red-shirt skaters were present in all the games.

The 1987 Thunderbirds consisted of Darlene Langlois, Arlene Sanders, Pattie Frazier, Nancy Grand, Debbie McCorkell, Gwen Miller, Tammy Contreras, and Lyle Morse for the women, and Ralphie Valladares, Mike Flaningam, Darryle Davis, Robert Smith, Joe Cardella, Bren Futura, Jerry Reis, David Arizmendez, Ray Robles, and Todd Stern for the men. The Thunderbirds only had two marquee names left from the past—Ralphie and Gwen, with Valladares way past his prime. Other than these two, all the other legacy skaters had retired.

Principal opposition skaters included Stephanie Garcia, Tammy Contreras, Vicki McEwen, and Gail Bowers for the women, and Larry Hamilton, Stevie Santillian, Freddie Lucero, and Harold Jackson for the men. Two former Thunderbirds mainstays, Patsy Delgado and Billy Marshall, made cameo appearances in 1987, skating just one game in Victorville with the Northern Devils.

In 1987 and 1988, the league was low on talent in both quantity and quality. Roller Games was down to three teams: The Thunderbirds, Northern Devils, and Western Outlaws. But there was barely enough skating talent to fill the rosters of two squads rather than three. Games were infrequent, and compensation was declining as well. Furthermore, without television, there wasn't much optimism about things getting any better anytime soon. Skaters had to hold down regular day jobs and juggle their schedules to accommodate the occasional derby appearances. For some who were getting up in years, the light schedule—with a few exciting travel destinations such as Hawaii and Canada—may have been a fitting balance. Griffiths was keeping Roller Games alive, albeit on a shoestring budget, in the hopes something else would come along. Soon it would, as Griffiths had one more trick up his sleeve. But first, he had to make it through 1988.

Chapter 38

For Those About to Rock (1988)

1988 THUNDERBIRDS

MIKE FLANINGAM, DARRYLE DAVIS, ROBERT SMITH, JERRY REIS, BREN FUTURA, RALPH VALLADARES
D.J. TERRIGNO, DARLENE LANGLOIS, PAULA WILSON, DEBBIE McCORKELL, GWEN MILLER, LYLE MORSE

"Jamming is 50% reaction and 50% pro-action." - Scald Eagle, Rose City Rollers.

988 was much like 1987, with just a few games (14 in total), all involving road trips, and no World Series. Without television in Los Angeles, Griffiths wisely focused on markets where the ESPN shows had been highly rated and where the team had yet to visit. The formula worked, and Roller Games was able to keep things together and execute its 27th consecutive season.

The Thunderbirds lineup was virtually the same as the prior year except for three new additions: Jim Terrigno, Robert "Ice-Box" Smith, and Billy Bibbus. Most of the opposition skaters were also like those in 1987. Those who were active in these years became the core skaters who participated in the next—and final—phase of Roller Games in 1989.

The 1988 season started in mid-January, with games at the University of Nevada, Reno on January 15, and at the University of Nevada, Las Vegas on January 16 vs. the Detroit Devils who were back to their classic name. In February, the Thunderbirds headed to the Midwest to meet the Philadelphia Warriors, with contests on February 4 in Springfield, Illinois; February 5 in Danville, Illinois; February 6 in Louisville, Kentucky; and February 7 in Indianapolis, Indiana.

Then in April, it was off to Utah on the 8th and 9th for two games with the Devils at the Salt Palace Arena in Salt Lake City, Utah. Then, to Reno for a game against the Golden State Bombers on April 30 at the University of Nevada in the Lawlor Events Center. These Golden State Bombers had no relations to the famous Bay Bombers.

On May 15, the Bombers and Thunderbirds were back in Vegas, this time at the Thomas and Mack Center at UNLV on May 15. The Bombers and Thunderbirds were the sports marquee names, much like the Yankees and Dodgers, or Lakers and Celtics. However, every time they met in the 1980s and forward, it damaged the reputation of classic roller derby and the once-famous team names, which before had garnered so much respect. It got even worse in the 2000s when Dan Ferrari's Bay Bombers and the Los Angeles Firebirds would compete. The same can be said of Bob Sedillo's Thunderbirds. Frankly, these games were much better than later contests, but were still nothing like those in the heyday. They were somewhere in-between.

In the warm months of August, Roller Games headed back to Canada for a three-game series on the 5th, 6th, and 7th in Regina, the capital of Saskatchewan. The Devils got the call for this series. In September, the Thunderbirds and Bombers were back in the Midwest for a game on the 24th at The Gardens in Louisville, Kentucky, and then on the 26th in Oklahoma City, Oklahoma.

According to Bill Griffiths Jr., "In February, Griffiths, Sr. got a call from Viacom. They were interested in putting the Thunderbirds back on television through their vast television holdings. The first meeting went very well and was attended by both Griffiths, Sr. and Bill Griffiths, Jr. The reps from Viacom had lots of questions. The Griffiths' assured Viacom that they were in fact the Thunderbirds that had been featured on ESPN just a year earlier. They gave Viacom all the facts and history, and mentioned that the Thunderbirds were going to be featured in the new Irene Cara music video, "Girlfriends". Cara was an '80s star with hits such as "Fame" and "What a Feeling". The day after the video shoot, there were clips on the news about the new music video featuring the Thunderbirds. The Griffiths' met with Viacom that day and things went well. Another meeting was set. A couple days later at the next meeting, Griffiths Sr. was asked, "Who is John Hall?" The Viacom reps stated that John had called them and said several "unpolite" things about Griffiths and his skaters. Viacom decided to not proceed based upon that phone call. A golden opportunity lost. Both Griffiths' and the skaters suffered. I believe that if the Viacom deal had gone to fruition, it would have rendered the Rock and RollerGames experiment moot. It would have never happened."

Except for the loss of a potential blockbuster deal with Viacom, 1987 and 1988 were better years than expected. Crowds were up and down but skaters were paid, and the league was stable. But without a television contract or a training facility, the league, as it was in 1988, was unsustainable and unlikely to continue much longer. However, something extraordinary was about to happen.

WAR

Chapter 39

Rock & RollerGames (1989)

WOMEN: JENNIFER VAN GALDER, RANDI WHITMAN, KRISTINE VAN GALDER
GWEN MILLER, DEBBIE McKORKELL, GINA GONZALES

MEN: MATT BICKHAM, ROBERT SMITH, BILL BIBBUS
DARRYLE DAVIS, RALPHIE VALLADARES, ADAM GONZALES

"On the heels of the successful union of rock music and professional wrestling – which helped resuscitate the moribund sport and launch a syndicated television phenomenon called "Wrestlemania" – another tired old game is putting on the glitz, joining forces with rock 'n' roll and being marketed to the MTV

> *generation. Roller Derby, gasping for life on and off for the past*
> *30 years, will be reborn this fall as "RollerGames," a weekly*
> *made-for-television extravaganza with a music-video look."* –
> *Los Angeles Times,* 1989

Sometime in the Fall of 1988, Bill Griffiths attended a meeting arranged by Burl Hechtman, the Vice President of Television for Motown Productions, with television producer, Michael Miller, and television promoter, David Sams. They pitched the idea of producing a rock and roll themed roller derby TV show that would be marketed to the young MTV demographic. Miller had produced the popular *Eye on L.A.* series and Sams had taken *The Oprah Winfrey Show* to new heights when he was Vice President of Creative Affairs at King World, among other accomplishments. These guys were heavy-hitters and Griffiths knew this had the potential to be something very lucrative.

The show was officially called *RollerGames*—with no space between the two words—and was marketed as *Rock and RollerGames.* The "purported" league was the World Alliance of Rollersports with the convenient acronym WAR. However, there was no league since WAR was strictly a fictional moniker used for marketing. This was a TV show, and it was managed and produced as such. The producers had little interest in carrying forward the traditions of roller derby from its celebrated past. They took control of a dying sport on life support and manipulated it by whatever means they thought would bring in the most viewers. More viewers translates into higher ratings, which translates into more advertising revenue. Of course, it's all about the money. Sams, Miller, and Griffiths thought their concepts would be highly successful. As it turns out, they achieved a high level of success, with *RollerGames* scoring outstanding ratings in its first and only season (1989-1990).

The consensus of most derby historians is that *RollerGames* was the lowest point in the history of the sport. For the most part, I agree, with the exception being that the classic style roller derby skated in the 2000s was an even more embarrassing incarnation of the sport, but that's for a later chapter. It is likely that after so many perceived failures throughout the history of roller derby—both Roller Derby and Roller Games leagues—these promoters felt the sport didn't sustain a broad audience without being updated and completely overhauled. Sadly, these folks didn't know the details of the history of the game they were so keen on manipulating. Details matter, and what you see on the surface isn't always an indication of the full truth. In nearly every case, when either of the main roller derby leagues faltered, it was not because of a lack of fan support. Often, failures were due to mismanagement by those in charge or cases of bad luck and bad timing. Whenever there was good skating and television to help promote it, on its own, roller derby drew impressive audiences wherever it went.

Sams and Miller had some unusual new ideas, and the concept of *RollerGames* was very different from traditional roller derby. They suggested there be four skaters rather than five per team on the track. The standard oval banked track was now a figure eight with a very steep banked section called "The Wall of Death." "Jetters", the new term for jammers, received extra points if they skated above the lines on the steep Wall of Death. They were then faced with the "Jet Jump", which would net the jetter six points if he or she cleared a 12-foot marker, and two if the jetter landed in front of it safely without falling. Neither of these obstacles added much to the spectacle, and seeing the same skaters pass through the same impediments over and over quickly became redundant and was not a sustainable aspect of the game. Rather than add to the entertainment value of the event, the Wall of Death and Jet Jump often exposed the limited abilities of some of the skating talent. Many so-called professionals looked clumsy in trying to navigate the jump and steep bank. Adversely, the more agile skaters routinely cleared these obstacles and after a while, viewers knew who would struggle and who would succeed. The figure eight track, while a novel idea, doomed the spectacle to be forever limited to just the one venue where the track had been constructed. The sheer size of the figure eight track would preclude its use for any future tours.

Like many long-time derby aficionados, when I first witnessed this new format, I was aghast. But I quickly learned of the alligator pit. In the case of a tie game, two designated skaters (one from each team) would skate around a waterhole full of alligators. The first person to make it around the pit five times, or throw his or her opponent into the alligator pit was deemed the winner. It wasn't just unsustainable; it was plain stupid. However, dumb sometimes sells and the debut show—the only one that ended in a tie and thereby involved the alligators—had huge ratings. Griffiths hated the gator idea, and the gater-skaters were not part of his personnel but hired professional alligator wranglers.

There also seemed to be a need to change just about anything, including long-standing terms such as "jammer" to "jetter". The penalty box was now the "penalty pod" and was sometimes referred to as "jail" by long-time referee Don Lastra. The rest of the game involved traditional roller derby fundamentals of scoring one point for every opposing skater lapped.

The two things that didn't change were: the Thunderbirds were still the good guys, and Little Ralphie Valladares was their marquee star. The team was often referred to as the "World-Famous; World-Champion" Los Angeles Thunderbirds, just like they had been throughout the 1980s. The name still carried some weight, and the audience was still composed of at least a small percentage of their national following from their 1960s and 1970s heyday, as well as the relatively recent season on ESPN, just three years prior. But most viewers were the targeted demographic of young folks that had most likely never witnessed a classic roller derby contest. In addition to the Thunderbirds, other teams consisted of the Rockers, Hot Flash, the Violators, Bad Attitude, and the Maniacs. One different twist in *RollerGames* compared to Roller Games is that there were three "white-shirt" teams. The Thunderbirds shared the position of fan-favorites with the Rockers and Hot Flash, while the evil "red-shirts" consisted of the Violators, Bad Attitude, and the Maniacs.

The Thunderbirds women's lineup included Gwen "Skinny-Minnie" Miller, "Electric" Randi Whitman, Gina "Go-Go" Gonzales, "Corker" Debbie McCorkell, and the rookie "T-Bird twins, Jennifer and Kristine Van Galder. The men featured "Stars and Stripes" Matt Bickham, Robert "The Ice Box" Smith, "BBBlockbuster" Billy Bob Bibbus, "Dynamite" Darryle Davis, Adam "Speedy" Gonzales, and "The Living Legend" Ralph Valladares. The pretty blonde Van Galder sisters got lots of camera time. David Sams found them at a Los Angeles restaurant and did the "I can make you a star" routine to convince them to skate. And they did. Like today's modern-day roller derby skaters, almost everyone in *RollerGames* had a nickname. In the past, many skaters had nicknames, such as "Skinny-Minnie", but not all skaters had one. *RollerGames* may well have started this trend. Of course, today's roller girls have taken this to a new level with their clever monikers.

Hot Flash was decked in bright pink and white jumpsuits and coached by Juan Valdez-Lopez. The men's team featured former Thunderbirds "Kahuna" Jerry Reese, "Hot Wheels" Billy Marshall, Bren Futura and Cass McEntee, "Iceman" Harold Caldwell, and "Pretty Boy" Ben Newberg. Captain "Sly" Fox led the women, which also featured "Tricky" Vicki McEwen, "Party" Pattie Frazier, "Sassy" Gina Valladares (daughter of Ralphie), "Irish" Mary Monahan, "Lightning" Lara Stafford, and "Terrific" Tammy Hansen.

The Rockers were coached by DJ Terrigno and featured a men's roster that included veteran former Thunderbirds "California Kid" Mike Flaningam and "Rockin" Ray Robles along with "Rollin' Rocker" Brian Jacobson, "Bam Bam" May, "Gentleman" Johnny Rodriguez, and "Wildman" Holly Masterson. The women also featured three former Thunderbirds: Dar the Star, "Lady D" Donna Young, and "Deadly" Debbie Van Doren, along with "Queenie" May Crommie and "Luscious" Lolly .

The "red-shirt" Violators were managed by Chuck "Skull" and led by "Mr. Mean" Harold Jackson, Roller Games great "Killer" Greg Robertson (who had started skating in the 1960s), veteran Tony "The Enforcer" Trujillo, newcomer Bill "The Hook" Hukriede, and speedster "Bullet" Bobby Cendejas. Cendejas was one of the better skaters who started in the 1980s. This was probably the strongest men's team in *RollerGames*. The women were headed up by "Sweet" Stephanie Garcia and supported by "The Flea" Paula Wilson, "Nasty" Nancy Wilkinson, Lauren "Sidecar" Halliwell, and Vicki "O" Orgill.

The unlikeable Georgia Hase was the manager of Bad Attitude, one of the Thunderbirds' biggest rivals. The men's captain was Bernie Jackson, who was the brother of Harold. His men's team featured Pete Christensen, Charlie Saunders, Todd Stern, Scott Castro, and former T-Bird David Arizmendez. The women were led by former Thunderbirds Patsy Delgado, veteran Gail Bowers, Lyle Morse, Marnie Smith, Margaret Christopher, and Sadie Cherestman.

Coach John "Guru" Drew led the Maniacs, and his go-to stars included the ageless "Little" Richard Brown (who turned pro in 1965) and "Sunset" Stevie Santillian, plus newcomers "Mercenary" Mike Dark, "Wildfire" Bob Ferris, "Crazy" Dave Mezero, and "Creepy" Kevin Ross. Only a red-shirt team would ever have anyone named "Creepy." The women's team featured "Spider" Denise Green, "the Blonde Bomber" Masako Anji, Liz Ard, and "Big Mo" Monica Garcia.

The "rock" part of the *Rock and RollerGames* equation was portrayed in the uniforms, which were styled as 1980s spandex rock and roll jumpsuits. Each halftime featured a rock or punk music act, including the likes of Warrant, Kool Moe Dee, Lita Ford, and Debbie Harry. Wally George famously did halftime commentary. George was a long-time right-wing radio host cut from the same cloth as Rush Limbaugh. His controversial radio show *The Hot Seat*, which started in 1983, had a large following. Former Playboy cover model Shelly Jamison was a sideline reporter. It was all very rock and roll, but the cheese factor was high.

Games were conducted and taped at the Super Roller Dome in San Pedro, California. Chuck Underwood handled the play-by-play, with David Sams providing color commentary. Behind the scenes, *RollerGames* was directed by the renowned Chet Forte, who in 1970, was the first director of *Monday Night Football* and helped that show become a huge success.

The nationally syndicated televised show was aired on Saturdays, mostly in a prime slot opposite *Saturday Night Live*. In some markets, it was broadcast on Saturday afternoon. Going up against SNL didn't seem to hurt ratings much at all since these two demographics were very different. KTLA, the station that had introduced the Thunderbirds to Los Angeles, carried the show at 11 a.m. Saturday mornings. Surprising as it may seem, the Thunderbirds were back in front of a vast national audience, just three years after the ESPN run ended. *RollerGames*, despite its flaws, was so popular that it was beating out *American Gladiators*, with nearly double the ratings. However, while *Gladiators* would last almost eight seasons, *RollerGames* lasted only one. With its popularity and so many big-hitters involved in all aspects of the show, why was it gone so quickly? Was Griffiths driving too hard of a bargain again? In this instance, Griffiths had little to do with the loss of this opportunity. *RollerGames* was hit with yet another sucker punch. The show's producers and distributors had financial problems unrelated to the popularity of *RollerGames* and filed bankruptcy before the completion of season one. As often is the case, vetting out the facts in cases involving personal or business finances is difficult, but it does seem possible that the high cost of producing *RollerGames* may have also been a factor in its demise.

Right before the first tapings, an incident occurred that could have created a mutiny. Bren Futura had skated with Roller Games since 1982 (7 years), nearly always as a "white-shirt" Thunderbird. He was well liked by management and a good veteran skater. He was excited about the new *RollerGames* format and the chance for national exposure. Bren had stepped away from the game briefly in 1985 and had missed participating in most of the ESPN shows from Vegas and San Diego. Things were going well until he found himself dating a young woman who, unannounced to him, was handling the contracts between Griffiths and the promoters. His new acquaintance shared the fact that the promoters were paying Roller Games a fee of $1,000 per skater, per game, yet Bren was being paid $200 per game.

"I got terminated by Bill Griffiths when he realized I found out he was stealing money from the skaters. Early on when *RollerGames* had started Bill Griffiths had a meeting with all the skaters telling us how he would handle everything between the promoter and the skaters because as he put it "they were not our kind of people." Shortly thereafter I met this young lady, and we started dating and I came to find out she was the one that worked for the promoter that ran the contracts between Bill and the promoter. I found out because she and I had just happened to start talking and she mentioned about how well-off I should be when the series was over now that we were skating two to three games a day for television purposes. I asked her what she meant by this, and I found out the promoters were paying Bill $1,000 per skater. We were supposed to be getting that, but instead, Bill was paying the top skaters about $200 – at least that's what he was paying me – and I knew some of the other skaters were making the same. So he was pocketing the rest. When I confronted him in the locker room, in front of everybody, I was told it was none of my business. Of course, this piqued the interest of the other skaters, but no one stood up to him except for me. Well, I sort of threw things around the place and was conveniently terminated, LOL," said Bren Futura

Bill Griffiths Jr. commented, "For the record, Griffiths was paid per skater, but that money was needed to cover not only the skater cost, but for insurance, training, and other overheads necessary to ready the personnel before and during the time of production."

On the surface, this looks grossly underhanded, and we don't know if similar deals were consummated during the history of Roller Games, but this was likely not the first. But before we blame Bill Griffiths, it would only be fair to look at the other side of this issue. Despite the fact that this situation seems cut and dried, it's not. Bill is no longer here to defend himself and so I have made it a priority to be as careful as possible when sharing unflattering stories about him. I should state that I was neither a friend nor enemy of Bill's; I was just a skater. I see both sides of the man who led Roller Games for so many years. I'm fully aware that many of his skaters and staff liked and admired him, while some did not – Bill was not perfect but I have yet to meet a person who is. I'll share my thoughts on one incident, but keep in mind this could apply to similar events as well.

In all aspects of life, the wise person steps back and tries to see the big picture. It is easy to get caught up with one side or another in any issue but to find the truth, you need to dig deeper. With that in mind, it's important to note that while Bill Griffiths ran Roller Games for more than half his adult life, he died with very little. Roller Games, just like Roller Derby, was an up and down roller coaster. I'm sure there were times when he made a killing, but there were also times when he lost his shirt. That's often how it goes when running a business. As an owner, you take tremendous financial risk and in return, you have the opportunity for significant financial rewards. In the case of *RollerGames*, and other nationally televised shows, the potential pay to all type of workers—in this case, skaters—is often higher than it would usually be. In this case, what Bill did was keep his skaters' salaries at or near the same levels he usually paid. The obvious question is why would he do that when the inflow of profit was so much higher than usual? I have personally experienced similar situations as a business owner myself. Once you raise someone's pay and things don't go as planned, it can be problematic to revert the raise. When you offer someone a raise, you should have strong reason to believe you can sustain the increase for the long term; otherwise, don't do it. It's a simple business principle. In this case, *Rock and RollerGames* was a brand-new venture. We all know that new ventures fail about 90% of the time, as did this one, and within a short period. Had this show been renewed for a few seasons, it would be a near certainty that the skaters' pay would have been substantially elevated.

The first telecast was a two-hour special that aired the weekend of September 16, 1989, which featured four of the six teams in a championship tournament. The Thunderbirds defeated Bad Attitude 53-52 in the debut game, which consisted of only two periods. In the other contest, the Violators defeated the Rockers 47-41, which set up the tournament championship featuring the Thunderbirds and Violators. The game went into overtime and was decided by the "gator skaters." The Violators won 81-80 to become the first champions of RollerGames. It was the only overtime game of the season.

The season only lasted 13 weeks, from September through December, before being cut short, so there was no final championship. The Thunderbirds ended up skating in seven games, winning five and losing two. The Violators skated six times, and won five games. Bad Attitude participated five times and went 2-3. The Rockers were featured in four games, and lost all of them. The Maniacs were featured in three games, and won just one. Hot Flash skated only twice, failing to win either of the contests. In Week 11, there was an All-Star Game pitting the West All-Stars (Thunderbirds, Rockers, Hot Flash) against the East All-Stars (Violators, Bad Attitude, Maniacs). Good vs. Evil. In this case, good prevailed, 129–119.

Fans of *RollerGames* are now left with YouTube videos of nearly all the episodes and some merchandise that was created for the series. This includes a magazine, a *Rock and Rollergames* soundtrack album, a Nintendo game, an arcade game, and a pinball machine designed by Steve Ritchie—the best-selling pinball machine designer in the world.

What could have been a great opportunity, not only for Roller Games but the entire sport of roller derby, turned out to be an ill-fated attempt to revive the game that did more harm than good. If the producers and backers had known more about the real potential of the game and its history, they might have chosen a different course. National television and high production values presented outstanding opportunities. What the sport didn't need was alligators, a wall of death, and a jet jump. A few storylines and altercations would have been acceptable and helpful for ratings, but *RollerGames* went too far with these aspects. The ratio of sports to entertainment was at an all-time low—much lower than even recent incarnations of Roller Games in the 1980s, before *RollerGames*.

One idea that came from *RollerGames* that had some merit is the figure eight track. Before my purist readers start screaming, let me explain why I feel this way and why it couldn't work in the long run. As a former skater, I was acutely aware that the hours spent circling a banked tracked (or flat-track at a roller rink) in one direction was throwing my body out of balance and developing some muscles more than others. The figure eight forces participants to skate in both directions and develops all leg muscles equally. It is also beneficial to coordination. I feel the ultimate roller-skating rink would be laid out in a figure eight, if space was available. I don't think the figure eight necessarily detracts from the tradition and excitement of the sport, as long as the turns are properly banked. However, no matter how attractive the idea of a figure eight track is, the space needed to create a track of this size is too large for most venues. Touring with this track would be very challenging and costly. In today's modern, legit roller derby, flat track has become the most popular form of the game. This is due to the prohibitive cost to purchase a banked track, as well as the ongoing costs to set it up for every event. An even bigger track, such as a figure eight, would undoubtedly be out of the question. The Thunderbirds' hallowed home, the Olympic Auditorium, would not have had the space to house the figure eight. Therefore, for all intents and purposes, this idea is just impractical.

Following the abrupt and unforeseen end of the TV series, Sams wanted to hold non-televised games in San Pedro at the Super Roller Dome using the track and its facilities.

"Sams had tried to steal Griffiths' skaters and never made final payouts. An out of court settlement was required to close the book on the debacle. The San Pedro facility was never used after the tapings," said Bill Griffiths Jr.

The revenue from the repackaging of the *RollerGames* episodes to international markets wasn't enough to sustain Griffiths and his league. As the 1980s came to a close and with the 1990s just beginning, Roller Games was once again on life support, with no television, no training facility, and aging talent.

I've interviewed many skaters who participated in *RollerGames*, as well as previous incarnations of Roller Games, and nearly all of them felt it was at or near their list of career highlights, despite the backlash it received. Another recurring comment was that *RollerGames* was a highly athletic, challenging competition that required their very best effort. In addition, almost all of them enjoyed the novelty of the unique figure eight track. It's always different being on the inside looking out, rather than the opposite.

Rock and RollerGames was the last hurrah for Roller Games. It had existed and, for the most part, thrived for 30 years—the longest tenure of any roller derby league. There were less than a handful of games to come in the 90s, and no TV.

1980's Recap: The tumultuous '80s featured a much lower quality of skating than did the '60s or '70s, but the Thunderbirds were showcased twice to substantial national audiences (ESPN and *RollerGames* syndicates). There were successful events held in numerous U.S. cities and states, including Madison Square Garden, as well as several international events. Roller Games made a triumphant return after the temporary closure at the end of 1974, and culminated in the '80s. There were a few other attempted roller derby leagues in the '80s, but none achieved the success of Roller Games. The Thunderbirds owned the title of "America's team", and no longer shared that billing with the Bay Bombers. Despite Roller Games' history of ups and downs (which no league ever dodged). At this juncture, Bill Griffiths and his family could legitimately claim the title of roller derby's second family. Leo Seltzer, the creator, and Jerry, his son, led the sport of roller derby for nearly 40 years. The Seltzer's will always be considered roller derby's first family.

Chapter 40

Motor City Madhouse (1990-1993)

1990 THUNDERBIRDS
ADAM GONZALES · DEBBIE McCORKELL · FAN · RALPH VALLADARES · GWEN MILLER
DARLENE LANGLOIS · BILLY BIBBUS · ROBERT SMITH · RANDI WHITMAN · GINA GONZALES · MIKE FLANINGAM

"Most never understood what it took to run a worldwide business with so many moving parts." – Bill Griffiths Jr.

The period of the 1990s and beyond was somewhat tragic. It is noteworthy for events such as the final Thunderbirds game in 1993, the passing of both Ralphie Valladares and Bill Griffiths, and failed comeback attempts. During this period, Roller Games was organized under the league name of Roller Games International or RGI for short. And while the highlights and glory years were in the past, there are many lessons to be learned from this period.

The end of *Rock and RollerGames* was also the end of Roller Games and the Thunderbirds. Over the next three years, there was a total of three games. Two of these were held in Alberta, Canada, in 1990. Griffiths hoped there was still some money to be made from the dwindling fan base created by the *RollerGames* TV show in 1989, so he scheduled three games in the Canadian cities of Vancouver, Edmonton, and Calgary. Ticket sales were so poor in Vancouver that the game was canceled. Griffiths, who was born and raised in Alberta, continued to promote the games despite low ticket sales. On August 8, the Thunderbirds went up against the Roller Games All-Stars at the 16,000-seat Northlands Coliseum in Edmonton, winning 60 to 59. Gina Gonzalez was the high scorer, with 13 points. Northlands was a major arena and home of the Edmonton Oilers of the NHL. It was made especially famous by an athlete who also wore skates—Wayne Gretzky. The following night, the same two teams clashed in Calgary in a doubleheader at the 20,000-seat Saddledome Arena, which is home to the Calgary Flames. The All-Stars took the first contest 56 to 48, but the Thunderbirds came back to win the final 53 to 52. These non-televised games did very poorly at the gate and were likely big money losers for Griffiths.

Plans had already been consummated for more dates in October, which included stops in Ontario, Quebec, and the Maritimes, but due to the poor attendance for the Alberta games, the tour was canceled. All the Canadian dates involved the same backers. The cause of poor attendance was the lack of TV. The promoters and Griffiths were trying to syndicate tapes of the 1989 figure eight track games through a company called LBS. Griffiths had expected at least

80 to 90 stations to pick up the games, but nothing came of it. It was not a good start for 1990s Roller Games.

The 1990 L.A. Thunderbirds were coached by the living legend Ralphie Valladares and included Debbie McCorkell, Gwen Miller, Darlene Langlois, Randi Whitman, Gina Gonzales, Adam Gonzales, Bill Bibbus, Robert Smith, and Mike Flaningham.

In 1991 and 1992, there were no scheduled games for the first time in the history of the league. During the Thunderbirds' hiatus, ESPN Classic TV aired Roller Games tapes taken from the 1978, 1979, and 1980 seasons. The games were shown from 1991 to 1993. The network worked out a deal with Griffiths for the rights to air these old games and fill time on their fledging station. What would have been even better was if they had aired games from the 1960s and early 1970s, games that could have been truly marketed as "classic." Much of the Roller Games content that you can currently find on YouTube stems from fans taping the rebroadcast games from this period. Fortunately, in the late 1970s, the league still featured a few veteran stars carried over from the golden years, as well as some developing talent.

The final Thunderbirds game took place on a cold winter evening on February 6, 1993 in Auburn Hills, a suburb of Detroit, Michigan. On this night, the moon was full and it was 23 degrees Fahrenheit outside. In what would turn out to be the very last contest for Roller Games, the Thunderbirds and the RGI All-Stars met at The Palace in Auburn Hills, which is home to the Detroit Pistons, among others. The 20,000-seat "palace" was packed on this night and was nearly sold out. At the time, the Detroit area was receiving TV broadcasts of revamped *Rock and RollerGames* tapes from 1989 and ratings were high, which is why Bill Griffiths booked the date. It was billed as a doubleheader, but in reality there was still eight periods total; four for each game.

The skaters didn't know this was be their final skate on the banked track for Roller Games, but some of them may have seen it coming. For this last game, the Los Angeles Thunderbirds took to the track with the following skaters: Darlene Langlois, Randi Whitman,

Debbie Garvey, Gwen Miller, and Lyle Morse for the women, and Bobby Cendejas, Mike Flaningam, Raymond Rose, Bill Bibbus, Mike Dark, and the Latin legend, Ralphie Valladares for the men.

The RGI All-Star Super Stars roster featured Lolly Waterman, Julie Martinez, Vicki McEwen, Denise Green, and Lory Weikel for the women, and David Arizmendez, Burnett Jackson, Harold Jackson, Ray Robles, and Jerry Reis for the men. Georgia Hase managed the All-Stars and was assisted by Chuck Skull.

Game one ended in a tie at 41 points per team. For the second half of the second game, the crowd was worked up because of the antics of Georgia and Skull, and the vicious tactics of the Jackson brothers. By the last (8th) quarter, fans had crowded the floor area around the track. By the final jam, many fans had climbed alongside the track and were hanging on the rails. Security presence was minimal, and it looked like it could get out of hand. Maybe the full moon was a factor?

For the final jam of the contest—the "blowoff" jam—the Thunderbirds sent out the California Kid, Mike Flaningam, who, other than Ralphie, had skated more games as a Thunderbird since 1980 than any other male skater. The All-Stars countered with Harold Jackson. He and his brother Bernie roughed up the California Kid and tried to throw him into the water feature, which was still being used due to the current TV broadcasts in the area. But in typical Thunderbirds style, the battered Flaningam slipped around the Jackson brothers to score the winning points. Those were the final points scored by a Thunderbirds skater. The Thunderbirds took the second and last game of the evening with a score of Thunderbirds 43, All-Stars 41. The scripted blow-off jam had gone almost as planned. The one hiccup was that before the Thunderbirds girls could throw Georgia Hase into the water feature at the end of the jam, the fans who had entered the track ended up throwing Hase into the water themselves! It was unscripted but a befitting way to end the reign of Hase, who had been one of the most despised villains in Roller Games history. Unfortunately, this game wasn't taped.

Not only was it befitting that Hase was thrown out by the very fans she had enraged, but even more befitting was the fact that even in their very last game, the Thunderbirds drew a near capacity crowd of almost 20,000. As it always seemed to be the case, when there was good television coverage of the games, the Thunderbirds could often go into a city and pack their largest arena.

In 1993, the Thunderbirds went 1-0-1, meaning one win, no losses, and one tie, and that was the end. Although it wasn't planned, with a packed house, Ralphie somehow still on the track, a full moon, and frenzied crowd, even Bill "Hoppy" Haupt couldn't have scripted a better finale.

The Aftermath

Chapter 41
This Bird Has Flown

"UP, UP AND AWAY." Little Ralphie Valladares, coach of the Los Angeles T-Birds sends his opponent flying as he goes on to score in recent ROLLER GAMES action.

"Ralphie Valladares was the first and last T-Bird
star." – The Author

Bill Griffiths, the song and dance man who always seemed to have another trick up his sleeve, was spent. His aging and depleted Thunderbirds were no longer marketable. The past decade of subpar skating, combined with an abundance of cheesy theatrics, had driven away much of the fanbase that had so loyally supported the Thunderbirds for 30 years. Griffiths had been sustaining his league on thin margins since reforming back in 1976. The major television deals in the 1980s were helpful, but they were too short-lived for Griffiths to realize enough profit to rebuild his reserves properly. The Detroit game netted a small profit but not enough to cover the losses from the Alberta games two years prior. Griffiths now did not have enough funds to promote more games and this time, no one came calling with any sweetheart deals. In fact, according to John Hall, Griffiths and Roller Games had been blacklisted by the National Arena Managers Association. It was over.

In 1994, Griffiths was 70 years of age. His best days were behind him. He had taken Roller Games as far as one man could. The achievements of Roller Games in both its phases (1960-1974 and 1975-1993) were nearly unparalleled in the sport of roller derby with the notable exception of Seltzer's Roller Derby. There was brilliance amidst failure, and so much squandered potential. In the history of roller derby, past or present, no team had ever been in the spotlight longer than the Thunderbirds.

Not long after the final game in Detroit, Bill Griffiths declared bankruptcy. John Hall, Ralph Valladares, and Debbie Heldon all received small checks as they were listed as creditors, but it was only a fraction of what he owed them. Thirty plus years at the helm of Roller Games International had left Bill nearly penniless, as well as his partners John and Ralph. The once mighty Thunderbirds had fallen and this time, they were unable to get back up.

In 1997, Bay Bomber legend Joan Weston died. She was considered by many the most significant female skater of all time. She spent one season with the Thunderbirds in 1974. Her final game was in 1995 at the Olympic Auditorium in a contest promoted by former skating great, Bert Wall.

November 13, 1998 saw the quiet death of a superstar. Just five years after he had skated his final game as a professional athlete, Ralph

Valladares passed onward surrounded by family and friends at his home in Pico Rivera, California. His life was cut short by complications from diabetes, including liver cancer. He was not yet 60 years of age.

Ralph Dwight Valladares was born in Guatemala on July 31, 1936. His family came to the United States when he was only 12 years old. His dream was to one day become a professional thoroughbred jockey. At 5 foot 2 inches, he was small in stature but still slightly too large to compete in horse racing. Luckily, he also loved to roller skate and was very good at it, winning several speed skating titles by the age of 16. Roller Derby got word of his prowess and by the time he turned 17, Ralphie was skating professionally for the Los Angeles Braves. He made the Roller Derby All-Star team in 1956, 1957, and 1958. In the early years of the Thunderbirds, Ralphie was already a veteran skater in the prime of his pro career. From the very start, Ralphie was the darling of LA fans. With his diminutive stature, he was perfectly cast in the role of a "good guy" fighting for his underdog Thunderbirds. If team records had been properly kept, Ralphie would hold just about every possible Thunderbirds record, if not only for his talent but certainly for his longevity.

He was a star in every sense of the word. In his prime (late 50s and early 60s) few could stay with him. His speed and agility were second to none. His nicknames included "The Guatemalan Flyer", "Little Ralphie", and "The Living Legend."

Ralphie was a tireless and effective trainer and led more training classes for Roller Games than anyone else. He also developed the skating talent in Australia and Japan and helped those ventures achieve great success.

Valladares was thrice married to skater Honey Sanchez. Yes, they were married and divorced three times. The two remained close throughout the years up until his death. The couple had a daughter, Gina, who also became a pro skater and Ralphie stayed in the game long enough to compete with and against her. He has two grandchildren, Megan Martinez and Josh Martinez, both of whom became skaters and participated in classic roller derby in the 2000s.

Ralphie skated in the very first Thunderbirds game in 1961, as well as the final game in Detroit in 1993. He was with Roller Games for all 33 years, and was a Thunderbird for nearly all 33 years. He spent thirty years with the L.A. Thunderbirds and the other three with the Australian and Tokyo Thunderbirds. During his seven years with the IRDL (Roller Derby), he spent five years with the Los Angeles Braves. Overall, in his career spanning forty years, Ralphie represented the city of Los Angeles for 35 years. He was a four-decade pro athlete from 1953 to 1993.

Ralphie's Latin roots endeared him to the Hispanic community of Los Angeles. He was the city's first Latin superstar and up until the arrival of Fernando Valenzuela, he was arguably the most well-known Latin personality. Although he arrived in L.A. nearly two decades before Fernandomania and remained a Thunderbirds star much longer than Fernando did with the Dodgers, he never gained the same notoriety due mostly to the inauthenticity of his sport. However, he was a household name in the Hispanic community throughout his tenure with the Thunderbirds.

Ralphie was to the Thunderbirds what Charlie O'Connell was to the Bay Bombers. While he was never as dominant as O'Connell, he was an exceptional skater in his younger years. Valladares skated 32 years with the Thunderbirds and with that fact in mind, it's incredible to think that his best years occurred in Jerry Seltzer's Roller Derby where he was one of the quickest, most agile skaters of the 1950s. Starting his career at age 17 with the Los Angeles Braves in 1953, Ralphie stayed with L.A. through the beginning of the 1958 season (except for brief stints with the Brooklyn Red Devils in 1954 and the Miami Westerners in 1955). In 1958 and 1959, he teamed up with Charlie O'Connell and they became an unstopped duo with the San Francisco Bay Bombers at a time when Roller Derby attempted to go entirely legit. The pair were overpowering and led their team to lopsided victories in nearly every game they skated. Charlie's defense and Ralphie's offense were just too much for the competition. They dominated so much that they were often pulled from games early to keep them somewhat competitive. The skaters I interviewed regarding this season all point to Ralphie and Charlie being the reason for the Bombers domination—they were that good. Ironically, their greatness may have led to the early demise of legit roller derby as fans stayed away when games became lopsided.

After seven years starring with Roller Derby, Ralphie came back to Los Angeles in 1960, but this time not as a member of the Braves but as the marquee skater for the new Los Angeles Thunderbirds of the newly-formed Roller Games for their inaugural 1961 season. Valladares continued to be a terrific skater throughout the 1960s, as well as the catalyst for the success Roller Games attained in both Japan and Australia. In the 1970s, he continued to be a solid skater, but he was not the Ralphie of the 50s and 60s. By the 1980s, he was an overweight shell of his former self, but still outperformed most skaters due to his knowledge and experience, combined with the demise of the league's talent. More than anything, Ralphie is remembered for his heroic skating for the Thunderbirds, especially when a game was on the line. He was the team's all-time leader in points and games skated. More importantly, he was the team's highly respected spiritual leader.

Ralphie had a glorious career with the Thunderbirds but like most skaters, he did not live a lifestyle that could be considered "healthy." He partied just as hard as he skated. Roller derby travel was far from first-class luxury. Long bus rides often led to seedy budget hotels, followed by late night card games complete with the ever-present cheap alcohol and cigarettes; it was a lethal combination. On the track, fragile bodies with far too little protection took a beating night after night. Burdened with all of the above and more, the immune system can become overworked. A small percentage of pro skaters reach average longevity.

Perhaps the saddest part of Raphie's early departure was that his Thunderbirds and the very game he had dedicated his life to was virtually extinct at the time of his death. He did not live to see RollerJam nor the surprising resurgence of the beloved sport in the new century. Ralph Valladares was one of the toughest, hardest-hitting, most legit skaters to ever grace a banked track. He would have been thrilled with the new crop of skaters and their version of the sport. Had he survived, he likely would have been training the skaters of today, just as his contemporary John Hall does. He was inducted into the National Roller Derby Hall of Fame posthumously in 2004.

Chapter 42

RollerJam

"Despite strong funding and four seasons of broadcasts on TNN, the venture (RollerJam) never became a 'live' attraction. Fabricated storylines and characters in the mode of professional wrestling were being featured more than actual competitive skating around season 3 and 4, raising the ire of many skaters and fans of true roller derby." – Wikipedia

ollowing a nine-year period in the 1990s, in which the sport of
roller derby went into oblivion and nearly a decade after *Rock
& RollerGames*, RollerJam made its debut in 1998 on national
television. This new incarnation of roller derby featured the use
of inline skates rather than traditional quads and was based in
Florida. A few Roller Games skaters participated, but this was not
a Roller Games production. Bill Griffith had planned to revive
Roller Games in the same year, but put those plans on hold upon
learning about RollerJam. Some of the former Roller Games skaters
who participated included Mark D'Amato, Richard Brown, Vicki
McEwen, and Patsy Delgado. Former Philadelphia Warriors star
Buddy Atkinson Jr. helped train the skaters as did Erwin "EG"
Miller, also formerly of Roller Games. Longtime Roller Games
referee Don Lastra participated as well. D'Amato became one of
RollerJam's biggest stars. Mark had always been a strong defensive
skater in Roller Games, but rarely in a starring role. However, he hit
his prime with "Jam" and was highly featured on and off the track.
The "suits" at RollerJam highly marketed his macho, menacing,
tattooed look. Sadly, he died at a very young age not long after this
period. Another skater who reached his potential in RollerJam was
Sean Atkinson, son of Buddy Jr., and a third-generation Atkinson
family pro. Sean never skated with Roller Games and had spent
most of his prime in obscurity since there were no televised games
in the 1990s before RollerJam. He was a big, strong, fearless skater
who wanted to make the most of this rare opportunity and gave it
his all. His hard-hitting style left him with severe back injuries that
linger today.

RollerJam only lasted about a year and a half despite decent
ratings. At the conclusion of the 20th century, it did not look like the
great American sport of roller derby would survive into the 21st century.

The "90's" generation of American youth who would one day
lead the current derby resurgence had mostly been exposed to the
1989 *Rock and RollerGames* and the 1998 RollerJam made for TV
productions. Both creations were highly scripted and have not been
looked upon favorably amongst roller derby historians. Much of the

backlash against classic roller derby by today's amateur skaters stems from their exposure to these productions, combined with their lack of exposure to true "classic derby" from the 1950s through the 1970s. *RollerGames* and RollerJam kept the sport alive and without them, today's revival may not have occurred. However, they have come to symbolize everything that current derby leagues try to avoid: a double-edged sword.

Chapter 43

RGI Relaunch Attempts

"Because of the gas crisis in 1972 and other issues, the International Roller Derby League shut down in 1973, but videos of the game were now appearing on tapes, and eventually on cable. And April Ritzenhaler in Texas saw some

of these, and with others in Austin formed Texas Roller Derby,
a banked track game for women in 2002. Eventually a group
of players broke away to form a flat track game, and the Texas
Rollergirls were born.....eventually, derby spread to many other
cities and countries, and today there are approximately 2,000
leagues around the world." – Jerry Seltzer, *Roller Derby Jesus.*

At the turn of the century, the Griffiths family, led at this time by Bill Griffiths Jr. (son of Bill Griffiths Sr.), made plans to relaunch RGI under the name RollerGames 2000. Griffiths Jr. negotiated a deal with the prominent William Morris Agency, but their good intentions never manifested, and not a single game was skated until 2004 when the Griffiths' leased their fast fading brands, Roller Games International and Los Angeles Thunderbirds, to promoter Robert Sedillo. Both parties were hopeful that the Thunderbirds would return to glory, but this period ended up expediting the demise of any remaining goodwill that Roller Games had built during the Thunderbirds heyday.

On March 22, 2003, former Roller Games and Roller Derby skater Lou Sanchez used the Thunderbirds name to promote a pair of matches at the Grand Olympic Auditorium, featuring the L.A. Thunderbirds vs. the San Francisco Bay Bombers, and the L.A. Stars vs. the Red Devils. The games had mixed results but featured some big names from the past. Ironically, back in the 1960s, a group of skaters led by Lou Sanchez and George Copeland broke away from Roller Games and formed another league. There was even a collaboration with Jerry Seltzer to re-establish a foothold in the Southern California areas. The new league was struggling when George got drafted to the war in Vietnam. Lou Sanchez was the remaining leader and with Copeland gone, the entire operation folded quickly.

Roller Games International

Chapter 44

Fiasco in Phoenix

"We do not choreograph or plan a winner. We play tough, fast, and hard. Our game is a sport. Our bouts are full on athletic competitions between tough, sexy women who take their game seriously." – Alotta Trouble, PHX Landsharks from the website "Girls With Guns."

In 2004, Bob Sedillo's debut game was an exhibition held in Glendale, Arizona—a suburb of Phoenix at the Glendale Arena, which was later renamed Gila River Arena, with a capacity of 18,000. It was billed as the "Duel in the Desert." In this event, the Thunderbirds women's team went up against the Phoenix Landsharks, composed of female skaters associated with the modern revival of the sport. The banked track was in poor shape and had no rails, just a rope where the guard rails are usually attached! Attendance was estimated to be between 500 and 1,000 fans, so the large venue looked nearly empty. Aside from the venue being too big, the turnout was as might be expected.

The bout was skated legit, which weighed heavily in favor of the Phoenix team, who was experienced in a legit modern-style roller derby. The Thunderbirds skaters were only informed that the game would be legit just before it started. Stephanie Garcia, Denise Dadras, Vicki McEwen, Denise Green, and Pam Schwab were some of the notable Thunderbirds skaters who participated. All of them were solid veterans, but were well past the age of 40 at the time. The remainder of the team consisted of three young rookie skaters who had little game experience, including Robyn Foster, who was injured during the bout. The head referee was Roller Games veteran Don Lastra, who had seen it all. The game was very physical, and the hometown Landsharks were not only considerably younger, but also in much better shape than the Thunderbirds. The Landsharks dominated from the start, taking the first period by a score of 25-3 and the second period by a similar margin. The game was not competitive. By the end of the first half, the Thunderbirds were battered and demoralized. Captain Vicki McEwen made the decision not the return for the second half of the contest. She spoke to the crowd at halftime on the microphone and complained that the track was "waxed" and therefore too dangerous to continue skating. Fans were outraged and demanded their money back. After a 40-minute delay and some discussions, a few of the veteran Thunderbirds came back to skate in the second half. However, the game became even more lopsided and the home team defeated the Thunderbirds by an estimated score of 60-4.

The Phoenix fiasco put another black mark on the already tarnished Thunderbirds, especially amongst the modern revival roller derby community. The once mighty Thunderbirds, the most storied team in the history of roller derby, was soundly thrashed by the Phoenix squad in the first-ever contest between old-school and new-school derby teams. On the surface, it looked as if the Thunderbirds could not compete with the likes of a modern roller derby squad. But looking deeper, this was not the classic era Thunderbirds, and even using the name seemed blasphemous. It's likely that a vintage Thunderbirds team with the likes of Terri Lynch, Sally Vega, Judy Sowinski, Honey Sanchez, and Liz Hernandez would have skated circles around the Landsharks. This makeshift Thunderbirds team was composed of over the hill veterans, none of whom had participated in the golden years of the team. It was a big mistake to arrange this contest, and the damage to the team's reputation was not underestimated. Couple this game with the debut of ESPN's "Cheap Seats", which comically lampooned Roller Games, and it became the lowest period in the history of the team.

Following the last Thunderbirds game that took place in Detroit in 1993, a pattern of ambitious promoters trying to capitalize on the name recognition of the Los Angeles Thunderbirds emerged. Eventually, these misguided efforts depleted the value of the brand to almost nothing.

Chapter 45

Cheap Seats

"The cynics take one look at a game, see a couple of monkey-business bits, and dismiss it all as patently phony. The apologists explain away these moments on behalf of show business." – Frank DeFord, *Sports Illustrated*

From 2004 to 2006, ESPN Classic aired the show *Cheap Seats*, hosted by Randy and Jason Sklar. The brothers lampooned cheesy sports broadcasts from the past—one of which happened to be latter-day Roller Games. Most of the games they mocked were from the 1985 and 1986 ESPN seasons, of which they owned the rights. By 1985, the level of talent in Roller Games was lower than at any time in the league's history, despite the national exposure provided by ESPN. In addition, the RGI cheese factor was at an all-time high and this added fuel to the fire and made for some humorous moments on the show. For Thunderbirds fans that dared to watch, it was uncomfortable at best. However, the show pointed out what most of us already knew: Roller Games had become a shadow of its former self and was surviving on memories from the past. The fact that Roller Games was regularly featured on this show spoke volumes about how low the once-respected operation had sunk.

Chapter 46

Sedillo Slo-Mo (2004-2008)

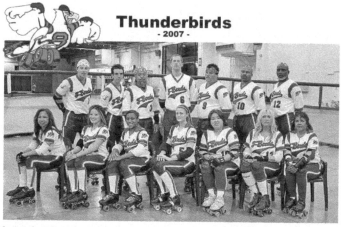

Thunderbirds
- 2007 -

Stephanie Garcia, Megan Martinez, Jo'na Sewell, Tara Halcomb, *Name Unknown*, Lali Outhoummountry, Carmen Thompson
Chris Martinez, Ricky Young, *Name Unknown*, Matt Devlahovich, Opie Simpson, Raymond Rose, Greg Robertson

*"It's easy to not take the theatrical versions of roller derby
seriously, particularly when you see the "fake" version of the
game being played in (contrast to) today's derby world of
legitimate, amateur competition." – Steven "WindyMan"
Rodriguez, RollerDerbyNotes.com*

ollowing the ill-fated Phoenix "Duel in the Desert," Bob Sedillo
promoted classic roller derby style Thunderbirds games for the next
five years. The games held during the period between 2004 and 2008
were underwhelming. It was the Los Angeles Thunderbirds in name
only. These were old-timer's contests. If you thought games from the
1980s and 1990s were suspect regarding talent and execution on the
track, these were on an entirely lower level. Many, if not most skaters
were 50 years of age or older. The sport of roller derby is fast, hard-
hitting, and dangerous. In this version, it was not fast or hard-hitting,
but it was dangerous only because the participants were much too old
to be participating. Most of the skaters had started their derby careers
in the late 1970s and 1980s and some of the skaters in Sedillo's RGI
began their careers as early as the 1960s! These '60's stars included
Carmen Thompson and Greg Robertson, both of whom participated
in nearly all the Sedillo RGI years, as well as a few others who partook
sporadically, such as Gwen Miller and Richard Brown. The was a
group of mostly 40 to 60-year-olds, playing a sport that many consider
to be as violent as the NHL. If you attended a game in this era, you
are likely a relative of one of the skaters. Most of the small crowds
were family members. For those luckless souls who may have been
attending their first roller derby contest, it was almost certainly their
last. Fortunately, these games were not televised and were seen by
relatively few people. Unfortunately, tapes of these games have been
uploaded to YouTube for all to see.

However, that's not to say that each game didn't have a few
worthy moments. The structure of the game, which is one of the
most entertaining of all sports, was still the same: There was a
banked track, participants wore quad skates, blocks were made (or
missed), and points were scored. Participants included both genders.
Occasionally, there was a jam executed that was entertaining and well
skated. But too often, this spectacle was merely embarrassing. The
worst moments involved scripted jams and fighting that the skaters
could no longer execute with proper finesse and agility—this was
slow-motion roller derby.

But all of this was not for lack of effort. Whether young or old, those who participated had a deep love of their sport and gave 110% on the track. There were a handful of rookies who developed into solid skaters but with their version of the sport—classic roller derby—quickly vanishing, there were few opportunities for even the best young athletes.

For long-time Thunderbirds fans, there was a natural curiosity in seeing some of their heroes in action 40 years after the prime of the sport. As for the real superstars who made comebacks during the Sedillo period such as the aforementioned Thompson, Miller, Brown, and Robertson, they were still the best skaters on the banked track and retained their grace and dignity, despite being many years past their prime. But the slightly younger crop of skaters who participated in later periods of Roller Games, including a few who never had star talent to begin with, often tried to do more than their aging bodies and limited talent would allow.

One of the highlights for the few long-time Thunderbirds fans who attended one of these games was witnessing the grandson and granddaughter of legend Ralphie Valladares on the track. Both Chris Martinez and his sister Megan were good skaters, having been trained by their parents David Martinez—a Thunderbirds skater, and Gina Valladares Martinez—the only child of Ralphie Valladares and Honey Sanchez. Had there been a roller derby queen, it would have been Megan, who was one of the most attractive women to have ever graced a banked track. And she could also skate!

Below is a partial list of the skaters who participated in Sedillo's league:

Former Roller Games skaters:

Carmen "Sugar" Thompson, Greg Robertson, Harold Jackson, Raymond Rose, Tony Trujillo, Stephanie Garcia, Bernie Jackson, Gail Bowers, Tammy Contreras, Lory Weikel, Darryle Davis, Stevie Santillian, Gwen Miller, and Richard Brown.

No previous Roller Games experience:

Henry Self, Dave Gerry, Dave Marez, Andrew Taylor, Joyce Hall, Jo'na Sewell, Nancy Barrera, Marnie Smith, Ricky Young, Matt Deviahovich, Opie Simpson, Chris Martinez, Tara Holcomb, Lali Outhommountry, Megan Martinez, Brian Novak, Lyle Glazer, Shar Cerrito, K.C. Evans, Pat Jones, and Earlene Brown.

A small highlight during this period was the 2003 *Charlie's Angels: Full Throttle* film in which Thunderbirds legend John Hall gave skating lessons, instructions, and advice to angels Cameron Diaz, Drew Barrymore, and Lucy Liu. John set up the skating scenes for this feature film and provided professional roller skaters to assist the actresses.

The Thunderbirds' last home game was at the Pomona Fairplex in 2008. Not long after that game, Bill Griffiths sued Sedillo's Pegasus Media Group for trademark infringement and no more contests were ever skated. Bob Sedillo died in 2009 and thus, completely ended the comeback attempt. It must be noted that Bob was a die-hard roller derby fan and invested (and lost) tens of thousands of dollars in his efforts to bring back his beloved sport. Following his death, the Thunderbirds brand reverted to the Griffiths family where it has been virtually dormant, except for a few flat track contests promoted by former Roller Games star, Stephanie Garcia in which the Thunderbirds name was once again used. None of the games held in the century (post millennium) were financially successful nor were they televised. Most roller derby fans had no idea these games even occurred.

Chapter 47
Unhappy Ending

"Vince McMahon got it all from Mr. William J. Griffiths. Mr. Griffiths executed sports entertainment with great skill." –
Larry McGinnis, Historian

At the age of 91, William John Griffiths Sr. died, ironically on Leo Seltzer's birthday, April 5, 2015. He ruled the roller derby world longer than anyone, past or present.

He was born in Edmonton and grew up in Alberta and British Columbia, Canada. Bill started in show business at an early age. He was already a talented tap dancer at age 4, and his parents got him into Vaudeville at age 5. His stage name was Sunshine Billy. From the ages of 5 to 8, he performed in British Columbia, Alberta, Washington, Idaho, Wyoming, Montana, and other areas.

He was that rare breed of student who participated in both theater and sports. At Britannia High School in Vancouver, he played on the rugby team, participating in a competition that is every bit as rough as roller derby. He was also in the drama club. These experiences served him well in later years, when he was the kingpin of Roller Games—a form of entertainment that merged a rugged sport with theater.

He served in the Royal Canadian Air Force as a radio operator during World War II, shortly after graduating from high school. When the war ended, Griffiths utilized the skills gleaned in the RCAF and had his own radio shows in Vancouver, Seattle, and San Francisco, in which he interviewed celebrities like Lucille Ball, Louis Armstrong, Frankie Lane, and Xavier Cougat. He even had his own Fan Club. He was one of the first TV announcers in L.A. performing live commercials on KTLA, KTTV, KHJ, and KCOP. He and his wife and two kids moved to LA in 1952.

He produced the theater version of *Don Juan in Hell* starring Paul Henried, Agnes Moorehead, Ricardo Montalban, and Edward Mulhare. The Broadway play toured the U.S. and was directed by John Houseman.

In his personal life, he was a diehard USC Football fan, attending home and away games with his family in the 1960s and 1970s. He learned to speak fluent Japanese, which came in handy when he spearheaded the Roller Games operation in Japan. He studied English-Japanese dictionaries before his first visit to Japan. When he returned, he took private lessons three days a week for a couple of years and became fluent in both speaking and writing.

According to his eldest son, Bill Jr., the skaters he was closest to included Ralphie, Red Smartt (and his wife, Joyce), Shirley Hardman, Dave Pound, Judy Arnold, Gwen Miller, and Stephanie Garcia.

His Thunderbirds, who always managed to finish games with a well-scripted "happy ending," were no longer active at the time of his death. Bill Sr., with help from Jerry Hill, Herb Roberts, John Hall, and Ralph Valladares, will be remembered for overseeing the longest running and most famous team in the history of the banked track sport—the Los Angeles Thunderbirds. His legacy is enshrined in the National Roller Derby Hall of Fame. Through his efforts with the Thunderbirds, he brought joy to millions of roller derby fans around the world.

Postscript

Chapter 48

Sports Entertainment

"The game is torn between the vulgar old-time buffoonery and the sometimes fast, tough, true speed and muscle that marks a real sport." – Frank DeFord

onservative sports purists may be offended by the mention of roller derby alongside more conventional sports such as baseball, football, and basketball. Admittedly, they have some justification for this. Simply put, the original professional sport of roller derby—unlike today's amateur versions—was staged to varying degrees. It was "sports entertainment" a combination of athletic competition enhanced with spectacular showmanship, theatrics, and storylines with the goal of attracting a broader fan base. And it worked—as long as it didn't go overboard and was at least somewhat believable.

The very mention of the word "fake" is offensive to most former pro skaters and most will staunchly defend the integrity of their beloved sport. You'd be hard-pressed to find skaters who didn't have a severe injury while participating in the Derby. Injuries are typically the first response when a derby skater is questioned about the legitimacy of the sport. There is no doubt that roller derby is a dangerous, violent, and often brutal sport: staged or not. And the athletic abilities of these performers cannot be questioned. Most skaters just wanted to be professional athletes and not actors.

When a well-known sportswriter, Damon Runyan, came out to roller derby's debut in Chicago on August 13, 1935, he convinced creator Leo Seltzer to change roller derby from a marathon skating session to a contact sport. He also encouraged Seltzer to exaggerate the hits and falls. It worked, and the impact was so tremendous that Mr. Runyan was later inducted into the Roller Derby Hall of Fame. From that moment forward, the roller derby incorporated this enhanced action, which helped grow the sport into national prominence. Leo Seltzer took his Transcontinental Roller Derby of 1935 into the world of sports entertainment. Fans loved it, and the game saw rapid growth.

Following this fundamental change, theatrics continued to increase naturally over time. Fans enjoyed the speed, finesse, and contact of the sport, just as they do when witnessing hockey or football. Skaters, as well as management, learned that adding extra-curricular activities created excitement for the audience and enhanced attendance numbers.

And what about other major sports? The NBA, NHL, and Pro Wrestling have all added and encouraged showmanship and sports entertainment to varying degrees, with outstanding success.

Professional Wrestling matches have pre-determined outcomes and highly theatrical, choreographed routines. Modern pro-wrestling leagues no longer even try to keep this a secret, and its fan base is still growing. In 2016 revenue topped $214 million!

Professional Hockey, namely the NHL, has historically encouraged fighting to enhance attendance. It is rare to attend a hockey game that doesn't have at least one altercation. Fans have come to expect this. And rather than quickly breaking up the fights as would occur in baseball, football or basketball, NHL referees step away from the action and let the skaters go at it for a while before breaking it up. It's just part of pro hockey, and other than the purists, very few fans or athletes complain about it. Aside from goal scoring, these fights often draw the most noise and excitement from the audience. Apart from these rather brief, electrifying interludes, the game of pro hockey is entirely legitimate. Any comparison of old-school Roller Derby with pro hockey ends here as Roller Derby went much further on the entertainment side of things. Unlike hockey, the "derby" action was often choreographed and winners and losers were pre-determined.

The demographics of a typical Roller Derby audience are of two categories: the very young, the very old, and the feeble-minded who believe everything on the track is legit. The second category includes fans of sound mind who enjoy the game for what it is: sports entertainment. When the game is executed well with top-level pros on the track, the believability and the potential for larger audiences increases. Keep in mind that it is these very antics of sports entertainment that allowed the sport to draw crowds at or above the NBA and NHL during its heyday. The exaggerated action is what brought many of us to the game initially, whether we knew it at the time or not. But that same element, if executed poorly, results in disenchanted fans who don't come back. Therefore, it is a balancing act.

The originator of the sport strongly desired to bring it back to its pure form, and in 1959, Leo Seltzer ordered his athletes to skate a completely legit game for the better part of the '59 season. Yes, the current crop of female flat track and banked track skaters were not the first to offer a legit version of roller derby. But when it was tried, the results were disastrous and fans left in droves. After that season, Roller Derby returned to its original format, and a disgruntled and disappointed Leo Seltzer dropped away from the game he had created and turned it over to his son, Jerry.

Jerry's game plan was to do whatever it took to return roller derby to the popularity it had experienced in the past—and he did just that. In a few short years, Roller Derby was more popular than ever before! He achieved this primarily by bringing the game back to its original, and some would say "natural state", with a combination of athletics and showmanship. Windyman.net wrote, "Leo's ambitious dreams to make people respect derby for its legitimacy didn't get people to buy tickets on a consistent basis. To turn the promotion around, Jerry made the decision to showcase the game's theatrics and celebrate its characters as much as the sport's players and their athletic abilities."

In looking at today's female roller derby, one might consider that the women have accomplished what Leo had fancied: a legit sport. But the big difference between then and now is the fact that in 1959, derby skaters were employed on a full-time basis. There was national television and packed arenas complete with a substantial revenue stream. It was a professional sport. There was much to lose by taking risks with an established fanbase. The Women's Flat Track Derby Association (WFTDA) doesn't have to pay its skaters nor try to maintain the likes of a pro sport. It may well be that roller derby, played on a legit basis, will someday reach a professional level and sustain their skaters with a livable income. However, this remains to be seen.

A significant reason Roller Derby gained such outstanding national popularity that rivaled the so-called mainstream sports was showmanship. When Leo Seltzer's mandate eliminated this component, the result was diminished attendance to less than half of what it had been before. To his credit, Seltzer wanted roller derby to become a wholly legitimate sport, and he took on tremendous financial risk to undertake this change. I think everyone who loves this sport needs to admire Leo for his efforts and also the efforts of today's amateur derby leagues.

Roller Games never undertook an effort to legitimize their action. On the contrary, Roller Games went the other direction and took showmanship to new levels. Because of this, the league developed a tarnished reputation amongst historians of the sport and diehard fans of the original Roller Derby. But when Bill Griffiths decided to make his entrance into the already successful Roller Games league, he knew all about the failures of Roller Derby when it attempted to become a legitimate game. He understood that Jerry Seltzer was quickly trying to get back to the style of game that had brought Roller Derby to prominence, including all its trappings of theatrics, pre-determined winners, fights, and more. Roller Games didn't invent the hyped up, choreographed, exaggerated, and pre-set game.

Some observers credit Bill Griffiths with genius as his style of play brought the popularity of roller derby to new heights, both nationally and internationally. Other say the antics of Roller Games eventually went too far.

In the early years of Roller Games, the games were skated in a manner very similar to Roller Derby. Most of the skaters in the original Roller Games league came directly over from Roller Derby. But as time went on, owner Bill Griffiths, a product of Hollywood show business, began to implement added showmanship and a few gimmicks, such as a midget mascot named Little Augie. He saw how crowds reacted to this and he gradually added a bit more spice. He and those around him began to craft more intricate storylines and encourage more mayhem. Some of these storylines were brilliant, and when appropriately executed, drove the crowds into a frenzy and they kept coming back to see what might happen next. Thus, ratings and attendance soared. The skaters pulled off elaborate jams and staging due to the high level of talent that existed in the game at the time. Skating in games with intricate choreography and storylines took a lot more mental focus compared to a more standard game typical of Roller Derby or very early Roller Games. One mental lapse by a skater could have dire consequences for the storyline. I had one such mental failure in a game in which I accidentally scored points when I wasn't supposed to, and it created a big problem. I was on a jam and at the time I was supposed to be taken down, there was no one there to do it. My only option was to take myself down by stumbling. I was confused and didn't recall precisely what was supposed to happen. After the game, I remember Ralphie furiously screaming at me and accusing me of doing it intentionally. He wasn't just a little upset. He had to restrain himself from punching me in the locker room. This is one example of what can happen when things went wrong on a "set" jam.

Now, let's look at the culture of major pro sports during the prime era of the L.A. Thunderbirds and S.F. Bombers, and how this may have influenced roller derby and vice-versa. From the birth of professional paid athletics up through the 1950s, pro sporting events valued tradition. Athletic competition alone, without any "enhancements", carried the day. The notable exceptions were Professional Wrestling and Roller Derby.

In the 1960s, there were signs of change. Elgin Baylor of the L.A. Lakers was one of the first NBA stars to add intentional flair and showmanship to the game. In the ultra-conservative Major League Baseball league, following the low scoring 1968 season dubbed "the year of the pitcher," the league lowered the pitching mound and shrunk the strike zone to increase scoring. This led to a significant increase in offense, which for the average fan, is a plus. In this decade, Roller Games, whose home-base in downtown Los Angeles was just nine miles from Hollywood, choose to add some spice in keeping with the times. It is important to note that this was roller derby and not the Metropolitan Opera.

Of all the major sports, the NBA may be the best example of the importance of showmanship and how it can impact attendance and fan support. Up through the 1960s and with only a few exceptions (such as Baylor), the NBA played their game "straight". Not surprisingly, both Roller Derby and Roller Games often outdrew the NBA in both attendance and TV ratings. Ten players on a 50 by 94-foot court lends itself to a less wide-open game in which defense is king. This may be the reason three-on-three leagues have become so popular today. Those of us who are avid NBA fans know that every season, the game changes dramatically come playoff time. Defense dominates these games and scores are lower. The reason for this is that teams play a more fundamental game in the playoffs, with an emphasis on defense very similar to the NBA of the early days. There are high stakes for winning and losing. However, regular season games are entirely different now. Early in the season and especially in the first three quarters of a contest, defenses are fairly "loose" and scoring is high. These loose defensive tactics allow more open space for the acrobatic showmanship of today's NBA. This started in 1967 with the outlaw American Basketball Association (ABA), which featured a colorful basketball and even more colorful performers. The ABA was trying its best to compete with the well-established NBA, and their contests were more fun and allowed their athletes to show their athletic skills in an entirely new manner. Winning was still a factor, but the main emphasis was on "the show." Connie Hawkins was the original prototype ABA star, followed by the great Julius Erving and others such as Rick Barry, Artis Gilmore, and Moses Malone. The ABA was very popular, and this eventually led to a merger with the NBA in 1976. Following the merger, the NBA continued to slowly integrate showmanship into the game and then in 1980, Magic Johnson came on the scene to lead the Showtime Lakers, and the NBA has never been the same.

Around the same time, the NFL began to take note of the changing times with a new emphasis on the passing game led by Don Coryell and the San Diego Chargers. His "Air Coryell" offensive scheme helped the Chargers lead the league in passing yards a record six consecutive years from 1978 to 1983. This influenced the entire league, which is now dominated by the passing offense and is much more exciting than running offense to all but the most die-hard traditionalist fans.

Therefore, it was in this sports cultural upheaval in which scoring and showmanship were the indisputable trends of the day that Bill Griffiths ramped up his show to include more theatrics, more mayhem and more scoring. It made sense, and it's very likely that Griffiths, Hall, and Valladares felt that these other sports were taking a cue from Roller Games. But the underlying issue for Roller Games, post-1975, is that the league had a diminished talent base. As the NBA, MLB, and NFL soared with acrobatics, more home runs, and longer passes, they also had better, bigger, and faster athletes. Whether Griffiths had the right idea in taking an already extreme form of sports entertainment to an even more exaggerated version can be debated, but what seems more apparent is that he may have miscalculated the ability of his "cast" to pull off these additional requirements. Imagine going to an NBA game where half of the attempted dunks were missed and where the players frequently stumbled awkwardly trying such acrobatic moves. That's analogous to what was happening in Roller Games. The top skaters could pull off and sell acrobatic moves and highly choreographed action, but many skaters simply were not ready for it. Therefore, the game suffered and the more Griffiths pushed the antics, the worse it got. It was quite tragic, but there was also a great effort by many to bring the game back to its former glory. John and Ralphie worked tirelessly to recruit and adequately train new skating talent and manage the game as best they could. There were many great skaters that excelled with this new format, and one of the best examples was Harold Jackson, whose athletic feats rivaled those of any sport. For all this effort, Roller Games saw an increase in fan support up through 1980, but fans eventually saw through the façade and attendance started to eventually fade.

Between 1961 and 1974, Roller Games was at its best. It was a highly entertaining and well-skated game with top pros on the track and dazzling storylines written behind the scenes that were well executed. During the 1960s, the fine line between entertainment and sport was roughly the same in both major leagues, Roller Derby and Roller Games, as was talent, popularity, and attendance. The proof of this can be found by watching videos of both leagues from this period. This is not to say that the Roller Games of Southern California circa 1960s wasn't more theatrical than the Roller Derby of the Bay Area—it was. But it struck a balance between athleticism and entertainment that worked in the Los Angeles market. On the East Coast, Roller Games' Philadelphia Warriors skated a "cleaner" game similar to Roller Derby, and it worked very well in that market.

The Warriors' success rivaled that of the T-Birds' during this period, despite skating a game with less theatrics.

These points will seemingly forever be debated amongst roller derby fans and historians, all of whom lament the eventual downfall of both leagues and often heap most of the blame on Roller Games. These conservative pundits are well-meaning and love the sport. There will always be differences of opinion. Roller Derby closed its doors at the end of 1973. Jerry Seltzer cited the gas crisis as the primary reason. Suffice to say, Roller Games had little impact on the demise of Roller Derby.

From 1970 to 1972, Roller Games slowly began to add more showmanship to its games, but within reason. Roller Games was also adversely impacted by the gas shortage, but carried on. During the gas crisis, they amped the showmanship up a bit more. In regards to the comeback period post-1975, there isn't a debate. In this era, Roller Games went over the top in a desperate attempt to recover and generate quick revenue, and this damaged the reputation of both the league (Roller Games) and the entire sport of roller derby.

A well-played roller derby game had outstanding entertainment value. Tickets were generally much less than for other sporting events, and the audience was highly entertained with a variety of action, including speed, hard contact, finesse, agility, altercations, and high drama. It was rare that fans didn't get their money's worth. And often the home team was victorious. Fans left with a smile. That's the way it was in Roller Games.

Chapter 49
Death of the Derby

"The lasting legacy of Roller Games is that it cemented roller derby as a true "sports entertainment" platform in America and across the world." – Steven "WindyMan" Rodriguez, RollerDerbyNotes.com

oller derby has a long history of well-documented bust and boom periods. In nearly every decade since its inception in the 1930s, the game has experienced near-fatal collapses, except in the 1960s— the hey-day of the sport.

The most surprising of all roller derby closures occurred on December 8, 1973, when Jerry Seltzer ceased operations of the original Roller Derby league, which was founded by his father and ran in various formats since 1935.

Since the main subject of this book is Roller Games and its premier team, the Los Angeles Thunderbirds, this chapter primarily focuses on the cyclical down periods of this league and its eventual downfall.

Roller Games had a lifespan of 33 years. During that time, there were four major downward cycles and two shutdowns:

1. Roller Games ceased operations at the end of the 1974 season.
2. After ESPN refused to renew the TV contract in mid-1986, Roller Games drastically reduced the number of games played.
3. Following the cancellation of *Rock and RollerGames*, Roller Games were finished.
4. At the conclusion of the Griffiths era, the final Thunderbirds game was skated in Detroit and the league never hosted another contest.

Roller Games survived slightly longer than the Roller Derby. Both leagues were met with diminished attendance due to the oil shortage, but Seltzer had to contend with a player strike that compromised his operations long before the oil shortage. By the time the crisis was in full effect, his league did not have the resources to continue.

The oil crisis, which is often cited for taking down the Roller Derby league, began in October of 1973, when Arab members of OPEC decreed an oil embargo. This was a political move by OPEC to target nations that supported Israel during the Yom Kippur War. The United States was one of these nations. The embargo lasted six months until it ended in March of 1974, but not before the price of oil had risen from $3 per barrel to nearly $12, globally. This embargo demonstrated the tremendous power the oil industry wields over the nations that rely on oil-based products, which was at that time (and is still today) virtually every nation on the planet.

While the oil crisis of 1973 was a factor in the demise of the Roller Derby, it also impacted – to a lesser extent – Roller Games, exposing the lack of long-term planning that both leagues were guilty of. At the time of the oil shortage, both leagues were one-man shows. Griffiths was the sole owner of Roller Games and Seltzer the sole owner/operator of the Roller Derby. Neither had put aside sufficient cash reserves to weather potential economic downturns and neither had been willing to bring in partners or expand to a franchise system like other sports leagues. The shortage of oil made it more expensive and difficult to travel anywhere, and this impacted almost all aspects of American life and business. People went out less, meaning fewer tickets were sold to concerts, movies, and sporting events — to name a few. However, other sports leagues did not close operations due to the shortage. They saw reduced profits, but their reserves and deep pockets helped them survive and continue to prosper. Once the crisis was over, things went back to normal. The oil crisis not only pushed the banked track game to near extinction, but it may have uncovered the cause as to why the Roller Derby didn't reach its potential — a lack of long-term planning. These were day-to-day operations with little if any foresight of their potential. Roller derby was a unique, exciting team sport. It drew a packed house nearly everywhere it had proper TV coverage. It was already popular, but it was poised to become the next big thing. One only needs to look to professional wrestling to see an example of the potential.

Years later, via his blog, *RollerDerbyJesus*, Jerry Seltzer proclaimed: "I made one huge mistake, running this enterprise as a family business with no partners. When the economy sunk us, I had no one to turn to for additional resources, so I had to shut it down."

It is important to note that the oil crisis impacted those lower on the economic scale more than others, and it was generally these folks who followed the game and filled the arenas. Ticket prices for the Roller Derby were lower than those of other sports, thereby decreasing profit margins. In the winter season, some arena operators passed on potential Roller Derby bookings due to the rising costs of heating fuel. Other sports continued to run their normal schedules as margins were higher.

When speaking about the final tour of Roller Derby in the Fall of 1973, following the embargo, Jerry Seltzer said, "On that tour, we had cancelations one after another."

When Roller Derby closed, Bill Griffiths purchased most of the assets and employed many of the star skaters from Derby. The opportunity to take over the markets once dominated by Derby and employ their marquee skaters was just too much to reject, despite the fact Griffiths wasn't in a strong financial position at the time. So, the mastermind of Los Angeles roller derby dove in head first. It was a business decision that carried with it significant risk. But that is the nature of all business. With a monopoly on the entire sport of roller derby, including access to double the number of skating pros, and just completing the two most successful years in "Games" history, why did Griffiths follow in the footsteps of Seltzer and shut it all down just a year later? Roller derby pundits will forever debate this topic, but here are six likely reasons for the demise, in order of magnitude and impact, in my opinion:

1. The departure of Jerry Hill – When Bill Griffiths bought out Jerry Hill in 1972, not only was he possibly over-extended financially but he became a "one-man show", taking on all of Jerry's responsibilities in addition to his own.

2. The purchase of Jerry Seltzer's Roller Derby – In just two short years, Griffiths bought out both Seltzer and Hill in separate transactions as well as increased his payroll tremendously. It proved to be more than he could handle.

3. The 1973-1974 Oil Crisis – This was in full swing in early 1974 when Griffiths already had his hands full with his expanded duties and obligations. Higher gas prices resulted

in a substantial decline in attendance. Roller derby was hit harder than many sports as its fan base was predominantly blue-collar folks who stayed home in droves.

4. The loss of TV Syndication – Television has always played a vital role in the success of roller derby. When Bill Griffiths failed to renew his syndication contract in 1974, it spelled eventual doom for the league. This item could have been placed at the top of the list, but it's likely all these other items contributed to the loss of TV as broadcasters could see a trending decline. Once the plug was pulled on television, attendance dropped dramatically and the league folded quickly.

5. Over-exposed Showmanship – Desperate to increase or at least sustain enough revenue to survive, Griffiths pushed the boundaries of showmanship vs. sportsmanship, increasing the number of scripted promotions, which alienated some fans and skaters. While it's true these promotions typically enhance attendance in the short term, a delicate balance between the proper dosage and overdose was needed. In 1974 (and in future versions of Roller Games), this balance was disrupted and resulted in the damage of the league's reputation and ultimately, lower fan turn-out. Unless extra caution is taken in regards to the sheer volume of scripted acts implemented, as well as their precise execution, the perceived integrity of the game is compromised and fans slowly move on.

6. The cyclical nature of the sport – By 1974, Roller Games had completed an unprecedented growth period of 13 years (1961-1973). Fan exposure to the game was at an all-time high. The very nature of the game, with its emphasis on theatrics over sport, makes over-exposure an ever-present obstacle to consistent, long-term success.

In the comeback years post-1975, revenue was limited and, thus, the talent on the track dipped significantly. This affected all aspects of the game, including the believability of the choreographed jams and the altercations. Many of the same routines that had worked so well in years past were not executed to the same precise degree, and the fans could see through it. Individual skater altercations increased during this period to bolster attendance. This worked for a while as attendance and ratings increased gradually from 1976 to 1980. But while some fans were coming in the door, others who grew tired of the lower skating level and corny antics departed. The second coming of Roller Games peaked in 1980, and then slowly declined afterward. But the 1980 peak was nothing compared to the summit of 1972. Back in those days, the Thunderbirds routinely packed the Olympic Auditorium, including selling out both the upper and lower levels. In the comeback years post-1976, the team never sold any tickets in the top level of the Olympic—it was always empty. Attendance at this time was no better than 50% of the glory years. Having skated myself during this comeback period, I can recall just how loud the Olympic would get with only the lower level full. I can only imagine what it would have been like when both levels were packed.

Veteran skaters were often disgusted with the level of skating in this period. You could see it on their faces as their eyes rolled when a rookie, pressed into action he or she wasn't quite ready for, messed up the jam (myself included). Most skaters wanted the focus to be more on skating and less on the sideshow. But as time went on, it was just the opposite. And this fiasco of so-called Roller Games increased until eventually, games were skated on a figure eight track with a "wall of death" and live alligators. It's important to note that the gators were never in the proximity of the skating action. It was David Sams' idea, but Bill Griffiths didn't agree and tried to get it taken out of the show. Unfortunately, Sams had creative control at that time. The gator sequences were shot with a second unit and directed by Mike Miller. There was no live audience, no skaters during the shooting, only stuntmen and gator wranglers.

The two derailments during the post-1974 comeback phase of Roller Games were both ultimately caused, first and foremost, by the loss of television exposure. ESPN abandoned Roller Games in 1986 after they couldn't come to terms with Bill Griffiths. Attendance and opportunities diminished significantly without TV until the RollerGames TV show manifested in 1989. After a successful season start, the show was canceled as the producers filed bankruptcy. Once again, when television vacated, it nearly shut down Roller Games. Following the loss of a national television outlet and the exposure that brings, the Thunderbirds skated only three more games before shutting down entirely in late 1993.

Chapter 50

Skating Lessons

"I loved the world of roller derby because I thought it was such an empowering metaphor, that you get out there and do it. It's such a rocker, athletic, capable, cool exhibitionist sport; it's about this great sort of camaraderie." – Drew Barrymore

What can modern-day leagues and promoters glean from these details on the rise and fall of a once powerful, profitable, dominant roller league? Lots! This section is aimed at league operators who desire to take their operations to a professional level.

Roller derby was a professional sport for more than 50 years. That is to say, the skaters were paid for their services. From 1961 through 1974, Roller Games skaters earned enough in wages to participate in skating "full-time." Some skaters made up to $50,000 a year. Keep in mind this is 30 to 40 years ago, so when accounting for inflation, $50,000 paid out in 1970 would be equivalent to $326,000 in 2018.

Today's leagues feature amateur competitions, not unlike that of high school or college sports programs. Some of these leagues desire to remain in the amateur category and hope to see their sport included in the Olympics one day soon. All of us who love the game are hopeful about this prospect. Other leagues aspire to compensate their skaters as paid professionals.

Going "pro" changes the dynamic of the business of roller derby drastically. It's not unlike a company that goes from a sole proprietorship to a corporation with stock offerings. Demands and responsibilities of league owners increase as do the pressures of running a business with paid employees or contractors. On the upside, there is the chance for significant profits and exposure for your league and the sport.

History has shown that the sport of roller derby can be hugely successful with attendance and revenue that rivals other major sports. During the period when derby was "professional," with paid participants, performed in large sports arena venues, and often televised, specific core ingredients were part and parcel of the success of the sport. These included youthful, well-trained athletic participants with high speed, hard-hitting action, a dedicated training facility, television coverage, teams composed of the men and women skating in separate periods, a banked skating track, quad skates, opposing skaters working in harmony to elevate the excitement level (showmanship), and articulate announcers. An additional component that could have further enhanced the chance for success was franchising.

I've included a more detailed summary of many of these

components below. The study and implementation of at least some of these items (the more, the better) could well be integral to the success of a professional roller derby league. The list is based on a comprehensive study of roller derby and its successes and failures. All current and future roller derby business promoters should, at the very least, consider these findings.

The Talent

This seems too obvious. The lack of top-level talent haunted Roller Games during its comeback period. It was a catch 22 situation in those rebuilding years as the league lacked the revenue to allow the employment of enough top-notch talent, so "filler skaters" were employed to save money in the hopes they might develop into decent skaters. Sometimes they did, while other times they didn't. But the learning curve was apparent to fans in the arenas and those watching on television. Jerry Seltzer's Roller Derby never had this issue. When things got tough financially, Jerry choose to bow out gracefully rather than lower salaries and craft make-shift squads with lesser talent.

Speed and Power

High-speed, hard-hitting, acrobatic athletics are the hallmark of most contact sports, and roller derby is no different. The faster the action, the more exciting it is for fans. When all the athletes on the track are in proper condition, the game is naturally fast. Two high-speed skaters dueling on a jam, the exciting whip to the jammer to generate even more speed, the spills, the hard blocks and ultimately, the passing of opposing jammers for points—these are the components of an exciting roller derby contest. But isn't this a given? Wouldn't any roller derby contest feature speed and power? The answer is, it doesn't always. In the later stages of Roller Games, the game had slowed to a crawl, especially if you compare it with the fast-paced 1950s and 1960s.

Television

This format is continually evolving and changing, but the fact remains that for a roller derby league to survive and thrive, it must find an outlet to broadcast its games to a broader audience than just those in attendance. High production value is a must. The Thunderbirds were leaders in this area, employing great camera crews and announcers and filming most of their games in a venue that was very conducive to beneficial television angles—the Olympic Auditorium. The international success of the Thunderbirds and the other home teams of Roller Games in Philly, Japan, and Australia was supported by an attention to detail regarding this vital medium. Predictably, whenever TV was absent, so were the fans. Can you imagine football, baseball, or basketball surviving without television distribution?

Women and Men

One of the best and most progressive aspects of roller derby was the inclusion of both genders. The sport was way ahead of its time and the very first to do this. Credit is given to the Seltzer family, specifically Leo Seltzer. However, it is important to keep in mind that although Leo would undoubtedly be considered as a forward-thinking individual, it also made sense at the box office as fans were excited to see women participate in a contact sport for the first time. Today, women participate in nearly every contact sport including MMA! But Leo Seltzer and his outstanding women skaters paved the way for this. The Thunderbirds continued this tradition with the likes of Shirley Hardman, Terri Lynch, Judy Sowinski, Gwen Miller, and so many others. Women have always been an integral part of the sport. The men added their own dimension of elevated power, speed, and excitement. Men's periods highlighted their unique brand of excitement; both similar and different from the women. When you put it all together, it was a one-of-a-kind spectacle that fans adored. I've never met a Thunderbirds fan who didn't have favorite skaters of both genders. The only legitimate reason to have an all women's or men's pro league is economics. When a game features four squads rather than two (two men's and two women's teams), the payroll cost for the talent is doubled. Ultimately, if the game ever returns to its former glory, I believe the league that reaches this plateau will feature both men and women. I think any roller derby historian will agree with this and concur that neither the Bombers, Chiefs, Pioneers, Warriors, or Thunderbirds would have thrived or even survived without the unique spectacle, excitement, and intrigue of multi-gender squads.

Banked Track

As a product of banked track derby, I must admit it is difficult for me to conceive of a roller derby league finding success without this seemingly crucial ingredient. Like most roller skaters, I started skating on asphalt surfaces. To this day, I still feel more comfortable and graceful skating on a flat surface. Although skating a banked track can be more challenging than a flat track, it can also be more fun and rewarding. The banked track is a veritable stage for the skaters. It has natural boundaries that are easy for fans to identify. The "bank" allows for higher speeds. The rails allow for acrobatic maneuvers and set an intriguing outside upper boundary.

And unlike hard, bone-breaking concrete, a banked track has a natural bounce and is much more forgiving. This not only means fewer broken bones, but also more infrequent long-term bone damage cases from repeated falls. Thus, skaters are more likely to take acrobatic falls that would be unwise on a concrete surface. But purchasing, housing and maintaining a good quality banked track is usually cost prohibitive for all but the most well-funded leagues. A track can run for $15,000 or more, not including the cost of renting a facility large enough to house it with room for fans to attend games. Therefore, the majority of today's leagues are not undertaking this cost and financial risk. However, when another league comes anywhere close to the fan support and revenue of roller derby's golden age, it's very likely a banked track will once again be featured.

Quad Skates

When rollerblade skates were all the rage in the 1990s, roller derby, which was traditionally played on quad skates (four wheels on each skate), was forced to consider allowing rollerblades into the competition. There were many reasons for this, but the two that stand out were the loss of potential sponsors who market rollerblades and the fact that most young skaters at the time were using "blades." RollerJam was the first major operation to utilize blades for most of the skating talent. Anyone who was familiar with classic roller derby would have immediately noticed the skating in RollerJam wasn't as smooth or fluid as it had been in the past. Blades on a banked track didn't seem to be working as well as hoped, and RollerJam was short-lived. Any league that wants pure skating talent to be at the forefront of their sport would not likely feature skaters on blades. Today's revival teams are almost all using quads exclusively, even though blades remain popular for street skating.

Franchises

Neither Roller Games nor Roller Derby branched out to franchising. Both Seltzer and Griffiths preferred more absolute control and simplicity than franchising would have allowed. Each man owned all the teams in his league. This, of course, is one of the main reasons roller derby wasn't taken too seriously by the media and the more discerning public. But more than that, running a one-person show isn't conducive to growth and expansion. When roller derby was at its peak around 1972, there was plenty of interest from investors who wanted to get in on the party. Ted Turner was just one of many who wanted to invest. This would have been an opportune time to expand with the value of both leagues at an all-time high. But both owners stuck with their tried and true formula, and if you've read this far, you know the results. Both leagues folded in the next three years. If a roller derby league ever wants to be in the "big leagues" of the sporting world, they'll have to consider franchising so that each team could have a separate owner. A group of savvy investors might start a league with eight franchises in cities which have a history of supporting roller derby, split into a simple East Coast/West Coast division to contain travel expenses in the beginning. If the initial eight owners showed success, additional investors would form a long line to get in on it. In this way, the potential for the initial investors would be tremendous.

Training Facilities

Proper training facilities and knowledgeable coaches are essential. Roller Games skaters trained at the Olympic Auditorium throughout the first and most successful phase of Roller Games. In the second phase, a training facility was opened by John Hall and Ralphie Valladares in Pico Rivera in 1976 where skaters could hone their skills until 1985, when the Rollerdrome closed. This unfortunate closing was the beginning of the end of the league. Without a training facility, a league cannot survive. Soon after the Rollerdrome closed, games became much slower paced with out of shape skaters. It had no chance.

Showmanship

If your game does not have some emphasis on showmanship, you won't elevate to a professional sport. The controversy is in deciding just how far to go with the "show" aspect of the game. Every league must confront this topic. No team or league ever pushed the limit further than the Los Angeles Thunderbirds of Roller Games, and they became the most successful roller derby team of all-time, considering their national and international fan support. Whether you're a fan of the infamous Thunderbirds antics or what some would call "side-show," those scripted bits brought out more fans than just about anything else. However, there is a delicate balance in this business of sport vs. show. Almost all the other top professional sports incorporate elements of showmanship to one degree or another. But where do you draw the line on the entertainment aspect? The answer should at least partially be based on how well trained and skilled the talent is. The execution of anything done strictly to enhance viewer satisfaction should always be done carefully. Roller Games was guilty of getting carried away with this aspect of the game. Roller Derby, on the other hand, while still staging and scripting many parts of their game, did it with more restraint. Their game was more believable, and the talent was such that the execution was impeccable. As I pointed out in the previous chapter, one critical aspect of the demise of the mighty Thunderbirds was the gross overuse of physical altercations; scripted sideshow dramas and pre-determined winners and losers. My advice to anyone running a current roller derby team, whether you are skating classic old-school derby or modern legit derby: build your initial fan base with 100% legit hard-hitting, fast action. Give this time so that you have a core fan base who profoundly understands your game, its rules, and intricacies. After a while, if you hit a plateau in your growth, allow your top skaters the freedom to add limited aspects of old-school roller derby showmanship. See if this helps build attendance. However, put a strict limit on the number of altercations in any game and don't do anything that isn't believable. Keep the exciting, competitive skating at the forefront. Until and unless you reach the level of professional paid athletes with television coverage, there is no reason to go further than some very basic showmanship. Too much will hurt the legitimacy of the sport with no real upside. If your goal is Olympic participation, avoid any theatrics altogether.

Appendix

Roller Games Timeline

1960's Chronology

1960 National Skating Derby dba Rollerskating Championships conceived of by Herb Roberts (June 1960)

1961 Thunderbirds debut at El Monte Legion Stadium with Dick Lane and KTLA TV (March 1961)

1961 League acquired by Bill Griffiths and Jerry Hill (late 1961)

1962 First game of National Skating Derby dba Roller Games skated at Olympic Auditorium (January 1962)

1963 Hawaiian Warriors founded as first Roller Games home team based outside of Los Angeles.

1966 Australian Thunderbirds established (1966-1968)

1968 Philadelphia Warriors home team established (1968-1974)

1968 Tokyo Thunderbirds established (1968-1970)

1968 Detroit Devils win World Series title

1969 *Sports Illustrated* publishes the article "The Roller Derby" by Frank DeFord on March 3

1970's Chronology

1970 Thunderbirds tour Mexico and sell-out ten straight games at 20,000 seat arena in Mexico City

1972 Canadian All-Stars established early 1972 (1972-1973)

1972 *Kansas City Bomber* released August 2

1972 51,000 witness Thunderbirds and Pioneers in Chicago on September 15

1972 Jerry Hill sells his ownership in Roller Games Fall of 1972

1973 Death of Shirley Hardman

1973 Oil Crisis begins in October

1973 Jerry Seltzer closes operations of Roller Derby at the end of the year

1974 International Skating Conference formed still dba Roller Games

1974 Roller Games absorbs personnel from Roller Derby; Charlie O'Connell and Joan Weston are Thunderbirds

1974 Eastern Warriors become the second team (other than the Thunderbirds) to win world title.

1974 Roller Games loses KTLA TV and syndication and National Skating Derby, Inc. closes (year-end)

1975 Handful of games held without TV, promoted separately by John and Ralphie, and Griffiths

1975 Major rule changes implemented, limiting jammers to one per team per jam

1975 *Rollerball* movie released June 25

1976 Griffith restarts Roller Games with Hall and Valladares as minor partners

1976 Thunderbirds Rollerdrome training center opens under John Hall and Ralph Valladares

1977 KCOP TV-13 begins televising Roller Games as *Roller Superstars* at the opening of 1977 season

1978 KHJ TV-9 takes over the airing of games; attendance boosted

1980's Chronology

1981 Bill Griffiths becomes leaseholder of Grand Olympic Auditorium

1981 Thunderbirds return to Australia but airline strike hurts gate

1983 Madison Square Garden draws large crowd but is last time Thunderbirds perform there

1985 ESPN carries Roller Games nationally

1986 John Hall leaves Roller Games

1989 U.S. television series *Rock and RollerGames* debuts

1990's Chronology

1993 Thunderbirds final game February 6, in Auburn Hills, Michigan

1998 Ralphie Valladares dies November 13, 1998

2000's Chronology

2000 Bill Griffiths Jr. relaunches Roller Games International in 2000 but no games scheduled

2004 Bob Sedillo takes over ownership of Thunderbirds. Holds games using former Games skaters 2004-2008

2004 Thunderbirds female squad (older skaters) lose lopsided game to modern roller derby team

2008 Last Thunderbirds game skated at Pomona Fairplex

2009 Bob Sedillo dies in December

2015 Bill Griffiths Sr. passes away at age 91 in April

Roller Games Stats - Official

Roller Games World Champions

1961 No Championship Series

1962 Los Angeles Thunderbirds defeat Texas Outlaws

1963 Los Angeles Thunderbirds defeat Texas Outlaws

1964 Los Angeles Thunderbirds defeat Detroit Devils

1965 Los Angeles Thunderbirds defeat New York Bombers

1966 Los Angeles Thunderbirds defeat New York Bombers

1967 Los Angeles Thunderbirds defeat Texas Outlaws

1968 Detroit Devils defeat Los Angeles Thunderbirds

1969 Los Angeles Thunderbirds defeat New York Bombers

1970 Los Angeles Thunderbirds defeat Detroit Devils

1971 Los Angeles Thunderbirds defeat Texas Outlaws

1972 Los Angeles Thunderbirds defeat Western Renegades

1973 Los Angeles Thunderbirds defeat Texas Outlaws

1974 Eastern Warriors defeat New York Chiefs

1975 Los Angeles Thunderbirds defeat Eastern Warriors

1976 No World Series (Los Angeles Thunderbirds claim world championship)

1977 No World Series (Los Angeles Thunderbirds claim world championship)

1978 Los Angeles Thunderbirds defeat Chicago Hawks

1979 Los Angeles Thunderbirds defeat Chicago Hawks

1980 Los Angeles Thunderbirds defeat Detroit Devils

1981 No World Series (Los Angeles Thunderbirds claim world championship)

1982 Los Angeles Thunderbirds defeat New York Bombers

1983 Los Angeles Thunderbirds defeat New York Bombers

1984 Los Angeles Thunderbirds defeat Texas Outlaws

1985 No World Series (Los Angeles Thunderbirds claim world championship)

1986 No World Series (Los Angeles Thunderbirds claim world championship)

1987 No World Series (Los Angeles Thunderbirds claim world championship)

1988 No World Series (Los Angeles Thunderbirds claim world championship)

Roller Games All-Time League Standings

"Statistics are used much like a drunk uses a lamppost: for support, not illumination." – Vin Scully

Team – Championship Wins / Appearances

1. Los Angeles Thunderbirds: 20 / 23
2. Detroit Devils: 1 / 5
3. Texas Outlaws: 0 / 8
4. New York Bombers: 0 / 5
5. Eastern Warriors: 1 / 2
6. Chicago Hawks: 0 / 2
7. Western Renegades: 0 / 1

Years with no championship game: 10

Thunderbirds in the Hall of Fame

Twenty-seven Thunderbirds have been inducted into the National Roller Derby Hall of Fame, and a total of forty-five Roller Games skaters have made it to the Hall.

1. Bill Griffiths, Sr.
2. Bob Lewis
3. Charlie "Specs" Saunders
4. Charlie O'Connell
5. Darlene Anderson
6. Dave Pound
7. Frankie Macedo
8. Gerry Murray
9. Jean Porter
10. Jerry Hill
11. Joan Weston
12. John Hall
13. John Parker
14. Judy Sowinski
15. Julie Patrick
16. Larry Lewis
17. Liz Hernandez
18. Margie Laszlo
19. Mary Lou Palermo
20. Ralph Valladares
21. Red Smartt
22. Ronnie Rains
23. Ronnie Robinson
24. Ruberta Mitchell
25. Shirley Hardman
26. Terri Lynch
27. Tony Roman

Roller Games Red-Shirt Skaters in the Hall Of Fame

(Never skated with the Thunderbirds)

1. Ann Calvello
2. Annabelle Kealey
3. Annis Jensen
4. Bob Hein
5. Bob Satterfield
6. Carol Meyer
7. Delores Tucker
8. Fred Noa
9. Jan Vallow
10. Judy Arnold
11. Judi McGuire
12. Leroy Gonzales
13. Loretta Behrens
14. Mary Gardner
15. Midge "Toughie" Brasuhn
16. Mike Gammon
17. Nick Scopas
18. Norma Rossner
19. Sid Harnesk

Ralphie Valladares – Team Chronology

Career History:

- 1954 – Brooklyn Red Devils and L.A. Braves (Roller Derby - IRDL)
- 1955 – Los Angeles Braves and Miami Westerners (Roller Derby - IRDL)
- 1956 – Los Angeles Braves (Roller Derby - IRDL)
- 1957 – Los Angeles Braves (Roller Derby - IRDL)
- 1958 – Los Angeles Braves and SF Bay Bombers (Roller Derby - IRDL)

- 1959 – San Francisco Bay Bombers (Roller Derby - IRDL)
- 1960 – San Francisco Bay Bombers (Roller Derby - IRDL)
- 1961 – Los Angeles Thunderbirds (Roller Games - RSC)
- 1962 – Los Angeles Thunderbirds (Roller Games - NSD)
- 1963 – Los Angeles Thunderbirds (Roller Games - NRL)
- 1964 – Los Angeles Thunderbirds (Roller Games - NSD)
- 1965 – Los Angeles Thunderbirds (Roller Games - NSD)
- 1966 – Australian Thunderbirds (Roller Games - NSD)
- 1967 – Australian Thunderbirds (Roller Games - NSD)
- 1968 – Los Angeles Thunderbirds (Roller Games - NSD)
- 1969 – Los Angeles Thunderbirds (Roller Games - NSD)
- 1970 – Los Angeles Thunderbirds (Roller Games - NSD)
- 1971 – Los Angeles Thunderbirds (Roller Games - NSD)
- 1972 – Los Angeles Thunderbirds and Tokyo Bombers (Roller Games - NSD)
- 1973 – Tokyo Bombers (Roller Games - JNRL)
- 1974 – Los Angeles Thunderbirds and Latin Liberators (Roller Games - ISC)
- 1975 – Los Angeles Thunderbirds (Roller Games - ISC)
- 1976 – Los Angeles Thunderbirds (Roller Games - RSS)
- 1977 – Los Angeles Thunderbirds (Roller Games - NSD)
- 1978 – Los Angeles Thunderbirds (Roller Games - NSD)
- 1979 – Los Angeles Thunderbirds (Roller Games - NSD)
- 1980 – Los Angeles Thunderbirds (Roller Games - NSD)
- 1981 – Los Angeles Thunderbirds (Roller Games - NSD)
- 1982 – Los Angeles Thunderbirds (Roller Games - NSD)
- 1983 – Los Angeles Thunderbirds (Roller Games - NSD)
- 1984 – Los Angeles Thunderbirds (Roller Games - NSD)
- 1985 – Los Angeles Thunderbirds (Roller Games – IRDL/CRD)
- 1986 – Los Angeles Thunderbirds (Roller Games – IRDL/CRD)
- 1987 – Los Angeles Thunderbirds (Roller Games - IRDL)
- 1988 – Los Angeles Thunderbirds (Roller Games - IRDL)
- 1989 – Los Angeles Thunderbirds (Roller Games - RRG)
- 1990 – Los Angeles Thunderbirds (Roller Games - RGI)
- 1991 – Los Angeles Thunderbirds (Roller Games - RGI)

- 1992 – Los Angeles Thunderbirds (Roller Games - RGI)
- 1993 – Los Angeles Thunderbirds (Roller Games - RGI)

Roller Games Lists - Informal

Thunderbirds Dream Team

Men:

1. John Hall (G.M./Coach)
2. Ralph Valladares
3. George Copeland
4. Ronnie Rains
5. Danny Reilly
6. Larry Lewis
7. Richard Brown
8. Punky Gardner
9. George Adams
10. Manny Servin

Women:

1. Terri Lynch
2. Jean Porter
3. Ruberta Mitchell
4. Julie Patrick
5. Judy Sowinski
6. Liz Hernandez
7. Carmen Thompson
8. Gwen Miller
9. Sally Vega
10. Honey Sanchez

Red-Shirt Dream Team

Men:

1. John Parker (G.M./Coach)
2. Dave Pound
3. Leroy Gonzales
4. Nick Scopas
5. George Adams
6. Jim Trotter
7. Lester Quarles
8. Harold Jackson
9. Jess Adams
10. Roger Schroeder

Women:

1. Shirley Hardman
2. Judy Arnold
3. Ann Calvello
4. Loretta Behrens
5. Toni Tagg
6. Darlene Anderson
7. Adeline Hocker
8. Candi Mitchell
9. Norma Rossner
10. Diane Syverson

L.A. Derby Dolls (2003-Present)

"Before roller derby was a grassroots sport played by tens of thousands of people around the world, it was a touring sports entertainment that thrilled a nation for decades." – Jonathan R., *New York Shock Exchange*

The Derby Dolls have kept banked track skating alive in Los Angeles since 2003. The Derby Dolls are one of only 14 banked track leagues currently operating (at the time of this writing) in the United States. The L.A. Ri-Ettes are their all-star team and compete against top teams throughout the country. As of 2018, they have been the reigning national champions seven years in row. Among the new generation of roller derby, the Derby Dolls are already a legendary team.

Hollywood

Both the movie and television industries have had affection for roller derby since way back to its inception. The first major movie that highlighted the game was *The Fireball* in 1950, starring a young Mickey Rooney. Roller Games was called upon by Hollywood to participate in numerous network TV shows and movies over the years. Many of the episodes occurred during the rebirth of the Thunderbirds post 1975. Being based in Los Angeles, the television and movie industry knew of the Thunderbirds to a much greater extent than they may have known the Bay Bombers. And the proximity to skaters and skating venues made it even more convenient. The Thunderbirds got most of the calls when Hollywood needed skating action. Some of the movies and shows that Roller Games participated in include:

- *Kansas City Bomber* (1972 film)
- *Six Million Dollar Man* (1977 TV)
- *The Roller Girls* (1978 TV)
- *Charlie's Angels* (1979 TV)
- *Chips* (1979 TV)
- *Real People* (1980 TV)
- *Sheriff Lobo* (1980 TV)
- *The Big Brawl* (1980 movie)
- *The Fall Guy* (1982 TV)
- *Fantasy Island* (1982 TV)

The Fifth Dimensions, a musical act with hits in the 1960s, inquired about buying a team franchise in 1995, when former skating star Bert Wall tried to launch a new league in 1995. The league held a few games at the Olympic but like many others, didn't succeed.

Various sources have claimed that Michael Jackson was a fan of the Thunderbirds. He liked to roller skate and the mere fact that he spent his pre-teen and teenage years in Los Angeles made it almost a certainty that he was exposed to Roller Games. He once said hello to John Hall when John was speaking with Lionel Ritchie. He and Ritchie had just finished an overnight editing supervision session on the "We are the World" production. John Hall stated, "I know that he did watch some games and that he knew who I was. He waved to me as I was talking to Lionel at my former editing facility "The Post Group" as he said goodbye to the editor upstairs. Lionel said that Michael knew of me and that Michael watched the games." Gary Stang, the long-time owner of San Diego Skateworld, who accompanied Roller Games on the 1980 tour of Mexico, once performed at a private birthday party for Michael Jackson. Gary showed Michael a few "artistic disco steps" and said Michael was a good skater.

The Refs

The lead referee in the early days of Roller Games was Al Costa, who worked from the early 1960s until 1967. John Hall often praised his work. He was Roller Games' best referee. Al had a brother named Lou Costa whom he trained and who eventually went on to referee Warrior games in Philadelphia for many years.

Roller Games' next top referee was Tony Lavore from the late 1960s up to the early 1970s. He was the brother of Detroit Devils captain, Toni Tagg (who later was on the Thunderbirds briefly in 1972). Their real family name was Taglialavore and they didn't want fans to know that they were related, so Anthony took the second half of their name and was called Tony Lavore. His sister, Antoinette, took the first half of the family name and was Toni Tagg.

John "Gooch" Gautieri was their next top referee. He started in the late 1960s and worked until 1971. He then became the U.S. representative of the Australian Kangaroos on the East Coast and Midwest and then became G.M. of the N.Y. Bombers in 1973. He had previously refereed for Seltzer's Roller Derby league in the 1950s.

Other notable referees of the 1960s and early 1970s include former skaters Sid Harnesk and Charlie "Specs" Saunders, both of whom worked from the late 1960s and early 1970s.

Don Lastra became the leading referee in the mid-1970s. He started in 1972. Lastra is perhaps the most well known referee in Roller Games history and remained with the league until the very end. Like every Roller Games zebras, he was at the center of countless confrontations between rival skaters. He took his fair share of poorly aimed shots from the fists of the game's greats (and not so greats).

Former skater Terri Toledo was also one of the top referees from 1976 to 1983. Tom Wersderfer, who provided much of the information for this section, refereed from 1983 forward.

There were many other referees for the Thunderbirds, including former skaters Ernie Lopez, Joe Stuart, Bob Marten (who became a red-shirt G.M.), Roberto Juarez (who became a red-shirt G.M.), and dozens of others.

References

http://slam.canoc.com/Slam/Wrestling/2014/06/18/22482666.html

http://www.latimes.com/local/obituaries/la-me-bill-griffiths-20150408-story.html

https://benchedathletes.wordpress.com/2015/05/01/bill-griffiths/

http://www.laobserved.com/archive/2015/04/bill_griffiths_impresario.php

http://kenlevine.blogspot.com/2009/09/memories-of-roller-derby.html

http://articles.latimes.com/1993-07-18/local/me-14540_1_roller-derby

http://dmboxing.com/the-olympic-auditorium-a-look-back-at-a-grand-venue-part-2-of-2/

http://www.nytimes.com/1983/02/26/sports/players-roller-derby-tour-tries-a-new-image.html

http://rollerderby.wikia.com/wiki/History_of_roller_derby

http://www.encyclopedia.com/media/encyclopedias-almanacs
-transcripts-and-maps/roller-derby

http://www.bankedtrack.info/index.html

http://www.wikiwand.com/en/History_of_roller_derby

http://www.rollerderbyhalloffame.com/id3.html

http://houseofdeception.com/Roller_Derby_History.html

https://ussporthistory.com/2014/10/27/the-roller-derby-origin-story/

http://www.derbylife.com/2015/08/a-brief-history-of-roller-derby/

https://ussporthistory.com/2016/03/10/women-in-the-roller-derby-
groundbreaking-athletes-or-entertaining-celebrities/

https://www.si.com/vault/1969/03/03/558511/the-roller-derby

http://people.com/archive/daring-darleen-has-to-skate-in-the-fast-
lane-to-keep-up-with-her-roller-games-hype-vol-13-no-23/

http://articles.latimes.com/1989-06-11/entertainment/ca-3058_1_
roller-derby-rollergames-variety-show

http://slumshollywood.blogspot.com/2012/03/queen-of-roller-games-
raquel-welch-in.html

https://www.frogmouthclothing.com/blogs/frogmouth-blog/
67525699-the-world-map-of-roller-derby-leagues

Special Thanks

John Hall
Ralph Valladares
Bill Griffiths, Jr.
Bill Griffiths, Sr.
Gary Powers
Phil Berrier
Bill Nagy
Buddy Atkinson Jr.
Sam Washington
Loretta Behrens
Ted Marolf
Tom Wersderfer
Jim McInernie
Peggy Fowler
Tory Christopher
Noonie Fortin
Bren Futura
Gina Valladares
Bobby Ice Box Smith
Steve DeBro
Steve Taylor

Larry McGinnis
John Drew
Juan Molano
Paul Hill
Judy Arnold
Robert Murdock
Jim Fitzpatrick
Paul Rupert
Hiroshi Koizumi
Joe Nardone
Jerry Seltzer

Index

Boyd, Betty 68
Brascia, Peter 166
Brasuhn, Midge \ 36, 42, 77, 80, 87,
    92, 96, 324
Brien, Kenny 127
Brooklyn Devils 138
Brown, Betty 31, 112, 119, 132
Brown, Earlene 43, 66, 142, 145,
    156, 285
Brown, Richard 43, 80, 92, 96, 97,
    98, 102, 109, 132, 141, 145, 160,
    161, 231, 250, 271, 283, 284, 326
Brown, Tim 92
Buckholtz, Bucky 63
Burton, J.J. 92
Butta, John 126

C

Caan, James 165
Caldwell, Harold 249
Calvello, Ann 86, 88, 89, 90, 91, 95,
    101, 108, 128, 134, 156, 182,
    191, 235, 324, 327
Campbell, Bobby 156
Campbell, Linda 212, 223
Canadian National Roller
    League 147
Candolero, Al 99
Cannella, Dave 92, 102
Cardella, Joe 238
Carr, Mary Ann 31
Carter, Julie 126, 127
Castro, Scott 250
Cattell, Jerry 141, 160
Cavin, Patti 31, 132, 156
Cendejas, Bobby 250, 260
Cerrito, Shar 285
Chakota, Chick 11
Chambers, Donnie 74, 80
Chambers, Neal 192
Chaney, Lynda 139

Charles, Ray 41
Chavez, Johnny 31, 73, 102
Cherestman, Sadie 250
Chicago Cyclones 62, 63
Chicago Hawks 73, 118, 193
Chicago Pioneers. *See* Midwest
    Pioneers
Chicago Thunderbirds 164
Cho, Debbie 156
Choyce, Carol 90, 102
Christensen, Pete 250
Christopher, Margaret 250
Christopher, Tory 211
Ciota, Jimmy 85, 95
Clark, Jean 127, 145
Cleveland Bucks 54
Coblentz, Dale 121
Cochu, Francine 43, 145, 146
Cohen, Sid 10
Congleton, Lynn 99, 137, 138, 141,
    160, 231
Conlon, Peggy 85
Contreras, Tammy 223, 238, 239, 284
Cooper, Vicki 156
Copeland, George 8, 11, 41, 43, 62,
    70, 73, 74, 274, 326
Corbin, Bob 90, 102, 110, 115, 119,
    127, 137, 138
Costa, Al 11, 329
Cox, Dave 88, 90, 110, 119, 127, 139
Crawford, George 121
Crews, Tom 42, 102, 119
Crommie, May 249
Curry, Bob 92

D

D'Amato, Mark 31, 271
Daniel, Georgeanna 127
Dare, Toni 80, 92
Dark, Mike 250, 260
Darrigo, Jan 126

KTLA 7, 11, 12, 20

L

Lamaestra, Rena 202, 212, 220
Lamastus, JoAnn 127
Lambert, Leroy 53
Lane, Dick 7, 8, 11, 12, 16, 17, 20, 22, 36, 41, 62, 131, 167, 174
Langlois, Darlene 183, 202, 212, 216, 220, 230, 238, 259
La Opinion 223
Lara, Abel 62, 114
L.A. Sentinel 222
Lastra, Don 330
Laszlo, Margie 156, 159, 323
L.A. Times 223
Latin Libertadores 99
Lavore, Tony 329
Leary, Ann 121
Lewis, Bob 26, 33, 54, 92, 114, 124, 125, 127, 323
    53
Lewis, Larry 31, 34, 37, 43, 82, 90, 92, 102, 110, 115, 118, 121, 196, 235, 323, 326
Lindsay, Jo 119
Lipschiltz, David 235
Lipsyte, Robert 9
Little Angie 53
Lockhard, Ed 127
Lockhart, Bob 127
Lolly, \"Luscious\" 249
Long Beach Falcons 70
Lopez, Ernie 11, 31, 42, 62, 73, 90, 96, 110, 121, 330
Los Angeles Braves 8
Los Angeles Sports Arena 26
Los Angeles Times 15, 65, 133, 246
Louisiana Superdome 223
Lucero, Fred 212, 214, 223
Lucero, Freddie 239

Lucy, Chavarria 92
Lynch, Cheryl 212
Lynch, Terri 11, 29, 33, 35, 62, 63, 66, 73, 74, 80, 81, 90, 98, 102, 110, 114, 115, 118, 119, 127, 137, 161, 187, 201, 279, 310, 323, 326

M

Macedo, Frankie 77, 145, 146, 183, 184, 187, 193, 203, 212, 235, 323
Madden, Pat 127
Madison Square Garden 65, 148, 149, 161, 218, 256
Majors, Lee 187
Maldinado, Irene 96
Maniacs 248, 250, 254
Manny, Servin 31
Manti, Stan 11
Maresca, Dee 16, 88
Marez, Dave 285
Marolf, Ted 183, 192, 202, 220, 229
Marquez, Carlos 31, 184, 212
Marshall, Billy 31, 33, 43, 115, 119, 127, 138, 203, 212, 214, 216, 220, 223, 239, 249
Marshall, Jennifer 31, 43, 119, 127, 139, 156
Marten, Bob 173, 330
Martinez, Chris 284, 285
Martinez, David 196, 223, 284
Martinez, Frank 31, 119, 127
Martinez, Josh 267
Martinez, Julie 223, 260
Martinez, Megan 267, 284, 285
Marziani, Louise 121, 146
Masako, Anji 250
mascots 53
match races 23, 25, 51, 53, 83, 89, 98, 124, 220
Materson, Holly 249
Matthews, Luther 119, 127

O

O'Connell, Charlie 66, 85, 104, 106,
    128, 134, 147, 148, 149, 154,
    156, 157, 158, 323
Ogbin, Cindy 99, 119, 160
O'Hara, Kelly 216
Olbermann, Keith 194
Oleson, Don 92
Oleson, Sandy 92
Olympic Auditorium 9, 11, 22, 25, 29,
    32, 41, 42, 48, 63, 172, 187, 199,
    202, 209, 222
Ontario Monarchs 145
Orgill, Vicki 250
Ott, Jim 11
Outhommoudntry, Lali 285

P

Palermo, Mary Lou 71, 74, 323
Parker, Janet 127
Parker, John 33, 36, 54, 77, 87, 89, 96,
    98, 110, 112, 121, 127, 209, 218,
    220, 323, 327
Patrick, Julie 8, 41, 62, 74, 90, 102,
    109, 110, 115, 145, 156, 323, 326
Payne, Eddie 35, 73, 74, 80, 102, 115
Peloquin, Michele 145
Perales, Marlene 73
Pete, Madden 126
Peter, Kelly 90
Peterson, B.J. 37, 110, 114, 119, 127
Petrasek, Larry 138
Philadelphia Warriors 94, 97, 99, 100,
    109, 161, 241
Phillipi, Bill de 31
Phillips, Carol 88, 110, 114, 145
Phillips, Cindy 220, 230
Phoenix Landsharks 278
Porter, Jean 8, 62, 323, 326

Pound, Dave 11, 34, 35, 50, 56, 71,
    80, 87, 99, 142, 156, 187, 204,
    288, 323, 327
President's Cup 56, 74, 105, 118, 126,
    135, 204
Purcell, Sarah 200

Q

Quarles, Lester 43, 54, 77, 109, 114,
    118, 119, 124, 125, 126, 127,
    138, 144, 327
Quebec Fleur de Lys 145, 146, 147
Quinn, Greg 31, 43, 119, 139, 141,
    156, 184, 196

R

Raffety, Tom 73
Rainer, Bob 127
Rains, Ronnie 37, 38, 39, 48, 50, 54,
    56, 66, 79, 88, 90, 92, 98, 102,
    104, 109, 114, 120, 124, 125,
    132, 136, 145, 156, 161, 184,
    187, 193, 196, 203, 212, 214,
    219, 323, 326
Randi, Whitman 230
Rapp, Gerry 63
Redmond, Victor 192, 212, 220
Redoble, Buddy 114
Reed, Patti 139
Reese, Jerry 249
Reilly, Danny 30, 31, 32, 33, 48, 50,
    74, 80, 85, 90, 92, 98, 102, 106,
    109, 112, 115, 118, 119, 127,
    135, 136, 137, 138, 139, 142,
    145, 149, 156, 159, 184, 187,
    193, 201, 203, 212, 214, 216,
    220, 326
Reilly, Jerry 31, 80, 85
Reilly's Renegades 136
Reinhart, Jerry 121

Resources

Thunderbirds website:
http://latbirds.net/

Thunderbirds FB Page:
https://www.facebook.com/LosAngelesThunderbirds/

Thunderbirds Instagram Page:
https://instagram.com/LosAngelesThunderbirds

The Author:
http://scott-stephens.com/

Roller Derby Hall of Fame:
https: www.rollerderbyhalloffame.com

CPSIA information can be obtained
at www.ICGtesting.com
Printed in the USA
LVHW092308200921
698320LV00003B/74